Fodor's 90
Philadelphia

Fodor's Travel Publications, Inc.
New York and London

Fodor's Philadelphia

Editor: Denise Nolty
Area Editors: Rathe Miller, Michael Schwager
Editorial Contributors: Joyce Eisenberg, Theodore Fisher, Sam Gugino, Chuck Stone
Art Director: Fabrizio La Rocca
Map Editor: Suzanne Brown
Cartographer: David Lindroth
Illustrator: Karl Tanner
Cover Photograph: Peter Beck/Uniphoto

Design: Vignelli Associates

Contents

Maps

Foreword

This is an exciting time for Fodor's, as we continue our ambitious program to rewrite, reformat, and redesign all 140 of our guides. Here are just a few of the new features:

★ Brand-new computer-generated maps locating all the top attractions, hotels, restaurants, and shops

★ A unique system of numbers and legends to help readers move effortlessly between text and maps

★ A new star rating system for hotels and restaurants

★ Restaurant reviews by major food critics around the world

★ Stamped, self-addressed postcards, bound into every guide, that give readers an opportunity to help evaluate hotels and restaurants

★ Complete page redesign for instant retrieval of information

★ FODOR'S CHOICE—Our favorite museums, beaches, cafes, romantic hideaways, festivals, and more

★ HIGHLIGHTS—An insider's look at the most important developments in tourism during the past year

★ TIME OUT—The best and most convenient lunch stops along the shopping and exploring routes

★ Exclusive background essays that create a powerful portrait of each destination

★ A mini-journal for travelers to keep track of their own itineraries and addresses

Although every care has been taken to ensure the accuracy of the information in this guide, the passage of time will always bring change, and consequently, the publisher cannot accept responsibility for errors that may occur.

All prices and opening times quoted here are based on information available to us at press time. Hours and admission fees may change, however, and the prudent traveler will avoid inconvenience by calling ahead.

Fodor's wants to hear about your travel experiences, both pleasant and unpleasant. When a hotel or restaurant fails to live up to its billing, let us know and we will investigate the complaint and revise our entries where the facts warrant it.

Send your letters to the editors of Fodor's Travel Publications, 201 E. 50th Street, New York, NY 10022.

Highlights '90 and Fodor's Choice

Highlights '90

Philadelphia certainly seems to be putting its best foot forward for the 1990s.

The landmark **Swann Fountain** in the Benjamin Franklin Parkway's Logan Circle, one of the most significant works of outdoor art in the city, is undergoing a privately funded $2 million restoration. The three figures in the 65-year-old fountain, each weighing about 4,200 pounds, are being completely dismantled and refurbished.

Fairmount Park's **Azalea Garden,** located behind the Art Museum, will bloom with hundreds of newly planted azaleas and rhododendrons this spring, the result of a three-year project by Pennsylvania Horticultural Society to enhance the 4-acre site. Also, new red oaks, red maples, and sweet gums are being planted along the parkway to replace 200 trees that had to be cut down because of soil compaction from the pounding of feet over the years.

In January 1989, new lighting replaced the "Christmas-tree" wiring system which had outlined the buildings along **Boathouse Row** for many years. Once again, the reflections of the various buildings twinkle and shimmer on the Schuylkill River—one of the city's loveliest sights. Just south of Boathouse Row, the Greek-Revival buildings of the **Fairmount Waterworks,** which have supplied water to the city since the early 1800s, are being restored to their original glory.

At the other end of the parkway, work continues on City Hall. Although the scaffolding around the William Penn statue atop City Hall was removed in 1987, it still encases much of the tower. The restoration should be completed in 1990, at which time the observation deck will reopen.

After being closed for more than two years, the 84-year-old Bellevue is back. Once the centerpiece of Philadelphia high society, the hotel was closed after an outbreak of Legionnaire's disease in 1976 and was threatened with demolition by the city administration two years later. A $150 million restoration of the building has been completed in the hopes of returning the **Hotel Atop the Bellevue** to a position of prominence among the city's luxury hotels.

Built 12 years ago, the 33-story **Rittenhouse** hotel finally opened in June 1989 on Rittenhouse Square, Philadelphia's classiest park. Rivaling both the Bellevue and the Four Seasons on Logan Circle, the Rittenhouse has 99 rooms and 180 condominium apartments with panoramic views of the square.

Other **new hotels** include the Independence Park Inn, the Omni, and the Thomas Bond House bed-and-breakfast, all of which are located in the historic district. The 290-room Ritz Carlton Hotel is scheduled to open in August 1990 as part of Two Liberty Place, a 58-story complex which will also include 80 stores and restaurants and an open-court food buffet.

It may be years before the $568 million **Philadelphia Convention Center** hosts any conventions, but planners for the center cleared a major hurdle in 1989. Despite criticism from many quarters that it was an economic boondoggle that would destroy two Philadelphia treasures—the Reading Terminal Market and Chinatown—the project did receive final approval from the City Council.

The **Penn's Landing** development project made great strides in 1989 as well. The contract for the project has been awarded, and work should begin shortly on the 37-acre area stretching along the Delaware River where William Penn first came ashore in Philadelphia. This $800 million project will have offices, stores, an atrium for entertainment and cultural uses, luxury condominiums, and a 1,200-room hotel. This is just one of many projects designed to transform and improve the Delaware waterfront in the near future.

Just across the Delaware in Camden, New Jersey, a $74 million **aquarium**—which will rival the one in Baltimore's Inner Harbor—is now under construction. The aquarium has prompted the revival of the Delaware River Ferry, which last ran in 1953.

The **30th Street Station,** Philadelphia's main train terminus and the second busiest in the Amtrak system, is currently undergoing a 2½-year face-lift. New restaurants, shops, and lighting are being added in the south concourse of the 55-year-old neoclassical building in the first step of a seven-year development plan that will include a 66-acre office-hotel complex.

At the airport, a long-overdue overseas terminal is currently under construction. It's part of the city's $315 million **airport renovation project,** which will include a new runway, improved terminals, additional parking, and a new luxury hotel. The new terminal should be completed in 1991.

Out on the highways, three years of reconstruction on the **Schuylkill Expressway** has finally ended. The project added lanes and ramps to the expressway and has made driving on Philadelphia's most important thoroughfare considerably safer and more pleasant. Work continues on the crosstown **Vine Street Expressway,** which will link the Schuylkill Expressway with I-95; it's scheduled for completion in spring 1991. The **Walnut Street Bridge,** a main link between West Philadelphia and downtown, is currently closed for reconstruction but is scheduled to reopen in November 1990.

Now that the One Liberty Place office tower at 17th and Market streets has broken the unwritten law which keeps all buildings in Philadelphia shorter than the William Penn statue on City Hall, the sky has literally become the limit. Of seven planned buildings that will dwarf City Hall, one is complete, four are under way, and two are in the proposal stage—including a 1,000-foot, 59-story trade center on the bank of the Delaware River.

In 1990, the **Philadelphia Orchestra,** under the direction of Riccardo Muti, will present its 90th season. Ground-breaking for the orchestra's new hall, at the southwest corner of Broad and Spruce streets, is scheduled for spring 1990. The new facility will be designed by architect Robert Venturi at a projected cost of $95 million. The orchestra's current home, the Academy of Music, will undergo a $20 million renovation and continue to be used by the Pennsylvania Ballet and the Opera Company of Philadelphia.

The **Philadelphia Museum of Art,** long the victim of insufficient city funding, was scheduled for a number of improvements in 1989 as the result of a successful $50 million fund-raising drive. The highlight of the museum's 1989 schedule was an exhibition of the Walter Annenberg Collection of Impressionist and Post-Impressionist Art, the greatest private collection of such art in the world.

Scheduled to open in 1990 is the Franklin Institute's $58 million **Futures Center.** The center, with an interior circular ramp, high atrium, and 300-seat Omniverse theater featuring a domed screen that surrounds the audience, will house eight permanent exhibits focusing on the 21st century. Among them: space, computers, health, trends, and products.

Nineteen ninety will also see the final step in a series of gradual transformations that have stretched over the past several decades at the **Philadelphia Zoological Gardens.** Visitors can look forward to the opening of the last of the zoo's natural habitats, a specially structured environment for carnivores, including big and small cats, red pandas, coati, and meerkats.

The **Academy of Natural Sciences** is adding an earth-science exhibit and a modern display of its mineral and gem collection.

The **Pennsylvania Academy of the Fine Arts** moved to new studio and school facilities at 1301 Cherry Street. The academy is also currently renovating its spectacular museum building, located a block to the west at Broad and Cherry streets.

On other cultural fronts, the **Philadelphia Dance Company** (a.k.a. PhilaDanco) celebrated its 20th anniversary; the **Black Theater Festival** celebrated its 10th season with three musical productions and readings of new plays; and regional theater presented its most abundant offerings in recent history. The run of *Les Misérables*, which ended at the Forrest in March 1989, shattered all Philadelphia theater records. In 1990 the Shubert will host a new production of *Phantom of the Opera*.

The vibrant **South Street** shopping and entertainment district is expanding to the south and the west, with a number of avant-garde art galleries, new-wave clothing shops, craft stores, and restaurants.

May 1989 marked the opening of the largest shopping mall in the region, **Franklin Mills.** Located in northeast Philadelphia, the mall has 230 stores, 1.8 million square feet of retail space, and is 1.3 miles from end to end. The extensive space is occupied by a number of "off-priced" outlets, a miniature golf course, batting cages, and a roller rink.

Fodor's Choice

No two people will agree on what makes a perfect vacation, but it's fun and helpful to know what others think. We hope you'll have a chance to experience some of Fodor's Choices yourself while visiting Philadelphia. For detailed information about each entry, refer to the appropriate chapters in this guidebook.

Special Moments

Rittenhouse Square on a rainy afternoon

The steps of the Philadelphia Museum of Art at dawn

Walking Forbidden Drive along Wissahickon Creek

Feeding time for the big cats at the zoo

Independence Hall any time

Taste Treats

Bassett's butterscotch-vanilla ice cream at Reading Terminal Market

Fresh soft pretzels with mustard from street-corner vendors

Pheasant wrapped in phyllo and covered with port-spiked demiglace at Ecco

Frozen yogurt at Scoop De Ville

Tasty kakes anywhere

Buffalo chicken wings at Silveri's

Off the Beaten Track

Bryn Athyn Cathedral

Laurel Hill Cemetery

After Hours

The chanteuse at Borgia Cafe

Cheesesteaks at Pat's (9th St. and Passyunk Ave.) at 3 AM

The view of Boathouse Row, the Waterworks, and the Philadelphia Museum of Art from West River Drive

The view of the William Penn statue atop City Hall from the top of Centre Square

Walking around Independence National Historical Park

Hotels

Hotel Atop the Bellevue *(Very Expensive)*

Four Seasons *(Very Expensive)*

Guest Quarters *(Very Expensive)*

Adam's Mark *(Expensive)*

Quality Inn Chinatown *(Moderate)*

Restaurants

Le Bec-Fin *(Very Expensive)*

The Fountain *(Very Expensive)*

Susanna Foo *(Very Expensive)*

Osteria Romana *(Expensive)*

Ecco *(Moderate)*

Marrakesh *(Moderate)*

Tokio *(Moderate)*

Roller's *(Moderate)*

Thai Garden *(Inexpensive)*

Van's Garden *(Inexpensive)*

Brandywine Valley

Longwood Gardens

Brandywine River Museum

Winterthur Museum and Gardens

Bucks County

Fonthill, Henry Chapman Mercer's concrete castle, and the Mercer Museum, both in Doylestown

Floating down the Delaware River in an inner tube rented from Bucks County River Tubing

Exploring River Road north of New Hope and staying overnight at a bed-and-breakfast

Lancaster County

A visit to a farmers market: the Central Market in downtown Lancaster or the Green Dragon Farmers Market and Auction in Ephrata

A drive along the back-country roads between Routes 23 and 340 to see the Amish farms and roadside stands

Lunch at a Pennsylvania Dutch restaurant

An overnight stay at a Mennonite farm

Philadelphia and Surrounding Area

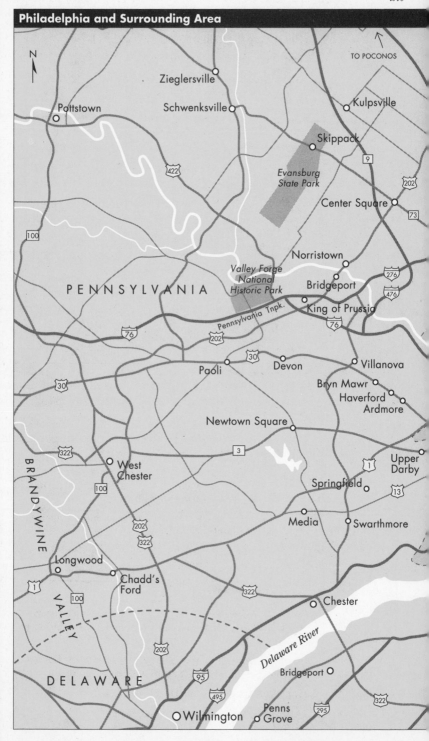

TO POCONOS

Zieglersville

Pottstown

Schwenksville

Kulpsville

Skippack

9

422

Evansburg
State Park

202

Center Square

73

100

Norristown

Bridgeport

276

PENNSYLVANIA

Valley Forge
National
Historic Park

King of Prussia

476

76

Pennsylvania Tnpk.

202

76

30

Devon

Villanova

Paoli

Bryn Mawr

Haverford
Ardmore

30

Newtown Square

3

322

West
Chester

Upper
Darby

1

BRANDYWINE

100

Springfield

13

202

322

Media

Swarthmore

Longwood

Chadd's
Ford

1

322

Chester

VALLEY

100

Delaware River

202

DELAWARE

Bridgeport

95

495

Penns
Grove

322

295

Wilmington

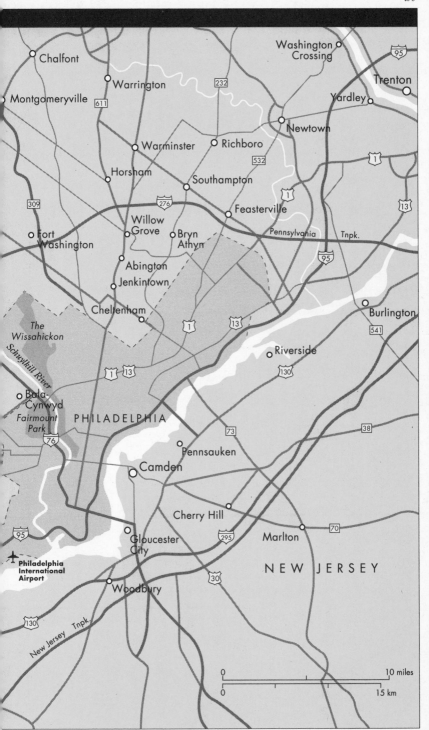

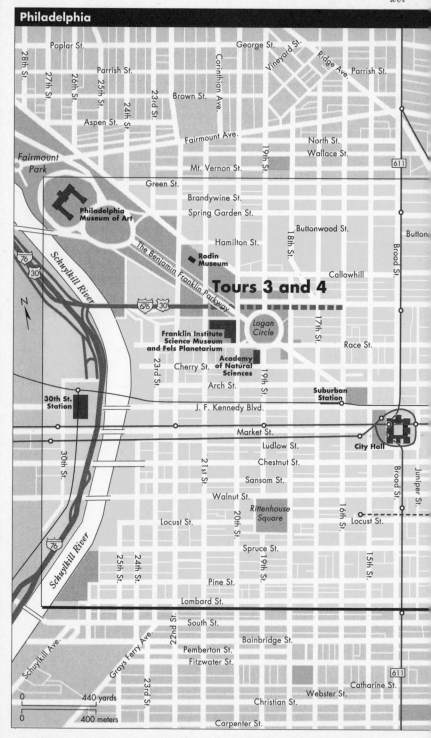

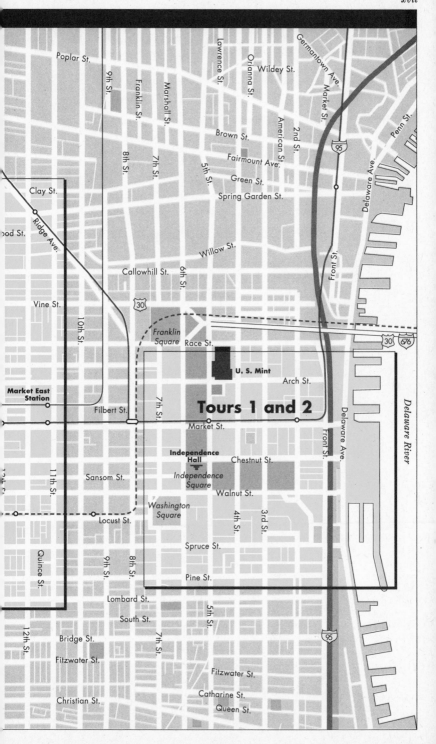

World Time Zones

Numbers below vertical bands relate each zone to Greenwich Mean Time (0 hrs.).
Local times may differ, as indicated by lightface numbers on the map.

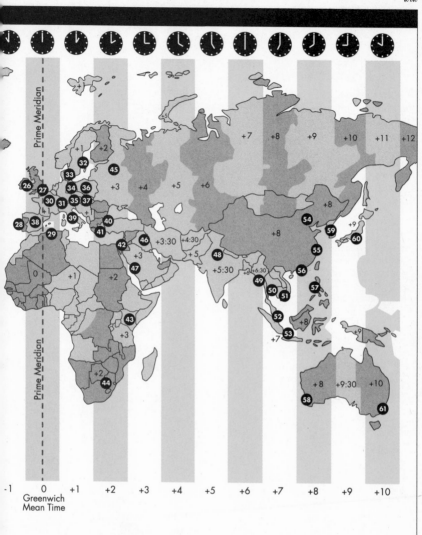

Introduction

by Chuck Stone

A senior editor of the Philadelphia Daily News, *Chuck Stone is professor of English at the University of Delaware.*

Yo, World!

Which is not a mere "hello," but a run-them-all-together salutation of "Hithere," "Howareya," and "Have-a-good-day."

Philadelphians claim credit for "Yo" as a greeting, although they concede it wasn't in vogue when Quaker William Penn founded Philadelphia or when the city's most distinguished citizen, Benjamin Franklin, prowled the streets in pensive solitude. Instead, a muscle-bound movie hero may be the source of its popularity.

In the movie *Rocky*, Philadelphians shout "Yo, Rocky!" as the underdog boxer jogs over some of the city's cobbled streets, through the open-air Italian market, up the Benjamin Franklin Parkway ("America's Champs Elysés"), and up the expansive steps of the Philadelphia Art Museum. Reaching the top, he raises his arms in a "V" in sweet anticipation of victory.

Today, many visitors try to imitate Rocky's dash up the 98 steps of this sandstone-color Greco-Roman building before entering to browse through its fabled art treasures. That irony is only one of the many examples of Philadelphia's *audacious uniqueness.*

Philadelphia is a fountainhead of superlatives cherished by both historians and tourists: the world's largest city-owned park, Fairmount Park; the oldest art school in America, the Pennsylvania Academy of Fine Arts; the first U.S. medical school to admit women, Women's Medical College of Pennsylvania; the oldest natural-science museum, the Academy of Natural Sciences; the oldest U.S. opera house still in use, the Academy of Music; the first library in America to circulate books, the Library Company founded by Benjamin Franklin; the world's largest sculpture atop a building, the statue of William Penn atop City Hall; the oldest black newspaper in America, the *Philadelphia Tribune;* the oldest African Methodist Episcopal church, Mother Bethel AME; and the nation's oldest street of continuous occupation, Elfreth's Alley, a narrow, one-block street of 33 Colonial homes in Center City (downtown).

All of these buildings still breathe architectural vitality. Or as that popular song cheerfully promises, "Everything old is new again."

But if love is a many-splendored thing, the name, Philadelphia, is a many-storied legend.

The "Philadelphia Lawyer," long a symbol of legal genius, was probably invented when a gout-ravaged, white-haired Philadelphian, Andrew Hamilton, successfully defended Peter Zenger in the nation's first libel case. The plaintiff was New York Governor William Cosby (no relation, of course, to a famous and cherished Philadelphia son, Bill Cosby).

The Philadelphia Story amused theatergoers with its inside peek at upper-class eccentricities.

The Philadelphia Negro, by W.E.B. duBois, set a standard for sociological research.

Philadelphia Cream Cheese enhances hors d'oeuvres (although the name alone doesn't claim to titillate taste buds).

And Philadelphians still yearn to make the world forget W.C. Fields's suggested impudence for his epitaph: "On the whole, I'd rather be in Philadelphia."

Classical-music lovers around the world pay homage to the Philadelphia Orchestra for its buoyant interpretations of Tchaikovsky. During the winter, the orchestra delights its fans in the Academy of Music's chandeliered splendor, a building modeled after La Scala Opera House. When summer comes, the orchestra moves to Fairmount Park's outdoor Frederic Mann Music Center where music lovers can lie on blankets under the stars and soar with the classics.

Musical diversity is a Philadelphia tradition.

Jazz still reflects the swinging sassiness of three Philadelphia jazz greats, Dizzy Gillespie, Stan Getz, and John Coltrane.

Popular music went through a golden period when South Philadelphia's "Golden Boys"—Frankie Avalon, Fabian, Jimmy Darren, and Bobby Rydell—seduced a whole generation into swooning to their love songs.

"Philly Sounds" still transform contemporary music with Teddy Pendergrass, the Ojays, the Stylistics, and the irrepressible Patti LaBelle, who can blow a hole in your soul every time she belts out a tune.

If Americans have "danced by the light of the moon," they owe that terpischorean pleasure to a Philadelphian. South Philadelphian Chubby Checkers popularized the "Twist" —and America's sacroiliacs have never been the same since.

Contrary to a Boston myth, the Philadelphia metropolitan area houses the nation's largest number of institutions of higher education, including a University for the Arts. *Parade Magazine* nominated Philadelphia's Central High School as one of the nation's 12 best high schools.

Given this explosive creativity, it's easy to understand why no city has nurtured the arts more lovingly. Visitors can share that affection when they visit the majestic Free Library with its Parthenon-like facade, the famed Rodin Museum, and the Pennsylvania Academy of the Fine Arts, a spectacular urban maharaja's palace.

But this "Athens of America" has also encouraged commerce to be an equally dominant force.

Four of the city's most distinctive buildings are the oval-front Philadelphia Merchants Exchange (1832) that majestically adjoins a cobblestoned street, the huge glass-paned dome that capacious Memorial Hall wears like a Victorian dowager's tiara, Independence Blue Cross's blue-glass-tinted headquarters, and the stately City Hall, an exquisite example of Second French Empire style.

Visitors to the nation's capital may have noticed the City Hall's architectural twin, the Executive Office Building, across the street from the White House.

Ironically, this same City Hall also became an excuse for resisting progress. An unspoken rule decreed that no building could be constructed higher than City Hall with its statue of William Penn on top. Eventually, Philadelphia's plow-resisting mentality succumbed to American ingenuity. Today, One Liberty Place fingers the sky as the city's tallest building, a spire-topped structure vaguely reminiscent of New York City's Art Deco Chrysler Building.

In the wintertime, Philadelphians follow convention. They lunch indoors. But when summer arrives, they lunch in their ubiquitous park. Fairmount Park winds through the city, an urban oasis from smoke-clogged, noisy traffic jams. Visitors can relax in its verdant serenity with noon-day picnics, softball tournaments, and family barbecues. A meandering Schuylkill River through the park also attracts a daily stream of neighborhood anglers and rowers from the city's 13 rowing clubs.

Because Quaker William Penn founded Philadelphia, Quakers quickly dominated the city's early political and commercial life. The Quaker City influence has diminished, but the memory lingers. Today, the nation's most enduring exercise in multiethnicity flavors the city's political and social life.

Although all of the city's founding fathers were WASPs, Philadelphia soon opened its arms to the world's "tired . . . huddled masses, yearning to be free." Successive waves of immigrants swarmed into Philadelphia as they did into New York City.

Mention the name of a neighborhood and Philadelphians will candidly identify its ethnic abundance: Italian South Philadelphia, black North Philadelphia, Irish Olney, Jewish Northeast, Puerto Rican Hunting Park, Chestnut Hill WASPs, Center City Chinatown, Vietnamese West Philadelphia, Polish Port Richmond, and Ukrainian Nicetown. Each enclave's lifestyles and restaurants exalt its ethnic heritage.

At the same time, the city's peoplescape is changing. Recently arrived yuppies are gentrifying black and Puerto Rican low-income neighborhoods within walking distance of Center City office buildings and the Art Museum. The relentless survival of ethnic neighborhoods, however, unfrocks a won't-lie-down-and-die spirit behind the city's name.

William Penn chose the name, "Philadelphia," a Greek word for "brotherly love." He hoped it would fill expectations for his "Holy Experiment"—"you shall be governed by laws of your own making, and live a free, and if you will, a sober and industrious people."

Since 1682, Philadelphia has diligently met all of those goals, even if the great journalist Lincoln Steffens dubbed it in 1903 "the worst-governed city in the country."

But Philadelphians have been forced to cope with the reality that their "City of Brotherly Love" is no more brotherly—nor even sisterly—than any other American city. Philadelphia has endured its share of white-black confrontations, other interethnic battles (early Colonialists roaming the streets, beating up the Germans and Quakers), and electoral decisions decided solely on race.

When the controversial ex-cop and colorful mayor, Frank L. Rizzo, held office, the Italian-American community provided his staunchest electoral base.

When the city's first black mayor, W. Wilson Goode, made a more perverse kind of history by approving the bombing of a neighborhood, black voters supported his reelection with 98% of their vote, even though an entire city block of black homes was incinerated and 11 blacks (including five children) were killed.

Every city should enjoy an interlude of greatness. Between 1949 and 1962 Richardson Dilworth and Joseph Clark dominated the city's politics, and "For one brief moment there was Camelot." Although the "Dilworth-Clark Renaissance" lasted only 13 years, it set a standard by which Philadelphia is still judged. These men dared to envision a people who would owe a higher loyalty to their city than their neighborhoods.

But Philadelphia's neighborhoods have triumphed because they are more than houses on a street. They are daily celebrations of life where families still sit on the marble steps of sentry-like rowhouses and gossip as the sun sets. They lounge in their bucolic backyards behind 12-room flagstone houses, attend religious services in Colonial-period churches, or just hang out on the street corner. "Yo, Angelo, your mother's lookin' for ya. Dinner's ready."

A *Washington Post* feature installed Philadelphia in the Culinary Hall of Fame with this observation of stunning authority: "There are four kinds of cuisine, Italian, French, Chinese and Philadelphia." Not only will the truth set you free, it will emancipate your taste buds. Succulent crabs are served in joyous heaps at world-famed Bookbinder's, Walt's, or DiNardo's. Cheesesteaks (as Philadelphian as the Liberty Bell), barbecue ribs (that will remind Southerners of home), hoagies (subs or hero sandwiches), pepper pot soup, Jewish deli corned beef, and Philadelphia's ubiquitous mustard-smeared pretzels cover the city's foodscape like a midwinter blizzard.

For food shopping, either the Reading Terminal Market in a cavernous railroad shed with its Amish farmers and Asian proprietors, or the outdoor Italian Market with barrel-by-carton sidewalk displays of fruits, vegetables, and exotic foods offer great money-saving values.

And then there's South Street, a one-thoroughfare adventure that combines the fascinations of New York's Greenwich Village and San Francisco's Ghirardelli Square. As Philadelphia *Daily News* writer Kathy Sheehan summed it up: "South Street must be the only street in America where, in one trip, you can do your laundry, watch live Jell-O wrestling, and buy a bridal gown, used books, natural foods, crazy hats, a mattress and box spring, wind-up toys, toilet paper, a VCR, key chains with condoms, Central American art, a box of wood screws, fresh flowers, used clothing, a fountain pen, window shades, water ice, margaritas, mint juleps, rolling papers, healing crystals, and Halloween masks."

Along the east bank of the Schuylkill River, boathouses are contoured by strings of white lights that brighten the dark night. It's a year-round festival of lights.

As the seasons change, so do the sports teams. Philadelphia's Eagles, the Flyers, the Phillies and the 76ers are supported by fanatically loyal fans. How fanatic? "Philadelphia fans will boo Santa Claus," a national newsmagazine once groused.

On New Year's Day, while Americans are recovering from night-before revelry and blearily watching football bowl games, energetic Philadelphians strut into the national limelight with their Mummers, gaudily plumaged string bands. After kicking up their frisky heels in an all-day parade of skits and dances, they dissolve into all-night neighborhood revelries.

But with all of Philadelphia's festive enticements, *caveat peregrinator* (let the tourist beware). As with any big city, Philadelphia does have a crime problem, although the efficiency of the PAVies might lead you to believe that illegal parking is the city's most serious offense.

PAVies (Parking Authority Vultures) will ticket your car if you pause one minute on a street to buy a hotdog or pick up a package. If you're parked in a "No stopping" zone, your car stands a good chance of being towed. Unsuspecting tourists have filled the columns of letters-to-the-editor with tales of horror because they erroneously assumed that the Philadelphia Parking Authority fanatics would exercise a reciprocal civility respected in their hometowns. In Philadelphia, PAVies don't. Beware of these ticket-writing zealots.

Yo, America!

Check out your "Cradle of Liberty" with its Independence Hall, Liberty Bell, Art Museum, cheesesteaks, Reading Terminal Market, ethnic neighborhoods, cobbled streets, hoagies, Center City boutiques, theaters, buoyant classical music, jazz nightclubs, the South Street cornucopia, and the neighborhood streets teeming with life.

As the rock groups at two simultaneous Live Aid concerts in London and Philadelphia sang, "We are the world, We are the children." In Philadelphia, we are the neighborhoods, we are the people—just like all of America.

1 Essential Information

Before You Go

Visitor Information

There are two centers to contact for free information on travel to Philadelphia and its environs: the **Philadelphia Convention and Visitors Bureau** (1515 Market St., Suite 2020, Philadelphia 19102, tel. 215/636–3300), and the **Philadelphia Visitors Center** (16th St. and John F. Kennedy Blvd., Philadelphia 19102, tel. 215/636–1666). You can also call the Visitors Center toll free (tel. 800/321–9563) to receive free brochures.

For further information on travel in Pennsylvania, contact the **Pennsylvania Division of Travel Marketing** (453 Forum Bldg., Harrisburg 17120, tel. 717/787–5453 or 800/VISIT–PA) for a free information packet.

Tour Groups

If you prefer to leave the driving to someone else, consider a package tour. Although you will have to march to the beat of a tour guide's drum, you are likely to save money on airfare, hotels, and ground transportation. For the more experienced or adventurous traveler, a variety of independent packages are available. Listed below are some options. Check with a travel agent or the Philadelphia Convention and Visitors Bureau for additional resources.

When considering a tour, be sure to find out exactly what expenses are included. Ask about tips, taxes, side trips, additional meals, and entertainment; ratings of all hotels on the itinerary and the facilities they offer; cancellation policies for both you and for the tour operator; and, if you are traveling alone, the amount of the single supplement. Most tour operators require that bookings be made through travel agents—there is no additional charge for doing so.

General-Interest Tours Cosmos/Globus Gateway (150 S. Los Robles Ave., Suite 860, Pasadena, CA 91101, tel. 818/449–0919 or 800/556–5454) takes you through Philadelphia on its "Historic East" package; other stops are Washington, DC; Virginia; and New York. "Historic Highlights" from **American Express Vacations** (Box 5014, Atlanta, GA 30302, tel. 800/241–1700, in Georgia, 800/282–0800) is similar, pausing at Gettysburg, Williamsburg, and Washington.

Package Deals for Independent Travelers

American Fly AAway Vacations (tel. 800/433–7300 or 817/355–1234) offers Philadelphia city packages with discounts on hotels and car rental. **Firstours** (12755 MN 55, Minneapolis, MN 55441, tel. 612/540–5000 or 800/223–6493) has two- and three-night packages with a choice of sightseeing trips. **American Express** includes a half-day sightseeing tour in its city package. Also check with **United Airlines** (tel. 312/952–4000 or 800/328–6877) for packages.

Tips for British Travelers

Passports and Customs You will need a valid 10-year passport (cost: £15). You will not need a visa if you are staying for less than 90 days, have a return ticket, and are flying with a participating airline. There are some exceptions to this, so for further information check with your travel agent or with the United States Embassy (Visa and Immigration Dept., 5 Upper Grosvenor St., London W1A 2JB, tel. 01/499–3443). No vaccinations are required.

Customs Visitors 21 or over can take in 200 cigarettes or 50 cigars or three pounds of tobacco, one U.S. quart of alcohol, and duty-free gifts to a value of $100. Be careful not to take in meat or meat products, seeds, plants, fruits, etc. Avoid illegal drugs like the plague.

Returning to Britain, you may bring home: (1) 200 cigarettes or 100 cigarillos or 50 cigars or 250 grams of tobacco; (2) two liters of table wine and, in addition, (a) one liter of alcohol over 22% by volume (most spirits), or (b) two liters of alcohol under 22% by volume (fortified or sparkling wine), or (c) two more liters of table wine; (3) 50 grams of perfume and ¼ liter of toilet water; and (4) other goods up to a value of £32.

Insurance We recommend that you insure yourself against health and motoring mishaps. **Europ Assistance** (252 High St., Croydon, Surrey CR0 1NF, tel. 01/680–1234) is a firm that offers this service.

It is also wise to take out insurance to cover loss of luggage (though check that this isn't already covered by any existing homeowner's policy you may have). Trip cancellation is another wise buy. The **Association of British Insurers** (Aldermary House, Queen St., London EC4N 1TT, tel. 01/248–4477) will give comprehensive advice on all aspects of vacation insurance.

Tour Operators Philadelphia is usually included on the itineraries of general tours.

Albany Travel (Manchester) Ltd. (190 Deansgate, Manchester M3 3WD, tel. 061/833–0202) offers a 14-night "Sights of the East" tour for the independent traveler that takes in Boston (three nights), New York (five nights), Philadelphia (three nights), and Washington, DC (three nights). Prices start at £1,042. It also has a "North-South Discovery" tour combining visits to Philadelphia, New York, and Washington with those to Orlando, Disney World, and Miami Beach. This tour lasts 14 nights; prices range from £999 to £1,096, depending on when you travel.

Speedbird (152 King St., London W6 0QU, tel. 01/741–8041) offers fly-drive holidays. Prices for a one-week stay including return airfare from London to Philadelphia and car hire start at £406.

Other travel agencies that will help you plan your trip to Philadelphia include:
Cosmosair plc (Tourama House, 17 Homesdale Rd., Bromley, Kent BR2 9LX, tel. 01/464–3400).
Jetsave (Sussex House, London Rd., East Grinstead, Sussex RH19 1LD, tel. 0342/312022).
Thomas Cook Ltd. (Box 36, Thorpe Wood, Peterborough PE3 6SB, tel. 0733/503202).

The independent traveler should check flight-only deals with the airlines. Try **British Airways** (tel. 01/897–4000), **Air France** (tel. 01/499-6511), and **Pan American World Airways** (tel. 01/409–4090). You may be lucky and find a round-trip fare to Philadelphia for as little as £199, if you can satisfy all the complex booking conditions; APEX fares start at £353. The small ads in newspapers are another good source for last-minute, low-cost flights.

Electricity 110 volts. You should take along an adaptor since American razor and hair-dryer sockets require flat, two-prong plugs.

When to Go

Late spring and early fall are the best times to visit Philadelphia. Like other northern American cities, Philadelphia can be uncomfortably hot and humid in the summer and freezing cold in winter (winter snowfall averages 21 inches).

However, any time is right to enjoy the special pleasures offered throughout the year. For sports fans, the schedule is packed with exciting competition year-round. In the **spring,** the city is at its most beautiful, when the cherry blossoms come into bloom, followed by azaleas, tulips, and dogwood. The city shows off with its Easter Parade and open-house tours.

In **summer,** the Philadelphia Orchestra gives free concerts at the Mann Music Center; there are also free performances at Penn's Landing and other outdoor plazas. The Freedom Festival celebrates the nation's birth and Philadelphia's part in it with hot-air-balloon races, restaurant extravaganzas, and special ceremonies.

Autumn offers Super Sunday, a giant block party, as well as numerous parades and the Army-Navy football classic. In **winter,** the highlight is the spectacular Mummer's Parade on New Year's Day. The orchestra, theater, and ballet seasons are in full swing; and the famous Philadelphia Flower Show takes center stage.

Climate The following are average daily maximum and minimum temperatures for Philadelphia.

Jan.	40F	4C	May	72F	22C	Sept.	76F	24C
	26	− 3		54	12		60	16
Feb.	41F	5C	June	80F	27C	Oct.	66F	19C
	27	− 3		62	17		50	10
Mar.	49F	9C	July	85F	29C	Nov.	53F	
	61F	16C	Aug.	83F	28C	Dec.	43F	6C
	43	6		67	19		30	− 1

Weather Trak provides information on 235 cities around the world—180 of them in the United States. To obtain the Weather Trak telephone number for your area, call 800/247–3282. The local number plays a taped message that tells you to dial a three-digit access code for the destination you're interested in. The code is either the area code (in the United States) or the first three letters of the foreign city. For a list of all access codes, send a self-addressed stamped envelope to Cities, Box 7000, Dallas, TX 75209, or call 214/869–3035 or 800/247–3282.

Festivals and Seasonal Events

Top seasonal events in Philadelphia start with the Mummer's Parade on New Year's Day. Other major events are the Philadelphia Flower Show in March, the spectacular July 4 fireworks, and the Thanksgiving Day Parade. For the exact date and further information about these and other events, contact the **Philadelphia Visitors Center** (16th St. and John F. Kennedy Blvd., Philadelphia 19102, tel. 215/636–1666).

Jan. 1: Mummer's Parade happens only in Philadelphia. An all-day event during which some 30,000 sequined and feathered paraders—members of string bands, "fancies," "brigades," and comics—march north on Broad Street to City Hall.

Late Feb.: Ebel U.S. Pro Indoor Tennis Championships attract many of the world's top men tennis pros. *The Spectrum, Broad St. and Pattison Ave., Philadelphia 19148, tel. 215/947–2530.*

Feb.: Black History Month features exhibits, lectures, and music at the Afro-American Historical and Cultural Museum, plus a number of other events around the city. *Afro-American Historical and Cultural Museum, 7th and Arch Sts., Philadelphia 19106, tel. 215/574–0380.*

Feb.: Philadelphia Boat Show displays more than 500 yachts, sailboats, and powerboats. *Philadelphia Civic Center, 34th St. and Civic Center Blvd., Philadelphia 19104, tel. 215/823–7400.*

Feb.: Mummer's String Band Show of Shows is a chance to see what you missed on New Year's Day. *Philadelphia Civic Center, 34th St. and Civic Center Blvd., Philadelphia 19104, tel. 215/823–7400.*

Feb.–May: Chinese New Year celebrations include 10-course banquets Tuesday through Sunday night beginning at 6:30 PM. Chefs come from China to prepare the feast. *Chinese Cultural Center, 125 N. 10th St., Philadelphia 19107, tel. 215/923–6767.*

Sunday nearest Mar. 17: St. Patrick's Day Parade displays the green along Benjamin Franklin Parkway. For information, call the Visitors Center (tel. 215/636–1666).

Mar.: Philadelphia Flower Show, the nation's largest indoor flower show, features acres of landscapes, flowers, and other exhibits. *Philadelphia Civic Center, 34th St. and Civic Center Blvd., Philadelphia 19104, tel. 215/625–8250.*

Mar.: The Book and the Cook teams the city's best chefs and the world's top cookbook authors in a four-day event. Meet the authors and sample their dishes. Held at area restaurants. For information, contact the Visitors Center (tel. 215/636–1666).

Mar.–May: American Music Theater Festival presents opera, musical comedy, cabaret-style revues, children's programs, and experimental works at indoor and outdoor theaters around the city. *Tel. 215/440–8282.*

Apr.: Philadelphia Antique Show offers museum-quality antiques, lectures, and appraisals to benefit the Hospital of the University of Pennsylvania. *103rd Engineers Armory, 33rd St. above Market St., Philadelphia 19104, tel. 215/636–1666.*

Apr.: Easter Promenade celebrates the holiday with a stroll down Walnut Street, and features music, entertainment, celebrities, and a fashion contest at Rittenhouse Square. *18th and Walnut Sts., tel. 215/686–2876.*

Apr.: Penn Relays is one of the world's oldest and largest amateur track meets. *Franklin Field, 33rd and Spruce Sts., Philadelphia 19104, tel. 215/898–6151.*

Apr.: St. Walpurgis Night Festival, the traditional Swedish welcome to spring, offers food, song, dance, and bonfires. *American Swedish Historical Museum, 1900 Pattison Ave., Philadelphia 19145, tel. 215/389–1776.*

Late Apr.–early May: Friends Hospital Garden Days boast 40 varieties of azaleas in bloom on 15 acres of the hospital grounds. *Roosevelt Blvd. and Adams Ave., Philadelphia 19124, tel. 215/831–4772.*

May: Philadelphia Open House is a two-week period during which selected private homes, gardens, and historic buildings in neighborhoods around the city—including Society Hill, Germantown, and the Main Line—open their doors to the public. *Tel. 215/928–1188.*

Mid-May: Israel Independence Day celebrates the birth of the State of Israel in 1948 with a bazaar, live music, and a Center-City parade. In 1990 it falls on May 20. *Tel. 215/922–7222.*

Third Thursday in May: Rittenhouse Square Flower Market has plants and flowers for sale, food, and a children's amusement corner. *18th and Walnut Sts., tel. 215/525–7182.*

Late May–early June: Devon Horse Show and Country Fair, first held in 1896, is a week-long event that draws up to 150,000 spectators. Top riders compete for more than $200,000 in prize money. *Devon Fairgrounds, U.S. 30, Devon 19333, tel. 215/964–0550.*

Late May: Jambalaya Jam celebrates New Orleans featuring such specialties as pralines, gumbo, jambalaya, and other Creole and Cajun food favorites; bands playing ragtime, Dixieland, and jazz music; and Louisiana crafts. On the Great Plaza at Penn's Landing. *Tel. 215/923–4992.*

June: Rittenhouse Square Fine Arts Annual, America's oldest (1931) and largest outdoor juried art show, exhibits paintings and sculpture by more than 100 Delaware Valley artists. *Rittenhouse Sq., 18th and Walnut Sts., tel. 215/636–1666.*

First weekend in June: Elfreth's Alley Days is the only time when residents of America's oldest continuously occupied street open their homes to the public. The occasion includes food, fife-and-drum music, and Colonial crafts. *Elfreth's Alley, between Front, 2nd, Arch, and Race Sts., tel. 215/574–0560.*

June: Mellon Jazz Festival presents the top names in jazz in a week-long series of concerts at the Mann Music Center, West Fairmount Park, and the Academy of Music, Broad and Locust streets. *Tel. 215/893–1999.*

Late June: CoreStates Pro Cycling Championship, the country's premier bicycle race, attracts the world's top cyclists. The 156-mile race begins and ends at the Benjamin Franklin Parkway and includes 10 grueling trips up the Manayunk "Wall." *Tel. 215/636–1666.*

Last weekend in June: America's Great Teddy Bear Rally gathers teddy bears and their owners for parades, festivities, and contests. The 1990 rally will have a bear talent show, an ailing-bear clinic, and paw readers. *Philadelphia Zoo, 34th St. and Girard Ave., tel. 215/243–1100.*

June–Aug.: Head House Crafts Fair. Set in a Colonial outdoor market, the fair has more than 40 artisans exhibiting jewelry, stained glass, leather, and quilts on summer weekends from noon to midnight Saturday, noon to 6 PM Sunday. *2nd and Pine Sts., tel. 215/864–0709.*

June–Aug.: Philadelphia Orchestra's Summer Season holds free concerts Monday, Wednesday, and Thursday evenings. *Mann*

Music Center, 52nd St. and Parkside Ave., Philadelphia 19131, tel. 215/878-7707 or 215/567-0707.

July: Freedom Festival. The city celebrates the nation's birth with several days of parades (including the Mummers), hot-air-balloon races, a drum-and-bugle competition, Independence Day ceremonies at Independence Hall, and the Old City Outdoor Restaurant Festival. It all culminates in a grand old-fashioned July 4 fireworks display. *Tel. 215/636-1666.*

July: Riverblues is a weekend waterfront festival featuring the top names in blues. *On the Great Plaza at Penn's Landing, tel. 215/636-1666.*

July-Aug.: Robin Hood Dell East presents top musicians and dancers in low-cost concerts. *Robin Hood Dell East, Strawberry Mansion Dr., Philadelphia 19132, tel. 215/477-8810.*

Late Aug.: Philadelphia Folk Festival, America's oldest continuous folk festival, consists of three days of concerts and workshops. Performers featured range from the relatively new and unknown to folk superstars. There's also food, crafts, folk dancing, impromptu jam sessions, and sing-alongs. Many "folkies" camp out on the grounds. *Old Pool Farm, Schwenksville 19473, tel. 215/242-0150.*

Sept.: International In-Water Boat Show, the largest in-water boat show on the East Coast, fills the 10-acre basin in Penn's Landing with yachts and other pleasure craft. *Penn's Landing, tel. 215/449-9910.*

Sept.: Puerto Rican Day Parade honors Philadelphia's Puerto Rican residents. *Tel. 215/636-1666.*

Last Saturday in Sept.: Von Steuben Day Parade, along Benjamin Franklin Parkway, honors the Prussian general who trained the Continental soldiers at Valley Forge. *Tel. 215/636-1666.*

Oct.: Pulaski Day Parade. The Polish American Congress honors a hero of the Revolutionary War, the Polish general known as the "father of the American Cavalry," with a parade up Broad Street. *Tel. 215/636-1666.*

Second Monday in Oct.: Columbus Day Parade includes both a parade on South Broad Street and a festival at Marconi Plaza, the parade terminus south of Oregon Avenue. *Tel. 215/636-1666.*

Oct. 31: Halloween is when several "haunted houses" open their doors to the public. Check newspapers for details.

Early Nov.: Philadelphia Craft Show is three days of exhibits and sales by 100 craftspeople from around the country. *103rd Engineers Armory, 33rd St. above Market St., tel. 215/636-1666.*

Nov.: Philadelphia Independence Marathon draws several thousand runners for the 26.2-mile race through Philadelphia neighborhoods to the finish line at Independence Hall. *Tel. 215/686-0051.*

Nov. or Dec: Dog Show. The Kennel Club of Philadelphia sponsors this event, which draws more than 3,000 entries. *Philadelphia Civic Center, 34th St. and Civic Center Blvd., Philadelphia 19104, tel. 215/823-7327.*

Late Nov.: Thanksgiving Day Parade features thousands of marchers, floats, and local personalities. The finale shows the arrival of Santa Claus to usher in the Christmas shopping season. *Benjamin Franklin Pkwy., tel. 215/636-1666.*

Dec.: Christmas Tours of Historic Houses take visitors around historic Fairmount Park and Germantown houses decorated with Christmas finery. *Tel. 215/763-8100 or 215/848-1777.*

Dec.: John Wanamaker's Light Show is a gala display with pipe-organ music held hourly in the Grand Court of the department store. *Wanamaker's, 13th and Market Sts., tel. 215/422–2450.*
Dec.: The Nutcracker. The Pennsylvania Ballet's production of the Tchaikovsky classic is a Philadelphia Yuletide tradition. *Academy of Music, Broad and Locust Sts., tel. 215/893–1935.*
Dec.: Washington Crossing the Delaware. The historic event that occurred on Christmas Day 1776—when Washington took the Hessian camp at Trenton by surprise—has since been reenacted 37 times. There are more than 200 participants—120 in four 40-foot replicas of Durham boats used by Washington and his troops. *Washington Crossing Historic Park, Washington Crossing 18977, tel. 215/493–4076.*

What to Pack

Pack light because porters and luggage trolleys are hard to find. Luggage allowances on domestic flights vary slightly from airline to airline. Most allow three checked pieces and one carry-on. Some offer the option of two checked and two carry-ons. In all cases, check-in luggage cannot weigh more than 70 pounds apiece or exceed 62 inches (total of length plus width plus height). Carry-on luggage cannot exceed 45 inches (length plus width plus height) and must fit under the seat or in the overhead luggage compartment.

Philadelphia is a fairly casual city, although men will need a jacket and tie in some of the better restaurants. Pack slightly dressy outfits for elegant restaurants, informal clothes for elsewhere. Jeans and sneakers or other casual clothing are fine for sightseeing. You'll need a heavy coat for winter, which can be cold and snowy. Summers are hot and humid but you'll need a shawl or jacket for air-conditioned restaurants. Many interesting neighborhoods and historic areas are best explored on foot, so bring good walking shoes.

Cash Machines

Virtually all U.S. banks belong to a network of ATMs (Automatic Teller Machines) which dispense cash 24 hours a day. Some eight major networks operate in the United States, the largest of which are Cirrus (owned by MasterCard) and the Plus System (affiliated with Visa). Some banks belong to more than one network. ATM cards are not automatically issued; you have to request them from your bank. If your bank doesn't belong to at least one network you should consider moving funds, for ATMs are becoming as essential as check cashing. Visa and MasterCard may also be used in the ATMs, but the service charges are usually higher than the fees on bank cards. Bank cards also impose a daily interest charge on the loan that begins on the day of the transaction. To locate a Cirrus affiliate in Philadelphia, call 800/4–CIRRUS; the Plus System number is 800/THE–PLUS. Check with your bank for fees and any limits on the amount of cash you can withdraw on any day.

Traveling with Film

If your camera is new, shoot and develop a few rolls of film before leaving home. Pack some lens tissue and an extra battery for your built-in light meter. Invest about $10 in a skylight filter and screw it onto the front of your lens: It will protect the lens and also reduce haze.

Film doesn't like hot weather. If you're driving in summer, don't store film in the glove compartment or on the shelf under the rear window. Put it behind the front seat on the floor, on the side opposite the exhaust pipe.

On a plane trip, never pack unprocessed film in check-in luggage; if your bags get X-rayed, you may lose your pictures. Always hand-carry undeveloped film through security and ask to have it inspected by hand. (For quick inspection, isolate your film in a plastic bag.) Inspectors at U.S. airports are required by law to honor requests for hand inspection; abroad, you'll have to depend on the kindness of strangers. The old airport scanning machines—still in use in some Third World countries —use heavy doses of radiation that can turn a family portrait into an early-morning fog. The newer models—used in all U.S. airports—are safe for anything from five to 500 scans, depending on the speed of your film. The effects are cumulative; you can put the same roll of film through several scans without worry. After five scans, though, you're asking for trouble.

If your film gets fogged and you want an explanation, send it to the National Association of Photographic Manufacturers, 600 Mamaroneck Ave., Harrison, NY 10528. It will try to determine what went wrong. The service is free.

Traveling with Children

Publications
: *Family Travel Times* is an 8- to 12-page newsletter published 10 times a year by TWYCH (Travel with Your Children, 80 Eighth Ave., New York, NY 10011, tel. 212/206–0688). Subscription includes access to back issues and twice-weekly opportunities to call in for specific advice. *Great Vacations with Your Kids: The Complete Guide to Family Vacations in the U.S.*, by Dorothy Ann Jordon and Marjorie Adoff Cohen (E. P. Dutton, $9.95), details everything from city vacations to adventure vacations to child-care resources.

Hotels
: The Four Seasons Hotel Philadelphia (1 Logan Sq., Philadelphia 19103, tel. 215/963–1500) allows children under 17 to stay free in their parents' room, runs holiday tea parties for kids, and provides a *Family Activities and Children's Services* brochure for guests. The **Guest Quarters Suite Hotels** in the Philadelphia area (tel. 800/424–2900) offer the luxury of two-room suites with kitchen facilities plus children's menus in the restaurants; children under 18 stay free in their parents' suite. Most **Days Inn** hotels (tel. 800/325–2525) charge only a nominal fee for children under 18 and allow kids 12 and under to eat free.

Home Exchange
: See *Home Exchanging: A Complete Sourcebook for Travelers at Home or Abroad* by James Dearing (Globe Pequot Press, Box Q, Chester, CT 06412, tel. 800/243–0495 or in CT 800/962–0973).

Getting There
: On domestic flights, children under two not occupying a seat travel free. Various discounts apply to children 2 to 12. Reserve a seat behind the bulkhead of the plane: They offer more leg room and can usually fit a bassinet (supplied by the airline). At the same time, inquire about special children's meals or snacks which most airlines offer. Ask the airline in advance if you can bring aboard your child's car seat. (For the booklet, *Child/*

Infant Safety Seats Acceptable for Use in Aircraft, write Community and Consumer Liaison Division, APA–400 Federal Aviation Administration, Washington, DC 20591, tel. 202/267–3479.)

Baby-sitting Services   Make child-care arrangements with the hotel concierge or housekeeper, or contact **Rocking Horse Child-Care Center** (6th and Walnut Sts., Curtis Center, Suite 25 LL, Philadelphia 19106, tel. 215/592–8257), which offers part- and full-time care for children ages 6 weeks to 6 years, with a maximum stay of 5 days. Of special interest to visitors: The "Bearly There" program that provides *hourly* care at $5 an hour for children 2 years and under; $4 an hour for ages 3 to 6.

Hints for Disabled Travelers

The **Visitors Information Center** (Bourse Bldg., 21 S. 5th St., Philadelphia 19106, tel. 215/923–6317) has free brochures for disabled travelers.
The **Information Center for Individuals with Disabilities** (20 Park Plaza, Room 330, Boston, MA 02116, tel. 617/727–5540) offers useful problem-solving assistance, including lists of travel agents that specialize in tours for the disabled.
Moss Rehabilitation Hospital Travel Information Service (12th St. and Taber Rd., Philadelphia 19141, tel. 215/329–5715) provides information on tourist sights, transportation, and accommodations in destinations around the world. The fee is $5 per destination; allow one month for delivery.
Mobility International (Box 3551, Eugene, OR 97403, tel. 503/343–1284) has information on accommodations, organized study, etc., around the world.
The **Society for the Advancement of Travel for the Handicapped** (26 Court St., Penthouse Suite, Brooklyn, NY 11242, tel. 718/858–5483) offers access information. Annual membership costs $40, $25 for senior travelers and students. For information, send $1 and a stamped, self-addressed envelope.
Travel Industry and Disabled Exchange (TIDE) (5435 Donna Ave., Tarzana, CA 91356, tel. 818/343–6339) is an industry-based organization with a $15-per-person annual membership fee. Members receive a quarterly newsletter and information on travel agencies and tours.
Greyhound/Trailways (tel. 800/531–5332) will carry a disabled person and companion for the price of a single fare. With 24 hours' notice, **Amtrak** (tel. 800/USA–RAIL) will provide redcap service, special seats, and a 25% discount.
The Itinerary (Box 1084, Bayonne, NJ 07002, tel. 201/858–3400) is a bimonthly travel magazine for the disabled.

Hints for Older Travelers

The **American Association of Retired Persons** (AARP) (1909 K St. NW, Washington, DC 20049, tel. 202/662–4850) has two programs for independent travelers: (1) The **Purchase Privilege Program** offers discounts on hotels, airfare, car rentals, and sightseeing; and (2) the **AARP Motoring Plan** offers emergency aid and trip-routing information for an annual fee of $29.95 per couple. The AARP also arranges group tours, including apartment living in Europe, through two companies: **Olson-Travelworld** (5855 Green Valley Circle, Culver City, CA 90230, tel. 800/227–7737) and **RFD, Inc.** (4401 W. 110th St., Overland

Park, KS 66211, tel. 800/448–7010). AARP members must be 50 or older. Annual dues are $5 per person or couple.

When using an AARP or other identification card, ask for a reduced hotel rate at the time you make your reservation or check in—not when you check out. Since restaurant discounts may be limited to certain set menus, days, or hours, present your card before being seated. When renting a car, remember that promotional rates on economy cars may be less than cars available with the AARP discount.

Elderhostel (80 Boylston St., Suite 400, Boston, MA 02116, tel. 617/426–7788) is an innovative 13-year-old program for people 60 and older. Participants live in dorms on some 1,200 campuses around the world. Mornings are devoted to lectures and seminars; afternoons to sightseeing and field trips. The all-inclusive fee for two- to three-week trips, including room, board, tuition, and round-trip transportation, is from $1,700 to $3,200.

National Council of Senior Citizens (925 15th St. NW, Washington, DC 20005, tel. 202/347–8800) is a nonprofit advocacy group with some 4,000 local clubs across the country. Annual membership is $10 per person or $14 per couple. Members receive a monthly newspaper with travel information and an ID card for reduced-rate hotels and car rentals.

Mature Outlook (Box 1205, Glenview, IL 60025, tel. 800/336–6330), a subsidiary of Sears, Roebuck & Co., is a travel club for people over 50, with hotel and motel discounts and a bimonthly newsletter. Annual membership is $7.50 per couple. Instant membership is available at participating Holiday Inns.

Travel Tips for Senior Citizens (U.S. Dept. of State Publication 8970, revised Sept. 1987) is available for $1 from the Superintendent of Documents, U.S. Government Printing Office, Washington, DC 20402.

Golden Age Passport is a free lifetime pass to all parks, monuments, and recreation areas run by the federal government. People over 62 can pick them up at any national park that charges admission. Driver's license or other proof of age is required.

Further Reading

Walking Tours of Historic Philadelphia, by well-known Philadelphiaphile John Francis Marion, is the best book of its kind. The Foundation for Architecture's *Philadelphia Architecture: A Guide to the City* contains maps, photos, biographies of noted Philadelphia architects, and detailed descriptions of almost 400 sites. *Sculpture of a City,* produced by the Fairmount Park Art Association, contains informative text and beautiful photos. *Philadelphia's Outdoor Art: A Walking Tour,* by Roslyn F. Brenner, is an excellent guide to the more than 50 works of art along Benjamin Franklin Parkway. *1787: The Day to Day Story of the Constitutional Convention* and Catherine Drinker Bowen's *Miracle at Philadelphia* both tell the story of the Constitution.

For biographies of seven Philadelphians, read *Philadelphia: Patricians and Philistines, 1900 to 1950,* by John Lukacs. *Principato,* by Tom McHale, is a family saga set in Philadelphia.

Other selections are *Country Walks Near Philadelphia,* by Alan Fisher; *Philadelphia One-Day Trip Book,* by Jane Ochevhausen Smith; *Philadelphia Preserved,* by Richard Webster; *Philadelphia—A Dream for the Keeping,* by John Guinther; *Country Inns, Lodges and Historic Hotels of the Mid-Atlantic States,* by Anthony Hitchcock and Jean Lindgren; *God's Pocket,* by Pete Dexter; *The Philadelphia Trivia Quiz,* by Bernard M. Stiefel; and *Philadelphia with Children,* by Elizabeth Gephart.

Arriving and Departing

"Temporary inconvenience; permanent improvement." That's been the catchphrase for Philadelphia transportation for decades. By and large, the transportation system has been getting better. The Center City commuter rail tunnel is operating; an express train connects the airport and downtown; the airport has been expanded and improved; and Interstate 95, the superhighway that stretches from Maine to Florida, now runs unbroken through Philadelphia.

But temporary inconveniences abound. Construction projects continue to tie up major arteries into and through the city. And there still aren't enough highway signs or exits to Center City off the major approach roads.

By Plane

Be sure to distinguish among nonstop flights—no changes, no stops; direct flights—no changes but one or more stops; and connecting flights—two or more planes, two or more stops.

Philadelphia International Airport (tel. 215/492–3181) is located in the southwest part of the city, 8 miles from downtown. It's served by **American** (tel. 800/433–7300), **Continental** (tel. 800/ 525–0280), **Delta** (tel. 800/221–1212), **Eastern** (tel. 800/327–8376), **TWA** (tel. 800/221–2000), **Midway** (tel. 800/621–2272), **United** (tel. 800/241–6522), **Northwest** (tel. 800/225–2525), and **USAir** (tel. 800/231–3131). International carriers are **Air Jamaica** (tel. 800/523–5585), **British Airways** (tel. 800/247–9297), **Lufthansa** (tel. 800/645–3880), and **Mexicana** (tel. 800/531–7921).

Luggage Regulations
Checked Luggage U.S. airlines allow passengers to check in two suitcases whose total dimensions (length plus width plus height) do not exceed 60 inches. There are no weight restrictions on these bags.

Rules governing foreign airlines vary, so check with your travel agent or the airline before you go. All the airlines allow passengers to check in two bags. In general, the two bags may not weigh more than 70 pounds. The size restriction on the first bag is 62 inches total dimensions, and 55 inches total dimensions on the second bag.

Carry-on Luggage Passengers on U.S. airlines are limited to two carry-on bags. For a bag you wish to store under the seat, the maximum dimensions are 9 x 14 x 22, a total of 45 inches. For bags that can be hung in a closet or on a luggage rack, the maximum dimensions are 4 x 23 x 45, a total of 72 inches. For bags you wish to store in an overhead bin, the maximum dimensions are 10 x 14 x 36, a total of 60 inches. Your two carry-ons must each fit one of these sets of dimensions; any item that exceeds the specified dimensions will generally be handled as checked baggage. Keep in mind that an airline can adapt these rules to circumstances, so on an especially crowded flight you may be allowed only one carry-on bag.

In addition to the two carry-ons, you may also bring aboard: a handbag (pocketbook or purse); an overcoat or wrap; an umbrella; a camera; a reasonable amount of reading material; an infant bag; crutches, cane, braces, or other prosthetic device upon which the passenger is dependent; and an infant/child safety seat.

Note that these regulations apply to U.S. airlines only. Foreign airlines generally allow one piece of carry-on luggage in economy class, in addition to handbags and duty-free goods. Passengers in first and business class are also allowed to carry on one garment bag. Check with the airline ahead of time to find its rules regarding carry-on luggage.

Luggage Insurance
Lost Luggage

Airlines are responsible for lost or damaged property only up to $1,250 per passenger on domestic flights, $9.07 per pound (or $20 per kilo) for checked baggage on international flights, and up to $400 per passenger for unchecked baggage on international flights. If you're traveling with valuables, either carry them with you on the airplane or purchase additional insurance for lost luggage. Some airlines sell additional luggage insurance when you check in, but many do not.

Insurance for lost, damaged, or stolen luggage is available through the airline, travel agents, or directly through various insurance companies. **Tele-Trip** (tel. 800/228–9792), a subsidiary of Mutual of Omaha, operates sales booths at airports, and also issues insurance through travel agents. Tele-Trip insures checked luggage for up to 180 days and for $500 to $3,000 valuation. For one to three days, the rate for a $500 valuation is $8.25; for 180 days, $100. The **Travelers Insurance Co.** will insure checked or hand luggage for $500 to $2,000 valuation per person for a maximum of 180 days. Rates for one to five days for $500 valuation are $10; for 180 days, $85. For more information, write The Travelers Insurance Company, Ticket and Travel Department, 1 Tower Square, Hartford, CT 06183. Both companies offer the same rates on domestic and international flights.

Before you go, itemize the contents of each bag in case you need to file an insurance claim. Put your home address on each piece of luggage, including carry-on bags. If your luggage is lost and later recovered, the airline must deliver the luggage to your home free of charge.

Smoking

If smoking bothers you, ask for a seat in the nonsmoking section. FAA regulations require U.S. scheduled and chartered airlines to provide seats in the nonsmoking section for any passenger who complies with the airline's check-in time requirements (usually 10–15 minutes before scheduled departure).

From the Airport to Center City

Airport Express trains run between the airport and downtown stations. Trains leave every 30 minutes from 6:10 AM to 12:10 AM. The trip takes about 20 minutes and costs $4.

Taxis are plentiful at the airport but are very expensive—around $17 plus tip. At $6 per person, "limos" (vans, not stretch limousines) are cheaper, but service is less frequent and most limos stop only at certain hotels and downtown points.

By Car

Getting to and around Philadelphia by car is often difficult and, at rush hour, it can be a nightmare. The main east–west freeway through the city, the Schuylkill Expressway (I–76), is often tied up for miles.

The main north–south highway through Philadelphia, the Delaware Expressway (I–95), is complete and all lanes are open. Because I–95 has no Center City exit northbound, motorists have to choose one of several alternative routes into town. The best bet is to exit I–95 at Broad Street and take Broad Street north to Center City.

To reach Center City heading southbound on I–95, take the Vine Street exit.

From the west, the Pennsylvania Turnpike begins at the Ohio border and intersects the Schuylkill Expressway (I–76) at Valley Forge. The Schuylkill Expressway, now undergoing renovation, has several exits in Center City. The Northeast Extension of the turnpike runs from Scranton to Plymouth Meeting, north of Philadelphia. From the east, the New Jersey Turnpike and I–295 access U.S. 30, which enters the city via the Benjamin Franklin Bridge, or New Jersey Route 42 and the Walt Whitman Bridge into South Philadelphia.

For routing information, AAA members can call the Keystone Automobile Club (tel. 215/569–4321).

Car Rentals

Renting a car in Philadelphia is not essential if you're staying in the city. With widespread public transportation like the PATCO High Speed Line, the Market-Frankford El, and 100 bus and trolley routes, major city attractions are easily accessible. Moreover, construction in several areas will tie up traffic in 1990.

Philadelphia's downtown grid makes driving easy for the out-of-towner. Major companies such as **Hertz** (tel. 800/654–3131), **Avis** (tel. 800/331–1212), **Budget** (tel. 800/527–0700), and **Dollar** (tel. 800/421–6868) have downtown and airport locations. Lower-price companies include **Enterprise** (tel. 215/521–3700) and **Ugly Duckling Rent-A-Car** (tel. 215/336–8459). Expect to pay $40 to $50 per day for a subcompact, usually with 100 free miles daily, from the major companies. Always ask for a reservation number when you call.

By Train

A major stop on **Amtrak's** Northeast Corridor line, Philadelphia is less than 90 minutes from New York City and only two hours from Washington, DC, and 80 minutes from Atlantic City. Amtrak trains stop at the 30th Street Station, 30th and Market streets. Another stop, North Philadelphia Station, is in a dangerous neighborhood; avoid it unless you have a special reason to get off there. Amtrak also serves Philadelphia from points west, including Harrisburg, Pittsburgh, and

Chicago. For Amtrak information, phone 215/824–1600 or 800/872–7245.

At 30th Street Station you can connect with Southeastern Pennsylvania Transportation Authority (SEPTA) commuter trains to two downtown stations—Suburban Station at 16th Street and John F. Kennedy Boulevard (near major hotels), and Market East Station at 10th and Market streets (near the historic district)—and to outlying areas.

By Bus

Greyhound/Trailways operates long-haul service out of a new terminal at 10th and Filbert streets, just north of the Market East commuter rail station. For information, call your local Greyhound number or 215/931–4000. NJ Transit (tel. 215/569–3752) stops at the Greyhound/Trailways terminal and offers service between Philadelphia, Atlantic City, and other New Jersey destinations.

Staying in Philadelphia

Important Addresses and Numbers

Tourist Information
The **Philadelphia Convention and Visitors Bureau** (tel. 215/636–1666) operates the Philadelphia Visitors Center at 16th Street and John F. Kennedy Boulevard, one block from City Hall. Open 9–6 daily. The **National Park Service** (tel. 215/597–8974) operates a Visitor Center at 3rd and Chestnut streets in the heart of the historic district. Open 9–5 daily. For a recorded message, call 215/627–1776.

Emergencies
Dial 911 for assistance. Or go to a hospital emergency room. The hospital closest to the historic area is **Pennsylvania Hospital** (8th and Spruce Sts., tel. 215/829–3358). The hospital closest to City Hall is **Hahnemann University Hospital** (Broad and Vine Sts., tel. 215/448–7963). Closest to Rittenhouse Square is **Graduate Hospital** (1800 Lombard St., tel. 215/893–2350).

Pharmacies
Downtown, **Corson's Pharmacy** (15th and Spruce Sts., tel. 215/735–1386) is open 9 AM to 10 PM Monday–Saturday, and until 3 PM Sunday. **Medical Tower Pharmacy** (255 S. 17th St., tel. 215/545–3525) is open 8:30 AM to 9 PM weekdays and until 5 PM Saturday.

Getting Around

The Southeastern Pennsylvania Transportation Authority (SEPTA) operates an extensive network of buses, trolleys, subways, and commuter trains.

By Subway, Trolley, and Bus
The Broad Street Subway runs from Fern Rock Station in the northern part of the city to Pattison Avenue and the sports complex in South Philadelphia. The Market–Frankford Line runs across the city from the western suburb of Upper Darby to Frankford in the northeast. Both lines operate 24 hours a day, albeit with service every 30 minutes between 1 and 5 AM.

With 10 routes, Philadelphia is one of the few U.S. cities that still operate trolleys. Route 23—the longest trolley ride in the nation —passes through some of the best neighborhoods and some of the worst on its 13-mile, one-hour-plus run between South Philadelphia and Chestnut Hill.

Buses comprise the bulk of the SEPTA system, with 91 routes extending throughout the city and into the suburbs.

The base fare for subways, trolleys, and buses is $1.25. Transfers cost 25¢. Exact change is required. Senior citizens (with a valid ID card) ride free during off-peak hours and holidays and pay half fare the rest of the time. For route information, call 215/574–7800. Be prepared for a busy signal and, once you get through, a long time on hold.

By Commuter Train Philadelphia's fine network of commuter trains serves both the city and the suburbs. The famous Main Line got its start—and its name—from the Pennsylvania Railroad route that ran westward from Center City.

All trains serve 30th Street Station (30th and Market Sts.), where they connect to Amtrak trains, Suburban Station (16th St. and John F. Kennedy Blvd., across from the Visitors Center), and the new Market East Station (10th and Market Sts.) beneath the Gallery at Market East shopping complex. Fares, which vary according to route and time of travel, range from $1.50 to $4 one way. These trains are your best bet for reaching Germantown, Chestnut Hill, Merion (site of the Barnes Foundation), and other suburbs. For information, call 215/574–7800. Be prepared for a busy signal and, once you get through, a long time on hold.

By Taxi Cabs cost $1.50 for the flag throw and then $1.40 per mile. They are plentiful during the day downtown—especially along Broad Street and near hotels and train stations. At night and outside Center City, taxis are scarce. You can call for a cab, but it frequently shows up late and occasionally never arrives. Be persistent: Calling back when the cab is late will often yield results. The main cab companies are **Yellow Cab** (tel. 215/922–8400), **United Cab** (tel. 215/625–2881), and **Quaker City Cab** (tel. 215/728–8000).

To the Airport Allow at least a half hour, more during rush hour, for the 8-mile trip between Center City and the airport. By car, the airport is accessible via I–95 south or I–76 east; follow the signs. You can easily get a taxi downtown, though this is the most expensive choice—the ride averages $17 plus tip. SEPTA's Airport Express train leaves the 30th Street, Suburban, Market East, and North Broad stations and takes about 20 minutes to reach the airport. Trains run every half hour between 6:10 AM and 12:10 AM; the fare is $4.50 ($5.50 if you buy your ticket on the train). For schedules and other information, call the Airport Information Desk (tel. 215/492–3181), or SEPTA (tel. 215/547–7800). More than a dozen limo companies leave from Center City hotels and charge about $6 a head. Among them are Deluxe Transportation (tel. 215/463–8787) and Econoline Limousine (tel. 215/725–3464).

Guided Tours

Orientation Tours Philadelphia has no orientation tours per se, but **Gray Line Tours** (tel. 215/569–3666) offers a 5½-hour "Grand Combination" tour of historic and cultural areas. Full-size buses leave from the Quality Inn on 22nd Street above the Benjamin Franklin Parkway.

Special-Interest Tours Independence Hall, the Liberty Bell, and other sites in historic Philadelphia are the main attractions offered by the city's tour operators. **Gray Line Tours** (tel. 215/569–3666) has a three-hour Historic Tour daily at 9:30 AM and 1:30 PM. Gray Line also has a 2½-hour Cultural Tour of the Art Museum and Fairmount Park beginning at 10 AM. Both tours leave from the Quality Inn on 22nd Street above the Benjamin Franklin Parkway.

Tracey Tours (tel. 215/457–8660) has guides in Colonial dress narrating 2½-hour minibus tours of the historic area. The buses leave from the Visitors Center, 16th Street and Kennedy Boulevard, at 10 AM and 1:30 PM. Or you can arrange for Tracey to pick you up at your Center City hotel.

Philadelphia Tours (tel. 215/271–2999) double-decker buses stop at a half dozen attractions daily. Reservations only.

ABC Bus and Walking Tours (tel. 215/677–2495) has six tours, including historic Philadelphia, the Italian Market, and Valley Forge. Reservations only.

Fairmount Park Trolley Bus (tel. 215/636–1666). Take a tour of the Benjamin Franklin Parkway and Fairmount Park in a bus dressed up as a Victorian trolley. The 90-minute narrated ride leaves the Visitors Center (16th St. and Kennedy Blvd.) every 20 to 30 minutes from 10 to 4. Stops include museums, the zoo, and Fairmount Park mansions. You can get on and off all day at no additional charge and receive discount admission at sites along the route. At press time the operation had been sold, and new schedules were not yet available. *Cost: $3 adults, $2 students, $1 senior citizens, children under 13 free.*

To combine lunch or dinner with a sightseeing cruise on the Delaware River, climb aboard the *Spirit of Philadelphia* (tel. 215/923–1419). This three-deck ship leaves Pier 24, between Spring Garden and Callowhill streets, for lunch cruises from noon to 2 PM and dinner cruises from 7 to 10 PM. Besides food, you get a band and singing waitstaff.

R & S Harbor Tours (tel. 215/928–0972) offers hour-long narrated tours of the waterfront aboard a 65-foot sightseeing boat, the *Rainbow*. It leaves Penn's Landing at Lombard Street on the hour weekdays from 10 to 3, and weekends from noon to 6. There is also a two-hour sunset cruise Thursday through Sunday at 7:30.

Reminiscent of a Mississippi riverboat, the 80-foot *Liberty Belle* (tel. 215/238–0887) offers lunch, dinner, and Sunday brunch cruises with a banjo player, sing-alongs, and a Cajun-style buffet. Moonlight cruises, during which oldies music is played, depart daily at 11 PM. Occasional private charters affect the daily schedule. Board at the Columbia Yacht Club, Linden and Delaware avenues in Northeast Philadelphia.

Walking Tours Several walking tours of historic Philadelphia are available. **Audio Walk and Tour** (tel. 215/925–1234) at the Norman Rockwell Museum, 6th and Sansom streets, offers go-at-your-own-pace tours of historic Philadelphia with cassette and tape player for rent and an accompanying map. The tour includes discounts at 21 museums and cultural spots.

For a candlelight stroll through Old Philadelphia, try **Centipede Tours** (tel. 215/735–3123). Guides in Colonial dress lead tour groups from the City Tavern at 2nd and Walnut streets every

Wednesday, Friday, and Saturday at 6:30 from May to October.

Theme tours and area tours given by the **Foundation for Architecture Tours** (tel. 215/569–3187) focus on architecture but touch on the history and development of each destination. Area tours include Chestnut Hill, Manayunk, Spruce Hill, and other neighborhoods. Theme tours include Art Deco, skyscrapers, the University of Pennsylvania campus, Washington Square, and Judaic architecture and influence. Most tours begin weekends at 2 PM and occasionally on Wednesdays at 6 PM.

Multilingual Tours   To accommodate Philadelphia's international visitors, some tour companies provide interpreters and foreign-language guides. For example, **Centipede Tours** (tel. 215/735–3123) can supply German-, French-, Spanish-, Russian-, Chinese-, Japanese-, or Italian-speaking guides for all parts of Philadelphia.

Carriage Rides   Numerous horse-drawn carriages wend their way through the narrow streets of the historic area. A half dozen companies give narrated tours using "vis-à-vis" carriages (with facing seats) or surreys. Tours last anywhere from 15 minutes to an hour. Some companies are out on the street from 10 AM to 2 AM. The cost ranges from $10 to $50. Carriages line up on Chestnut and 5th streets near Independence Hall and at Head House Square, 2nd Street between Pine and Lombard streets. You can reserve a carriage and be picked up anywhere downtown. Carriages operate year-round, though a city ordinance prohibits them when the temperature is below 20 or above 94 degrees Fahrenheit. After numerous complaints from area residents, all horses are now diapered. Carriage operators include **Ben Franklin Carriages** (tel. 215/634–0545), **Philadelphia Carriage Company** (tel. 215/922–6840), **76 Carriage Company** (tel. 215/923–8516), and **Society Hill Carriage Company** (tel. 215/627–6128).

2 Portraits of Philadelphia

Portrait of an Amish Family

by Carolyn Meyer

You'll spot Jacob Stoltzfus working his fields with a team of horses as you drive the back roads of Lancaster County. You will certainly encounter his somber black buggy on one of the traffic-choked highways. You might exchange a few words with his wife, Becky, in her plain dark dress and white cap, if you happen to stop by their farmhouse to buy fresh eggs or inspect the homemade quilts she has for sale. If you're on the right road at the right time, you might see their younger children playing in the yard of a one-room schoolhouse. And on certain Sundays, you may pass the farmhouse where the Stoltzfus family and other Amish people gather to worship.

Stoltzfus is the most common of a dozen Amish family names; Jacob and Becky and their children are fictitious but typical of the more than 16,000 Amish (pronounced AH-mish) in this area. Their roots and religious tradition reach back to 16th-century Europe. Every detail of their lives, from their clothing to the way they operate their farms, is an expression of their faith in God and their separateness from "the world"; every detail is dictated by the *Ordnung*, the rules of their church.

Becky Stoltzfus, like Amish women of any age, wears a one-piece dress in a dark color (bright colors and printed patterns are forbidden). The sleeves are long and straight, her full skirt hemmed modestly halfway between knees and ankles. The high, collarless neck is fastened shut in front with straight pins; buttons and safety pins are forbidden although the Ordnung of some church districts allows hooks and eyes. Over her shoulder she wears a shawl the same color as her dress, pinned in front and back to the waistband of an apron also in the same color. Since apron strings tied in a bow are considered frivolous and therefore forbidden, her apron is also pinned. She wears black stockings rolled below the knee, and black low-heeled oxfords. At home in warm weather Becky and her family go barefoot.

Soon after her daughters were born, Becky made sure they wore the white organdy prayer cap. When Katie turned 12, she changed to a black cap for the Sunday preaching; after she marries she will wear the white cap all the time. The head coverings may look identical to outsiders but subtle differences tell the Amish a great deal about one another. The width of the front part, the length of the ties, the style of the seams, the way the pleats are ironed all indicate where the woman lives and how conservative or liberal her church district is.

Becky has never cut or curled her hair nor has she let it hang loose. She pins it in a plain knot at the back of her neck. She parts little Hannah's hair in the middle, plaits it, and fastens the two little braids in the back. When Becky is away from home she wears a black bonnet with a deep scoop brim over her prayer cap.

The clothes Jacob wears are also carefully dictated by the Ordnung of his church district. For Sunday preaching he wears a *Mutze*, a long black frock coat with split tails and hook-and-eye closings but no collar or lapels. His vest is also fastened with hooks and eyes.

Jacob's broadfall or "barn-door" trousers have no fly, just a wide front flap that buttons along the sides; they have no creases and no belt—homemade suspenders hold them up. There are buttons on his shirt, the number specified by the Ordnung. Colored shirts are permitted, but stripes and prints are out. Neckties are forbidden.

When he's not dressed up, Jacob hangs up his Mutze and puts on a *wamus*, a black sack coat with either a high round neck or V-neck and neither lapels nor outside pockets. Sometimes the wamus has hooks and eyes, but more liberal church districts allow buttons. Buttoned sweaters are sometimes permitted and there are also buttons on the long greatcoats some of the older men wear in cold weather.

In winter Jacob and his sons wear broad-brimmed black felt hats; in summer they switch to straw. Ben and Ezra, Jacob's younger boys, have been wearing hats with three-inch brims since they were little. Sam, the oldest son, wears a hat with a crease around the top of the crown, a sign (along with his sprouting beard) that he is newly married. The hat is a status symbol among the Amish. The grandfather's hat is higher in the crown than the father's and its brim is four inches wide. At the top of the hierarchy, the bishop who preaches at the Sunday service is recognizable by his hat's high rounded crown and its brim, the broadest in the district.

The width of an Amish man's hat brim also signifies his degree of conservatism: The broader the brim, the more conservative the wearer. Young rebels like Jacob's middle son Joe sometimes trim their hat brims to just a little less than the prescribed width.

Jacob's long beard is as much the mark of an Amishman as a broad-brimmed hat. He shaves only his upper lip, since mustaches are against the rules. He cuts his hair straight around well below the ears. Ben and Ezra have theirs parted in the middle with bangs across the forehead. Cutting it short—up to the earlobe, as Joe did—is another form of rebellion.

The style of the Amish buggy is as carefully prescribed as the style of his hat. The Stoltzfus family owns a black carriage with a gray top and big wooden wheels. The battery-powered side lamps, reflectors, and bright orange triangles have been added as required by Pennsylvania state law. The iron-tired wheels are precisely set, toed in slightly, farther apart at the top than at the bottom. A gear assembly at the pivot of the front axle adds stability. The brakes are operated by hand, an iron block pressed hard against the rear tire. This kind of brake is prescribed by the Ordnung; different groups permit different kinds of brakes. The Ordnung tells the buggy owner whether or not he may have roll-up side curtains or sliding glass doors, and if he is allowed a dashboard, a whipsocket, and other variations. The Stoltzfus family also owns a farm wagon and young Joseph was given his own horse and open one-seater when he turned 16.

The waiting list is long for handmade buggies. Carriage-making used to be a non-Amish occupation but the growing Amish population, the toll of wrecked carriages, and the need for approved work in addition to farming have brought some Amish into the trade. The carriage maker is in a more liberal church district that allows power tools.

Incidentally, the Amish can—and do—ride in cars owned by non-Amish people, travel on trains, buses, even airplanes and taxis. But they are not allowed to *own* a car. Teenage Amish boys sometimes manage to buy a car and hide it out of sight of their families. They are not subject to the rules of the Ordnung until they have been baptized, an event that takes place in their late teens or early 20s after they've had time to sow some wild oats.

No electric wires lead from the power lines along the road into the neat, well-kept buildings of the Stoltzfus farm, a difference that distinguishes Amish farms from their non-Amish neighbors'. The farms are small, no more than 50 or 60 acres, which is all that can be handled by a farmer limited to horsepower. Tractors, like electricity, are taboo among most of the Amish.

The Stoltzfuses' house is spacious and uncluttered. There is no wall-to-wall carpeting to vacuum; plain, unpatterned linoleum covers the floor. There are no curtains to wash or draperies to clean; although some church districts allow plain curtains on the lower half of the windows, this district permits only dark green roller shades. There are no slipcovers to launder or upholstery to shampoo, because upholstered furniture is not allowed.

Becky has a large kitchen where the family eats around a big wooden table. Afterward Becky and Katie and Hannah clean up the kitchen, washing the dishes and putting away leftover food in the gasoline-operated refrigerator. A one-cylinder engine in the cellar chugs noisily, powering the water pump, but many Amish families still rely on windmills or water power. A creek that runs through a farm also supplies water. Although labor-saving devices are generally forbidden, Becky does have a washing machine that runs by gasoline. Her refrigerator is also gasoline powered. Her stove burns kerosene; she would prefer bottled gas, but that is forbidden by the Ordnung of her district. She uses a treadle sewing machine and sews by the bright and steady light of a gasoline lamp.

About once a year, it is the Stoltzfuses' turn to host the every-other-Sunday preaching service. As many as 175 people may attend: There are 90 members in the district, and double that number counting unbaptized children. The removable partitions built into the downstairs walls are folded back and furniture moved aside. The district's backless oak benches are brought in and set up in rows. For that one Sunday morning the entire district fills the big house for the long service, staying on for a hearty lunch that Becky has been preparing for days.

Jacob and Becky Stoltzfus are fluent in English but the language they speak among themselves is Pennsylvania Dutch, a German dialect related to the dialects spoken in the part of Germany from which their Amish ancestors came. It is primarily a spoken language and spelling varies with the writer. "Dutch" actually means *Deutsch*, or German, and some scholars call the dialect "Pennsylvania German." Many Pennsylvanians of German descent speak the dialect, but among the Amish it is the "mother tongue," the first language an Amish child learns to speak and another mark of separation from the world.

When Hannah, Becky's youngest child, starts school, she will learn to speak and read and write in the language of "the world." Jacob and Becky want their children to know English, because their survival depends on good business relationships with English-speaking people. Sometimes when the Amish converse in English, they resort to dialect translated literally into English. The results are the quaint expressions that amuse tourists and inspire souvenir manufacturers to decorate switchplates and cocktail napkins with "typical Amish" expressions like "Outen the light" and "Throw Papa down the stairs his hat."

About the same time Hannah Stoltzfus starts to learn English, she will also be taught High German, the language of religion. The family Bible is written in High German and she and her brothers and sisters must learn to read it. By the time they are baptized in their late teens, they will be able to understand most of the Sunday sermon and to join in the prayers and hymns. Most Amish can't carry on a conversation in High German and have no need to unless they are ordained church officials who must preach sermons and pray. But everyone needs to be able to read and to listen.

The outsider may not notice the inconspicuous building on a back road where Ben and Ezra and Annie Stoltzfus attend school, along with eight grades of children in one room taught by a young Amish woman with only an eighth-grade education. Amish children are not sent to public school and Amish schools go only as far as the eighth grade. That's time enough to learn the basics of reading, writing, and arithmetic! The *real* education for their lives takes place at home, on the farm.

At age five, Hannah Stoltzfus would be old enough for kindergarten if the Amish had one. But they believe children should be at home with their parents until they are six. Annie loves school and wishes she could continue, but her brothers can hardly wait until their 14th birthdays, the end of school for them. Schools are built to serve children within a 2-mile radius so that no one has far to walk. Some children go to old one-room schoolhouses once owned by the public-school district. When districts consolidated, the Amish bought the obsolete schools and remodeled them—not modernizing them but ripping out the electric wiring. Since none was available near the Stoltzfus farm, the Amish fathers in that area built a plain cinder-block structure with big windows to take advantage of natural light.

Stepping into an Amish schoolhouse is like entering a time machine and emerging 70 or more years in the past. At 8:30 the teacher pulls the rope to ring the old-fashioned bell on the roof. Ben and Ezra and Annie come early, after they've finished their farm chores, so they have a chance to play before school begins. When the bell rings, the children line up and file through the big front door into the cloakroom. They hang their hats and jackets on pegs, line up their lunch boxes, and go quietly to their carefully refinished old-fashioned desks.

The school day begins with the roll call. During peak periods of farm work, the Amish close down the schools for a few days; they stop earlier in the spring than the public schools. They make up for the time by taking only a short Christmas break and celebrating none of the national holidays. Except in the case of illness, everyone stays home to work or goes to school to learn.

Next, the teacher reads to the pupils from the German Bible and then everyone recites the Lord's Prayer in German. Except for the lessons in reading German Scriptures and prayers, the teacher speaks English exclusively in the classroom.

Beside the teacher's desk is a "recitation bench." There are more than 30 students in the eight grades and each class of three or four or five comes forward by turns to recite its lessons. There is no competition to come up with the answer first and they all respond in a singsong chorus.

Because it is essential to the work of a farmer, arithmetic is considered very important. Picking readers for the pupils was not easy. The parents want the subject matter to be farm children, not city life; they want the stories to teach a moral lesson; fairy tales, myths, and fantasies are taboo. The Amish think most modern readers are too worldly, showing families with clothes, cars, and too many material possessions. Outsiders would consider the books they use hopelessly outdated.

During the 15-minute morning recess, Ezra and Ben and the other boys resume their baseball game. One of the rules of the Amish schoolyard is that children are never allowed to stand around by themselves; everyone must be included in the group. Annie and the older girls play blindman's bluff; the younger ones, joined by their teacher, race around in a game of tag.

During recess and lunchtime, the yard rings with conversation in English, Pennsylvania Dutch, and mixtures of the two. Parents disagree about which language should be used in the schoolyard. More pragmatic parents want their children to become as fluent as possible in English. The more traditional argue that using English when it's not necessary helps to drive a wedge between the Amish child and the Amish community.

The Amish want their children to learn to work together as a group, not to compete as individuals. Preserving tradition is a goal; reasoning abstractly is not. Asking too many questions is not acceptable. Discipline is strict; the only voices heard in the schoolroom are those of the teacher and the pupils who are reciting. The Amish expect pupils to master the material unquestioningly: Memorization replaces reasoning in a culture dominated by oral tradition. Rapid learning is not considered an advantage; thoroughness is valued more. Teachers believe that intellectual talents are a gift from God and that children should be encouraged to use the gift by helping others in the school.

Before the day is over, there is time for singing. Singing is a vital part of the Amish tradition, important in their religious life and in their social life as well. There are no harmonized part-songs for the Amish; unaccompanied unison singing is the universal rule. The Amish have their own style of singing, in which the leader (*Vorsanger*) sings the first word and everybody else joins in for the rest of the line.

When it's time to go home, students put away their books, sweep out the room, line up the desks neatly, wash the old-fashioned slate blackboards, and clap the erasers until they are clean. In cold weather they carry in the wood for the stove and take turns cleaning out the ashes and banking tomorrow's fire.

For years public-school authorities were in conflict with the Amish. Truancy laws were enforced and Amish fathers were often arrested and jailed for refusing to send older children to school. But in 1972 the United States Supreme Court ruled that the Amish are exempt from state compulsory education laws that require a child to attend beyond the eighth grade, claiming that such laws violate the Constitutional right to the freedom of religion.

Today, the Amish accept the idea of sending their children to school for eight years to learn what they need to survive in the 20th-century rural economy. But what an Amish child really needs to know to survive in the Amish culture he learns from his parents and from other adults in the community. Most of the practical knowledge of farmers and housewives is acquired not in books but in a family apprenticeship.

The marriage of Jacob and Becky Stoltzfus is a very practical affair. The Amish are quite realistic about their expectations. They do not marry for "love" or "romance" but out of mutual respect and the need for a partner in the kind of life they expect to live. The farmer needs a wife and they both need children. Marriage is essential to the Amish community; divorce is unknown; separation is rare. Marriage is the climax of the rite of passage that begins with baptism, the signal of the arrival of adulthood and sober responsibility. It signifies that young people have really joined the community.

From the time they reach the age of *Rum Schpringe* ("running around"—about 16 for boys, a little younger for girls) and for the next half-dozen years until each marries, Joe Stoltzfus and his sister Katie do much of their socializing at Sunday night singings usually held at the farm where the preaching service took place in the morning. Singings are functions of the church district which helps keep dating and eventually marriage within the group. In Lancaster County, young people from several church districts with similar interpretations of the Ordnung may get together for a joint singing. Although the main activity is singing hymns, these occasions are more social than religious.

At the more conservative singings, boys sit on one side of a long table in the barn and the girls sit on the other, and between joking and teasing they take turns in the role of Vorsanger. The hymns they sing are the "fast tunes" (some of them familiar Protestant hymns) rather than the "slow tunes" or chants sung at the preaching service. At around 10 o'clock the singing ends and the girls serve snacks. The couples, now paired off—Joe is with Leah Zook, as usual, and Katie has somehow ended up with Reuben Beiler—start home.

Although outsiders believe that the social life of an Amish teenager begins with a singing and ends with a buggy ride home at a respectably early hour, Amish dating is actually much livelier. Among the more liberal groups, the old-fashioned singings can turn quickly into rowdy, foot-stomping hoedowns. A few bring out harmonicas, guitars, and other forbidden instruments; older boys haul in cases of beer. Few outsiders attend these events.

On the "off Sunday" when there is no preaching service, Joe and Leah and other young unmarried people go courting— but always in secret. Before they marry, they are never seen together in public as a couple except as they leave a singing or a barn dance.

Bundling, the practice of courting in bed fully clothed, is usually attributed to the Amish. Actually it is an English word with no equivalent in Amish dialect and the custom dates back to New England where it had more to do with keeping warm in a cold house than with sex. No one is quite sure whether the Amish do or don't, but the consensus is that the girl's parents, rather than the Ordnung, have the final say. Leah's father and Jacob Stoltzfus have both said "no."

There is a saying that if a boy can persuade his girl to take off her prayer cap, she'll have sex with him. Evidently that doesn't happen often because the rate of premarital pregnancies among the Amish is quite low. Premarital sex is forbidden, birth control is taboo, and sex education is non-existent. The Amish child growing up on a farm isn't ignorant of the reproductive process, but human "facts of life" usually remain somewhat mysterious until the age of marriage.

When Jacob's son Sam married Sarah Beiler, their wedding was held after the harvest in November; December is the second most popular month for weddings and there are traditionally only two possible days in the week for the ceremony: Tuesday and Thursday. Sarah chose Thursday. There was no honeymoon but every weekend throughout the winter the couple went to visit relatives. Now they're living on the Stoltzfus farm.

The average age at marriage of Amish couples has been rising because of the problems of accumulating enough money to establish a household and to acquire land. Many Amish parents retire while they are still relatively young, especially if they have a son who needs a farm. Sam and Sarah have moved into the "grandfather's house," a section of Jacob's farmhouse built to accommodate a second generation. In a few years, when Sam assumes full responsibility for the farm and has children, he and Sarah will move into the larger part of the house and Jacob and Becky will move into the grandfather's house.

Recently Sam told his parents that a new little "woodchopper" or "dishwasher" is expected, the first grandchild of

Jacob and Becky. A new generation of the Stoltzfus family and for the Amish community is on the way.

The roots that nourish Amish beliefs and bring vitality to Amish tradition reach back hundreds of years. Theirs is a complex story of persecution from without and division within. Remembrance of the past is a part of the present for the Amish every day of their lives, not something reserved for Sunday worship and special ceremonies.

To understand the Amish as something more than a quaint anachronism, turn back the calendar to 16th-century Europe. The poor, by far the majority, were exploited by the rich and powerful few. The Roman Catholic Church wielded tremendous influence and many blamed the church for society's ills. When Martin Luther launched the Protestant Reformation in 1517, he had many opponents in addition to the Roman Catholic Church. One was Ulrich Zwingli, a radical Swiss Protestant, who in turn opposed Conrad Grebel. Grebel's followers wanted to establish free congregations of believers baptized as adults who made a confession of faith and committed themselves freely to a Christian life. Backing Zwingli, the Great Council of Zurich announced that babies must be baptized within eight days after their birth or the parents would be exiled.

This marked the beginning of Anabaptism, which means "rebaptized." Regarded as radically left wing, the Anabaptist movement posed a threat to both Roman Catholic and Protestant establishments. Anabaptist leaders were imprisoned, beaten, tortured, and killed until, by the end of the 16th century, nearly all the Anabaptists of Switzerland and Germany had been put to death.

But the movement spread through Central and Western Europe. Menno Simons, a former Roman Catholic priest, became one of those persecuted for Anabaptist preaching. His followers were called Mennonites. (In Switzerland they were known as the Swiss Brethren.) And although they were hounded by Catholics and other Protestants, dissension began to grow among the Mennonites themselves. A principal source of disagreement was the interpretation of the *Meidung*, the practice of shunning church members who had broken a rule. Shunning was based on St. Paul's advice to the Corinthians to avoid keeping company and eating with sinners. The Mennonites interpreted this to mean the member was to be subjected to Meidung only at communion. But Jakob Ammann, a young Mennonite bishop, insisted that the Meidung meant that the rule-breaker must be shunned totally; even his wife and family must refuse to have anything whatever to do with him until he repented and had been forgiven.

The controversy grew and in 1697 the stubborn and fiery Jakob Ammann broke away from the Mennonites. His followers, known as the Amish, were as stubborn and inflexible as Ammann himself and they became known for their unwillingness to change. Although differences in details of clothing were not a primary issue, they did become symbolic of the split. The Amish became known as the *Haftlers* (Hook-and-eyers) while the more worldly Mennonites were called the *Knopflers* (Buttoners).

Meanwhile, King Charles II of England granted a large province in the American colonies to William Penn. A devout Quaker, Penn believed he could offer refuge, freedom, and equality to the persecuted. Penn arrived in 1682, and the following year Francis Daniel Pastorius of the Frankfort Land Company brought the first group of Mennonites to Pennsylvania. They established themselves in Germantown, northwest of Philadelphia. The first Amish immigrants left Switzerland and the Palatinate of Germany in 1727, settling near Hamburg north of Reading. When Indian raids threatened that community, the Amish moved toward the southwest.

By the start of the Revolutionary War, about half of the 225,000 Pennsylvania colonists were German, but only a small minority were Amish and Mennonite. Although the Germans were excellent farmers, Benjamin Franklin dismissed them as "stupid boors." The English scorned them and tried to Anglicize them. But the Amish and Mennonites were determined to hold on to their religion, which was a way of life that included their language and their plain dress.

The Amish of Pennsylvania were all of one conservative mind until 1850, when a schism divided the Amish into two main factions. The more progressive group built meeting houses which earned them the label "Church Amish," to distinguish them from the stricter "House Amish" who continued to worship in their homes. Since then, innumerable splits have been caused by various interpretations of the Meidung (as happened in the days of Jakob Ammann) or by different details of the Ordnung—by Haftlers who want to live more like Knopflers but still remain Amish.

Every society changes to some extent and in every society there are a few people who cannot adjust. The Amish are no exception. Many leave; there is generally a shortage of young men in the Amish community because most of the dissidents who leave are male. But some exert pressure for changes in the Ordnung that result in splits. Today there are 7 Amish, 21 Mennonite, and 9 Brethren groups in the Lancaster area.

The ultimate control exerted by the Amish to keep the members in strict adherence to the Ordnung is the Meidung. No one will speak to the person, eat with him, conduct business with him, or have anything whatever to do with him while he is under the ban. It can last for a lifetime, unless the sinner mends his ways, begs for forgiveness, and is readmitted to fellowship by a unanimous vote of the congregation.

Visitors are sometimes surprised to learn that "Pennsylvania Dutch" and "Amish" are not synonymous. Many of the early settlers of Pennsylvania came from Germany at Penn's invitation; many were farmers, most were Protestant, and they spoke the same dialect. Despite these similarities, the Amish refer to all non-Amish as "English." These English are the Pennsylvania Dutch who permit hex signs on their farms (the Amish do not) and whose ancestors decorated useful items such as furniture and dishes with colorful peasant-style designs. The work of Amish craftsmen is competent but plain.

The Amish are generally friendly and hospitable people. Tape recorders and cameras are not welcome but a visitor sincerely interested in the Amish people who does not act like an interrogator can quietly learn something about their unique way of life.

The Search for Intelligent Life

by Paul Fussell

Well, not exactly a newcomer. I've been living here four years now, long enough to regard the scaffolding on City Hall tower as a permanent part of the architecture, long enough not to expect drivers to yield the right of way at pedestrian crossings, long enough to accept the litter, if not the dog ca-ca, as a natural part of the environment.

But even though I've been here awhile, living in Center City, I'm still poking around trying to see whether Philadelphia is culturally more like London, or Calcutta, or Sauk Centre, Minn. Coming to a conclusion isn't easy because no one knows for sure what "culture" is or how you might experience it or why it's a good thing to have. Some people think you can get it at a specific outlet, like Lincoln Center in New York or The Kennedy Center in Washington. Others—Matthew Arnold, for example—think it's not a commodity at all, but a state of mind, not easily come by and acquired by a prolonged immersion in "the classics," whatever they may be. A Nazi storm trooper in a popular German play of the 1930s thought he could detect it easily and was prepared to protect his loved ones from its pernicious influences. "Whenever I hear the word 'culture,'" he said, "I release the safety catch on my pistol." Today the word can cause plenty of confusion, as the *Inquirer* unwittingly reveals each Sunday by titling one of its sections "Entertainment and the Cultural Arts." This awards equal time to symphony and opera and dance and country music and prole movies, thus suggesting that the "Cultural Arts" include anything not edible or portable or obviously utilitarian that readers can be enticed to spend money on.

And the *Inquirer* may be right. For T. S. Eliot, culture included much more than art, music, and beautiful letters. It embraced, he said, "all the characteristics and interests of the people." For the British that included, he maintained, the dart board and (ugh) "boiled cabbage cut into sections." If that's what culture means, I'd have to look into cheesesteaks and soft pretzels with mustard, Frank Rizzo's impressive bod and the pitiable performances of the Iggles. But for me culture still means what it meant before anthropologists began using the term to include everything. For me it still designates things that don't make money, that engage your mind and imagination, that address your aesthetic sense and gratify your curiosity and connect you with the past. Culture invites you to think about time and history. It means things that government is disinclined or embarrassed to subsidize. It means those things that insti-

tutions are always begging for funds to house and maintain
and exhibit. It is comparable to those things a philistine
school board, considering the annual budget, would stigma-
tize as "frills."

Before moving to Philadelphia I lived in Princeton for many
years, and there "my city" was New York, an easy cultural
commuting distance away. I'd visited Philadelphia a few
times, once for an opera, once for a road-show play, once for
some soccer at Veterans Stadium, once for a not-so-hot seafood dinner. But because I knew very little about
Philadelphia and its cultural operations, I consulted the es-
timable *Places Rated Almanac* (1981 edition). This rated
American urban areas on the basis of their presumed
cultural attractiveness according to various criteria, not all
of which were plausible. From the *Almanac* I learned that
Philadelphia ranked seventh among metropolitan areas for
its number of actors. But the problem is that Philadelphia's
are now mostly waiters. ("Hi. My name is Gary. We have a
number of specials tonight I'd like to tell you about.") I
learned also that Philadelphia's public library system
ranked seventh in the United States, beaten not just by
New York and Chicago and Boston (no surprise there) but
astonishingly enough, by Cleveland and—shock!—Cin-
cinnati. Another of the *Almanac's* measures of cultural ad-
equacy was the number of authors in residence. New York
had a reputed 4,382, Philadelphia only 449, just above De-
troit (395). There weren't many dancers here, but a lot of
painters and sculptors and a vast number of musicians and
composers, giving Philadelphia a ranking for music fourth
in the nation, just behind New York, Los Angeles, and Chicago. Considering all its criteria of cultural desirability
together, the *Almanac* concluded that Philadelphia ranked
seventh in the country, a ranking earned in very large part,
I'd say, by the efforts of Stokowski, Ormandy, and Muti.
Above Philadelphia: New York, Washington, Chicago, Boston, Los Angeles, and San Francisco. Below it: Denver,
Minneapolis, Dallas, Buffalo, Baltimore, Houston, and Atlanta, not to mention Fort Smith, Ark., Greeley, Colo., and
Laredo, Texas. At the bottom of the list of 277 places
ranked is poor Lafayette, La., apparently a locus of bowling
alleys, fast-food dispensaries, porno theaters, and dirt
auto-racing tracks.

Now, if you need a shot of civic pride, look into the
second edition of the *Almanac*, dated 1985. Philadelphia is now ranked sixth in the country as a
metropolitan area rich in the arts and—hold your hats—
first in the country (out of 328 metropolitan areas) in higher
education. Eat your heart out, Boston: You're only 14th.

But as I confronted such statistics and tried to make sense
of them, I remembered something more about Philadelphia, and it was mighty encouraging. Long ago, when I was
returning to the States after living a year in London and en-

cumbered with a whole lot of household stuff to bring back, friends advised encountering U.S. Customs in Philadelphia rather than New York. "People are nicer there," they said, and they were right. No one at the Philadelphia airport displayed open envy or contempt because of my good fortune in spending a year abroad. No one was rude for the fun of it. The sensitive questioning of the customs officer allowed me to bring in all my stuff without any trouble at all. This was a memorable experience of Philadelphia niceness, and since then I've had many more.

But there's a problem with niceness. It exacts cultural costs. I hadn't lived here very long before I sensed a deadly critical vacuum in Philadelphia. The most awful things—books, plays, restaurants, buildings, public utterances—passed without complaint or satire or abuse. I got the impression that Philadelphians really cared as little about a strenuously earned excellence as about spotless streets, a safe, well-run mass transit system, and an uncorrupt judiciary.

Because no one seems to care enough, literary culture in Philadelphia has suffered a notable erosion. The major book publishers have decamped, and with them the agents and most of the editors and writers. The book trade has been largely taken over by chains, mass-market bookstores where no one has heard of Flaubert or Veblen, let alone Montaigne or Sir Thomas Browne. And books are not authoritatively reviewed here. In one Sunday book-review section of the *Inquirer* recently, there were 10 full reviews. All were either by *Inquirer* staff people, some apparently recruited from the mail room, or by freelance writers. There were no national authorities whatsoever reviewing books, and this left the unhappy impression that the amateur and the parochial were good enough for Philadelphia. Not that the *Inquirer* hasn't some good, sharp critics, such as Carlin Romano on books, William B. Collins on theater, Elaine Tait on restaurants, and pre-eminently Thomas Hine on architecture and urban imagery. But the general critical tone in Philadelphia is soft and nice, rather like the local pretzel, and that's no way to encourage a culture for grown-ups.

If literary culture here seems in decline, theater is, of course, in a worse state. The curse here is the lack of a permanent, stable repertory company with knowledge and taste. By this lack Philadelphia betrays its cultural inferiority not just to New York, but to San Francisco and Washington, not to mention New Haven and Cambridge, Mass. One of my bitter disappointments in moving here was discovering that whatever it does, the immensely expensive Annenberg complex at the University of Pennsylvania does not consider it a duty to stage plays in the historical repertory, which means not only that I can't profit from repeated attendance at *Antony and Cleopatra, Major Barbara, Six*

Characters in Search of an Author and *Krapp's Last Tape*, but that, worse, the local students can't. I think they're being cheated.

Having said that, I must recognize that there's wonderful stuff here, even if it takes some nosing around to find it. That's because Philadelphia culture is decentralized. You don't find it all in one place, or even in one district. If this were New York, the building of The Pennsylvania Academy of the Fine Arts on Broad Street would probably have been torn down years ago and its contents consolidated with those of the Philadelphia Museum of Art. The same with the Rodin Museum. And Philadelphia's culture is unique for another reason. It's rather shy. New York has the pompous Morgan Library, looking like a rich man's palace designed to awe beholders. Philadelphia has The Rosenbach Museum and Library, established in a town house on a quiet domestic street. It seems the same here with the least important cultural things. It took me some time to notice, passing almost daily, that Firstrust Savings Bank on Rittenhouse Square provides a lending library for its clients. But there's little indication in front that there you can borrow books as well as money. That suggests Philadelphia's cultural style at its best: Don't shout, just quietly and modestly deliver something good. And wait for the cultural clients to find it.

A decentralized culture like Philadelphia's has large and subtle advantages. Other cities' "cultural centers" give the impression that culture can be assembled all in one place. That makes it seem a luxury isolated from real life and thus fit to be ignored. But when it's spread all around, you can't help meeting some of it all the time, passing and perhaps dropping in to the Balch Institute or the Atwater Kent or the Afro-American or American Jewish museums, or the Historical Society of Pennsylvania or The University Museum, or noticing the delightful group of "Dutch Renaissance" buildings on Walnut Street between 19th and 20th streets. And the more you walk around, the more you're likely to notice that there's an oboe repair shop on Pine Street.

The Gideon Bibles placed in hotel rooms offer specific "how-to" advice for alleviating common spiritual and psychological maladies. Like, "If you are weary and discouraged, read Matthew 11:28-30," or "When your friends seem to go back on you, read I Corinthians 13." In the same way, here are some nuggets of cultural therapy for Philadelphians, all possible because of a happily decentralized culture.

● When you feel that residence in or around Philadelphia is beginning to blunt your sense of humor, as well as of beauty, go to the Art Museum and contemplate Oldenburg's hypertrophied cherry wood multiple plug, hung up near the ceiling. You will smile.

• While at the museum, if you feel the need of a sexual lift combined with artistic refreshment, seek out Duchamps's *Etant Donnés*. More or less X-rated, it has to be kept from the children and thus is not easy to find. But it's eminently worth the search and inquiries.

• When you are persuaded that these days "young people are no good," devoted only to drink and drugs and dumb movies, go hear a recital by the devoted kids at The Curtis Institute. And when you've convinced yourself that the federal government and its agencies are distinguished by no artistic instincts whatsoever, go hear the Curtis students in a free noontime recital at, of all places, the Federal Reserve Bank on 6th Street, presented in its own civilized, comfortable, small auditorium.

• When you feel that despite your costly education your ability to entertain two conflicting ideas simultaneously is feebler than it should be, go to the corner of 15th and Market streets and study, really study, the *Clothespin*. Or is it lovers embracing? Is it a clothespin becoming lovers or lovers becoming a clothespin? Or both at once?

• When you feel that Philadelphia radio offers little but proletarian call-in shows, turn to WFLN (95.7 FM) for 24 hours of intelligent music, with lots of Baroque from midnight to morning.

• When you're overcome with the depressing conviction that Philadelphia is hopelessly provincial, ruinously out of touch with Europe and Asia and the world's significant history, join the Alliance Française and speak French, and after that drop into the Rosenbach and contemplate the manuscript of Joyce's *Ulysses*. Then look into The University Museum. If you were sent by *The Last Emperor*, try exercising your imagination on the crystal ball which once delighted the Dowager Empress.

• If your experience of contemporary politics, and especially tax policy, has persuaded you that the rich and famous of all places are necessarily selfish swine and always have been, spend an hour in "The Titanic and Her Era" exhibit at the Maritime Museum on Chestnut Street. There you can reacquaint yourself with the fact that boundlessly rich men within living memory sacrificed themselves, when the chips were down and the odds very bad, so their wives and children could live. It's a mind-expanding experience to wonder if you would do the same, and if not, why not.

• When wearied and bored by the sight of the new business architecture all over town, which gives the impression that plate glass and aluminum are interesting, stroll across the Schuylkill and regale yourself with the facade of the original Drexel Institute Main Building (Chestnut at 32nd). You will enjoy the sexy muse or angel or whatever at the top. They don't make them like that anymore. Contemporary women have breasts that good, but no wings.

3 Exploring Philadelphia

Orientation

by Michael Schwager and Rathe Miller

Michael Schwager writes articles and books about subjects ranging from Philadelphia history to computers. His articles have appeared in the New York Times, The Writer, *and many other publications. Rathe Miller is a Philadelphia writer and editor. His work appears in the* Philadelphia Inquirer, Philadelphia *magazine, and other local and national publications. Their joint work has appeared in the* Philadelphia Inquirer Magazine, *the* Philadelphia Inquirer, *and the* Boston Globe. *They have lived in the Philadelphia area for a total of 77 years.*

"On the whole I'd rather be in Philadelphia." W. C. Fields may have been joking when he wrote his epitaph, but if he were here today he could make the statement seriously. They no longer roll up the sidewalks at night in Philadelphia. An entertainment boom, a restaurant renaissance, and a cultural revival have helped transform the city.

The birthplace of the nation has become a city of superlatives. Philadelphia has the world's largest municipal park, the best public collection of art in the United States, the widest variety of urban architecture in America, and the highest concentration of institutions of higher learning in the country.

In addition, Philadelphia is a city of neighborhoods: Shoppers haggle over the price of tomatoes in South Philly's Italian Market; families picnic in the parks of Germantown; street vendors hawk soft pretzels in Logan; and all over town, kids play street games such as stickball, stepball, wireball, and chink.

Philadelphia's compact 2-square-mile downtown (William Penn's original city) is nestled between the Delaware and the Schuylkill rivers. Thanks to Penn's grid system of streets—laid out in 1681—the downtown area is easy to navigate. The traditional heart of the city is Broad and Market streets (Penn's Center Square), where City Hall now stands. Market Street divides the city north and south; 130 S. 15th Street, for example, is in the second block south of Market. North–south streets are numbered, starting with Front (First) Street, at the Delaware River, and increasing to the west. Broad Street is equivalent to 14th Street.

The city extends north, south, and west from downtown into more than 100 neighborhoods covering 130 square miles. The Benjamin Franklin Parkway breaks the rigid grid pattern by leading out of Center City into Fairmount Park, which straddles the Schuylkill River and the Wissahickon Creek for 10 miles. It's a distance of 30 miles from one end of the city to the other.

Sections of Philadelphia range from posh old-money enclaves to inner-city slums. The downtown is comparatively safe during the day. After dark, exercise caution, especially in areas like Market Street east of Broad Street; 13th Street; and the neighborhoods ringing the downtown. Ask hotel personnel about the safety of places you're interested in visiting. At night, cabs are safer than walking.

Philadelphia has too many attractions to see in one day. Unless you severely limit your itinerary, figure on spending several days. We have divided the downtown into four walking tours. Tour 3 can be done in a day—if you move fast. Each of the other three takes more than a day of sightseeing.

Tour 1. Historic District

Numbers in the margin correspond with points of interest on the Tours 1 and 2 map.

This tour covers "the most historic square mile in America." Most of the sites are part of **Independence National Historical Park,** administered by the National Park Service. Except as noted, all have free admission, the same telephone number (tel. 215/597–8974), and the same hours: daily 9–5. In summer, some buildings—we'll tell you which—remain open into the evening.

Admission to Independence Hall, the Bishop White House, and the Todd House is by guided tour only. Tickets for the Bishop White and Todd houses can be obtained at the Visitor Center on the day of your visit. No tickets are required for tours of Independence Hall; admission is first come, first served. From early May to Labor Day, you may wait from 15 minutes to an hour for the Independence Hall tour.

❶ Start the tour at the **Visitor Center** (3rd and Chestnut Sts.). Operated by the National Park Service, the center has a large counter staffed by several park rangers who answer questions and distribute maps and brochures on Independence National Historical Park and other sites in the historic area. The main attraction is a video-computer exhibit that gives Constitutional perspectives on contemporary issues such as gun control, drug testing, sex discrimination, and the national speed limit. Shown in two 300-seat auditoriums, the 28-minute movie *Independence*, directed by John Huston, dramatizes events surrounding the birth of the nation. The center's bookstore specializes in books about the Revolution, the Constitution, and Colonial times. For $1.50 you can buy a reproduction of a 1787 map of Philadelphia; for $525 you can buy a replica of the silver-plated inkstand used for the signing of the Declaration of Independence.

❷ Directly across 3rd Street is the **First Bank of the United States,** the oldest bank building in the country and headquarters of the government's bank from 1797 to 1811. Symbolizing the hope of prosperity for the new republic, the pediment carving depicts a cornucopia and an oak branch on either side of an American eagle. Executed in 1797 by Clodius F. Legrand and Sons, it is made of mahogany and is one of the few remaining examples of 18th-century wood carving. No other outdoor wooden sculpture from that period is known to have survived in such excellent condition (it has withstood acid rain better than the bank's marble pillars). *Not open to the public.*

Next to the bank is a wrought-iron gateway topped by an eagle. Pass through it and you step out of modern-day Philadelphia and into Colonial America.

A red-brick path alongside manicured lawns and ancient oaks and maples leads to the first group of historic buildings, Carpenter's Court, which includes **Carpenter's Hall.** Built in 1770, **❸** this was the headquarters of the Carpenters' Company, a guild founded to teach carpenters architecture and to aid their families. In September 1774 the First Continental Congress convened here and addressed a declaration of rights and grievances to King George III. Re-creations of Colonial settings include original chairs and candle sconces and displays of 18th-century carpentry tools. The building, with features such as a tile floor and marble fireplaces, is still owned and operated by the Carpenters' Company. *320 Chestnut St., tel. 215/597–8974. Open Tues.–Sun. 10–4.*

Next door are two buildings of interest to military history buffs **❹** —the **Pemberton House** and **New Hall.** Dioramas in Pemberton House (the Army–Navy Museum) depict highlights of the Rev-

olutionary War. Authentic weapons on display include pow-
derhorns, swords, and a 1763 flintlock musket. The second-
floor exhibit puts you behind the cannon of an 18th-century bat-
tleship. New Hall (the Marine Corps Memorial Museum) is a
small museum displaying weapons, uniforms, and medals dating from 1775 to 1815. *Chestnut St. east of 4th St., tel. 215/597–
8974. Open daily 9–5.*

⑤ Leave Carpenter's Court and continue west on the red-brick
path across 4th Street to the **Second Bank of the United States.**
Built in 1824 and modeled after the Parthenon, the Second
Bank is an excellent example of Greek Revival architecture.
Housed in the building are portraits of prominent Colonial
Americans by noted artists such as Charles Willson Peale, William Rush, and Gilbert Stuart. Peale's portrait of Jefferson is
the only one that shows him with red hair. The permanent exhibit, "Portraits of the Capital City," opened in 1988, has a life-
size wooden statue of George Washington by William Rush; a
mural of Philadelphia in the 1830s by John A. Woodside Jr.; and
the only known likeness of William Floyd, a lesser-known sign-
er of the Declaration of Independence. *420 Chestnut St., tel.
215/597–8974. Open daily 9–5.*

⑥ As you continue west on the red-brick path, you pass **Library
Hall,** the library of the American Philosophical Society. A research library for historians, it contains such artifacts as a copy
of the Declaration of Independence handwritten by Thomas
Jefferson, William Penn's 1701 Charter of Privileges, and Benjamin Franklin's will. Exhibits in the lobby change frequently;
recent ones have included Modern Physics in America (on four
physicist members who were involved in the Manhattan Project); Scientific Broadsides (posters from the 19th century); and
the History of Astronomy. *105 S. 5th St., tel. 215/627–0706.
Open weekdays 9–4:45.*

Crossing 5th Street, you arrive at **Independence Square,**
where, on July 8, 1776, the Declaration of Independence was
first read in public. Although the square is not as imposing today, you can still imagine the impact that this setting had on the
Colonials.

⑦ The first building on your right is **Philosophical Hall** (104 S. 5th
St., tel. 215/627–0706), the headquarters of the American Philosophical Society. Founded by Benjamin Franklin in 1743 to
promote "useful knowledge," it is the oldest learned society in
America. The membership, which is limited to 500 Americans
and 100 foreigners, has included Washington, Jefferson, Lafayette, Emerson, Darwin, Edison, Churchill, and Einstein. The
building (dating from 1785) is closed to the public except by appointment.

⑧ Next is **Independence Hall.** Opened in 1732 as the State House
for the Colony of Pennsylvania, this was the scene of many early events in the nation's history. The Second Continental
Congress convened here on May 10, 1775. In June 1775, George
Washington accepted appointment as general of the Continental Army. A year later Virginia delegate Richard Henry Lee
offered a resolution declaring "that these United Colonies are,
and of right ought to be, free and independent States." On July
4, 1776, the Declaration of Independence was adopted. The
Articles of Confederation were signed here in 1778 and the
Constitution was formally adopted on September 17, 1787.

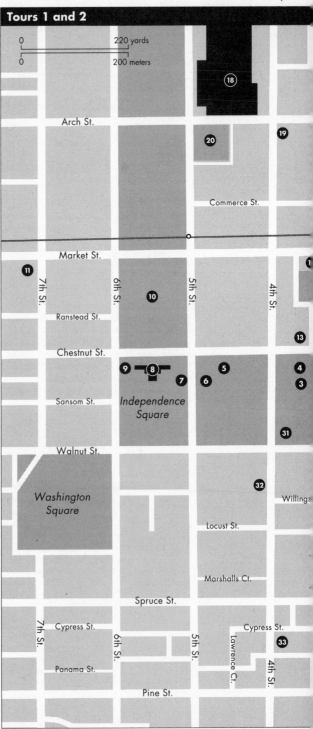

Arch Street Friends
Meeting House, **19**

Betsy Ross House, **17**

Bishop White
House, **30**

Carpenter's Hall, **3**

Christ Church, **14**

Christ Church Burial
Ground, **20**

Congress Hall, **9**

Elfreth's Alley, **15**

Fireman's Hall
Museum, **16**

First Bank of the
United States, **2**

Franklin Court, **12**

*Gazela of
Philadelphia,* **24**

Graff House, **11**

Head House
Square, **35**

Hill-Physick-Keith
House, **33**

Independence Hall, **8**

Liberty Bell, **10**

Library Hall, **6**

Moshulu, **26**

New Market, **36**

Pemberton House and
New Hall, **4**

Penn's Landing, **21**

Penn's Landing
Trolley Company, **27**

Philadelphia
Contributionship for
the Insurance of
Houses from Loss by
Fire, **32**

Philadelphia Maritime
Museum, **13**

Philadelphia
Merchant's
Exchange, **29**

Philosophical Hall, **7**

Port of History
Museum, **25**

Powel House, **37**

Second Bank of the
United States, **5**

Thaddeus Kosciuszko
National Memorial, **34**

Todd House, **31**

United States Mint, **18**

USS *Becuna,* **23**

USS *Olympia,* **22**

Visitor Center, **1**

Welcome Park, **28**

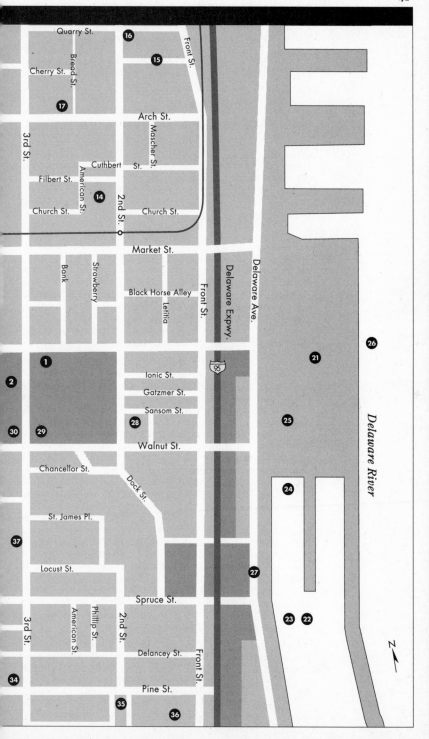

The site of these events was the first-floor Assembly Room, which has been painstakingly restored and now displays many historic items. Especially notable are the inkstand, designed by Philip Syng and used for signing the Declaration and the Constitution; and the chair from which Washington presided over the Constitutional Convention. After the Constitution was adopted, Franklin said about the sun carving on the chair, "I have the happiness to know that it is a rising and not a setting sun." Also on the first floor is the Pennsylvania Supreme Court chamber, with judge's bench, jury box, and prisoner's dock.

The 100-foot Long Room on the second floor was the site of banquets, receptions, balls, and suppers. The east wing of the building is Old City Hall, home of the U.S. Supreme Court from 1791 to 1800. Free tours start there every 15 to 20 minutes; admission is first come, first served. The tour lasts 35 minutes, including a 10-minute orientation, but you may have to wait in line up to an hour during the busy season from early May to Labor Day. *Chestnut St. between 5th and 6th Sts., tel. 215/597–8974. Open daily 9–5; early July–early Sept. 9–8.*

9 The west wing of Independence Hall is **Congress Hall,** formerly the Philadelphia County Courthouse and the meeting place of the U.S. Congress from 1790 to 1800. On the first floor is the House of Representatives, where President John Adams was inaugurated in 1797. On the second floor is the Senate chamber, where George Washington was inaugurated for his second term in 1793. Both chambers have been authentically restored. *6th and Chestnut Sts., tel. 215/597–8974. Open daily 9–5.*

North of Independence Hall, one block up the mall, is
10 Philadelphia's best-known symbol, the **Liberty Bell.** Ordered in 1751 and originally cast in England, the bell cracked during testing and was recast in Philadelphia by Pass and Stow in 1753. To keep it from falling into British hands during the Revolution—they would have melted it down for ammunition—the bell was spirited away by horse and wagon to Allentown 60 miles north. The subject of much legend, the bell cracked when tolled at the funeral of Chief Justice John Marshall in 1835. It was repaired but cracked again in 1846 and then forever silenced. You can touch the 2,080-pound bell and read its biblical inscription, "Proclaim liberty throughout all the land unto all the inhabitants thereof." It was called the State House Bell until 1839, when a group of Abolitionists adopted it as a symbol of freedom and renamed it the Liberty Bell. After being housed in Independence Hall for more than 200 years, the bell was moved to a glass-enclosed pavilion for the 1976 Bicentennial. The new home is an incongruous setting for such a historic object, but it does display the bell 24 hours a day. While the building is open, rangers and volunteers tell the story. After hours you can press a button on the outside walls to hear a recorded account of the bell's history. *Market St. between 5th and 6th Sts., tel. 215/597–8974. Open daily 9–5; early July–early Sept. 9–8.*

With independence still on your mind, walk one block west on Market Street to 7th Street. At the southwest corner is a re-
11 construction of the **Graff House,** where Thomas Jefferson wrote the rough draft of the Declaration of Independence in June 1776. Jefferson rented rooms from bricklayer Jacob Graff. The bedroom and parlor in which he lived that summer have been re-created with period furnishings. The first floor has a

Jefferson exhibit and a seven-minute film, *The Extraordinary Citizen*. The display on the Declaration of Independence shows changes Jefferson made in the writing. The first draft had an antislavery clause, which did not survive debate. *7th and Market Sts., tel. 215/597-8974. Open daily 9-5.*

Time Out On 5th Street across from the Liberty Bell Pavilion is the **Bourse,** Philadelphia's former stock exchange and now a festive complex of shops, offices, and eateries. The third floor has a dozen restaurants, including a salad bar, a deli, a pastry shop, a Chinese fast-food restaurant, and an American restaurant. You can eat your food at a table overlooking the Grand Hall of this magnificently restored 1895 building, or in the outdoor café.

⓬ Now walk east to 316 Market Street, the entrance to **Franklin Court.** First notice the post office, the only one in the country where employees wear Colonial dress. Letters mailed here are hand-stamped with the cancellation "B. Free Franklin." Pass through the archway and you'll see a steel-girder superstructure in the shape of Franklin's last house, which stood on the site. Down the long ramp is an underground museum, which has displays and a 20-minute film on Franklin's life and achievements. Beside the post office are four other restored homes once owned by Franklin. No. 318 has architectural and archaeological displays of the houses themselves and artifacts found in the court. No. 320-322 was the print shop and office of the Colonial newspaper, *The Aurora*, published by Franklin's grandson Benjamin Franklin Bache. *314-322 Market St. (or enter from Chestnut St. walkway), tel. 215/597-2760. Open daily 9-5; early July-early Sept. 10-6.*

⓭ When you leave the underground museum, you'll be facing the entrance of the **Philadelphia Maritime Museum.** Pay particular attention to three main exhibits: "The Titanic and Her Era" has artifacts from the ill-fated liner, such as Mrs. John Jacob Astor's life jacket and the discharge book of Frederick Fleet, the lookout who first spotted the fatal iceberg. "The Ironclad Intruder" displays journals, paintings, and artifacts about the USS *Monitor*, the Union's ironclad ship of the Civil War; the display includes the ship's 1,500-pound anchor. "Man and the Sea" has ship's models, marine art, navigational instruments, shipbuilders' tools, weapons, and figureheads. *321 Chestnut St., tel. 215/925-5439. Donation: $1. Open Mon.-Sat. 10-5, Sun. 1-5.*

⓮ Walk one block east on Market Street and a half-block north on 2nd Street to **Christ Church,** where noted Colonials, including 15 signers of the Declaration, worshiped. The congregation was organized in 1695 on this site; the present church—a fine example of Georgian architecture—was completed in 1754. The bells and the steeple were financed by lotteries run by Benjamin Franklin. Brass plaques mark the pews of Washington, Robert Morris, Betsy Ross, and others. (The church burial ground, two blocks west, is No. 20 on this tour.) *2nd St. north of Market St., tel. 215/922-1695. Open Mon.-Sat. 9-5, Sun. 1-5. Services Sun. at 9 and 11.*

⓯ Continuing north on 2nd Street for a block and passing Arch Street, you come to a small street on the right. **Elfreth's Alley** is the oldest continuously occupied residential street in America, dating back to 1702. The street has 33 houses. The Elfreth's Alley Association has restored No. 126, a Colonial craftsman's home, with authentic furnishings and a Colonial kitchen. On the first weekend in June, residents celebrate Elfreth's Alley Days by dressing in Colonial garb and opening their houses to the public. The rest of the year, only No. 126 is open. *Off Front and 2nd Sts. between Arch and Race Sts., tel. 215/574-0560. Open daily 10-4, Mar.-Dec.; weekends 10-4, Jan. and Feb.*

16 Walk back to 2nd Street, turn right, and a few footsteps take you to the **Fireman's Hall Museum.** Housed in an authentic 1876 firehouse, the museum traces the history of firefighting, from the volunteer company founded in Philadelphia by Benjamin Franklin in 1736 to the professional departments of the 20th century. The collection includes early hand- and horse-drawn fire engines (such as an 1815 hand pumper and a 1907 three-horse Metropolitan steamer); fire marks; uniforms; and other memorabilia. You can even stand in the wheelhouse of a fireboat and steer it. A film traces the human side of firefighting. *147 N. 2nd St., tel. 215/923-1438. Open Tues.-Sat. 9-5.*

17 Walk south on 2nd Street and turn right to 239 Arch Street, the **Betsy Ross House.** In this three-story brick house, seamstress and upholsterer Betsy Ross supposedly sewed the first American flag. A Quaker, Ross lost her first two husbands in the Revolutionary War. Owned and maintained by the City of Philadelphia, the eight-room house is crammed with artifacts such as a family Bible and Betsy Ross's wardrobe and yardstick. Alongside the house is brick-paved Atwater Kent Park, with a fountain, benches, and the graves of Betsy Ross and her third husband, John Claypoole. *239 Arch St., tel. 215/627-5343. Open daily May-Oct. 9-6, Nov.-Apr. 9-5.*

Continuing west on Arch Street, you'll see an eight-foot-high bust of Benjamin Franklin made of 80,000 pennies donated by Philadelphia schoolchildren and children of city firefighters.

18 Across 4th Street, the **United States Mint** stands just two blocks from the first U.S. mint, which opened in 1792. Built in 1969, this is the largest of the three U.S. mints, and is also the largest mint in the world. A tour shows how blank discs are turned into U.S. coins. The visitors' gallery has an exhibit of medals from the nation's wars, including the Medal of Honor, the Purple Heart, and the Bronze Star—once made at the mint. Also on display are bullion boxes used to transport gold bars during the days of the Pony Express: The boxes had special locks that counted the number of times they were opened. The David Rittenhouse Room on the mezzanine level has a display of U.S. gold coins. Seven Tiffany stained-glass mosaics depict coin making in ancient Rome. A shop in the lobby sells special coins and medals—in mint condition. *5th and Arch Sts., tel. 215/597-7350. Open weekdays 9-4:30, also weekends spring and summer.*

19 Catercorner is the **Arch Street Meeting House,** built in 1804 for the Philadelphia Yearly Meeting of the Society of Friends. It is still used for that purpose—aside from weekly services, 13,000 Quakers congregate here for five days each March. A small museum in the church presents a series of dioramas and a 14-minute slide show depicting the life and accomplishments of William Penn, and from April 15 to October 30, Quaker guides give tours. *4th and Arch Sts., tel. 215/627-2667. Open Mon.-Sat. 10-4; services Thurs. at 10 and Sun. at 10:30.*

㉒ A block west on Arch Street is the **Christ Church Burial Ground**, resting place of five signers of the Declaration and other Colonial patriots. The best-known graves are those of Benjamin Franklin and his wife, Deborah. According to local legend, throwing a penny on Franklin's grave will bring you good luck. A peaceful, cloistered spot in the center of the city. *5th and Arch Sts. Open daily late spring, summer, and early fall 9:30–4:30, weather permitting.*

Tour 2. Society Hill and the Waterfront

㉑ You start Tour 2 at **Penn's Landing,** the spot where William Penn stepped ashore in 1682. This is the hub of a 37-acre park that stretches from Market Street on the north to Lombard Street on the south. The development of this area—an ambitious effort to reclaim the Delaware River waterfront—began in 1967; extensive work in 1990 is expected to close some sections. Plans include condominiums, offices, more recreation areas, hotels, and restaurants. In warm weather, the Great Plaza at Penn's Landing—an outdoor amphitheater—is the scene of concerts, jamborees, festivals, and other special events; pick up a calendar at the Visitor Center (3rd and Chestnut Sts.) or the Tourist Information Shop (2nd and Chestnut Sts.). Walk along the waterfront and you'll see scores of pleasure boats moored at the marina, and cargo ships chugging up and down the Delaware. Philadelphia's port, which includes ports in New Jersey and Delaware, is one of the world's largest freshwater ports, generating $2 billion a year in revenue and 99,000 jobs.

㉒ One ship docked at Penn's Landing played a key role in American maritime history. The USS *Olympia* was Commodore George Dewey's flagship at the Battle of Manila in the Spanish-American War. Dewey entered Manila Harbor after midnight on May 1, 1898. At 5:40 AM, he told his captain, "You may fire when ready, Gridley," and the battle began. By 12:30 the Americans had destroyed the entire Spanish fleet. The *Olympia* was the last ship of the "New Navy" of the 1880s and 1890s, the beginning of the era of steel ships, and it is the only remaining ship from the Spanish-American War. You can tour the entire restored ship, including the officers' staterooms, engine room, galley, gun batteries, pilothouse, and conning tower. *Penn's Landing at Spruce St., tel. 215/922–1898. Admission: $3 (includes USS* Becuna). *Open daily 10–4:30, summer 10–5.*

㉓ Opportunities to board a submarine come infrequently, but you can follow the *Olympia* with a tour of the adjacent **USS Becuna.** This "guppy class" sub is 318 feet long and had a crew of 88. It was commissioned in 1944 and conducted search-and-destroy missions in the South Pacific. After World War II it became a training vessel; by the time it was decommissioned in 1969, it had made 10,000 dives. Note the crew's cramped quarters as you step through the narrow walkways, climb the ladders, and glimpse the torpedoes in the torpedo room. Especially appealing to kids. All guides are World War II submarine vets. *Penn's Landing at Spruce St., tel. 215/922–1898. Admission: $3 (includes USS* Olympia). *Open daily 10–4:30, summer 10–5.*

㉔ Docked a block north is the ***Gazela of Philadelphia,*** formerly *Gazela Primeiro*. Built in 1883, this 177-foot square-rigger is the last of a Portuguese fleet of cod-fishing ships. Still fishing as late as 1969, it is the oldest and largest wooden square-rigger still sailing. As the Port of Philadelphia's ambassador of goodwill, the *Gazela* sails up and down the Atlantic Coast to harbor festivals and celebrations. It is also a sail-training ship and a museum. The all-volunteer crew of 35 works all winter to restore it and sail in summer. Climb aboard to view the crew's living quarters, the hold where fish were kept, the galley, spars and rigging, and captain's and officers' quarters. *Penn's Landing between Walnut and Spruce Sts., tel. 215/923–9030. Open Memorial Day–Labor Day daily 10–6; rest of year, weekends noon–5.*

㉕ A few steps from the *Gazela* but back on solid ground is the **Port of History Museum.** Built for the U.S. Bicentennial in 1976 by the Commonwealth of Pennsylvania, the museum features ever-changing displays of fine art, crafts, and design. Recent shows have included "National Sculpture Society Celebrates the Figure," "Sea Finland" on the waterways and ships of Finland, and the Pennsylvania Academy of Fine Arts fellowship exhibition. Some of the permanent collection—such as ship models and African sculpture—are occasionally displayed. *Penn's Landing at Walnut St., tel. 215/925–3804. Admission: $2. Open Wed.–Sun. 10–4:30. Call for information on current exhibit.*

㉖ Docked in the river a block north is the 394-foot-long *Moshulu* (Penn's Landing at Chestnut St., tel. 215/925–3237). The largest steel sailing ship still afloat, it is now a restaurant (*see* Chapter 6) and maritime museum.

㉗ In the middle of Delaware Avenue are the tracks of the **Penn's Landing Trolley Company.** You can board an authentic turn-of-the-century trolley at Dock Street or Spruce Street for a 20-minute round-trip along the Delaware River waterfront. The conductor provides a guided tour as you ride. *Delaware Ave. at Spruce St., tel. 215/627–0807. Fare: $1 adults, 50¢ children under 12. Runs 11–dusk weekends and holidays from Apr. 12 to Dec. 7; also Thurs. and Fri. from June 19 to Labor Day.*

㉘ Watch out for traffic as you leave the trolley, and head back to Front Street at Sansom Street. As you walk west on Sansom Street, you'll spot **Welcome Park,** site of the slate-roof house where William Penn lived briefly and where he granted the Charter of Privileges in 1701. (The *Welcome* was the ship that transported Penn to America.) On a 60-foot-long map of Penn's Philadelphia carved in the pavement in the park sits a scale model of the Penn statue from atop City Hall. The wall surrounding the park displays a time line of his life, with information about his philosophy and quotations from his writings.

Time Out Stop for a bite to eat or a drink at the historic **City Tavern** (2nd and Walnut Sts.), where the fathers of our country hung out and where waitstaff in Colonial dress now serve traditional American dishes.

㉙ A half-block west on Walnut Street, the **Philadelphia Merchant's Exchange** (3rd and Walnut Sts., tel. 215/597–8974) stands behind Dock Street, a cobblestone thoroughfare that is closed to traffic. Designed by the well-known Philadelphia architect William Strickland and built in 1832, the Greek Revival structure served as the city's commercial center for 50 years. It was both the stock exchange and a place where merchants met to trade goods. In the tower, a watchman scanned the Delaware and notified merchants of arriving ships. Now it's the regional offices of the National Park Service and the interior is not open to the public.

30 Just a few steps farther west on Walnut Street is the **Bishop White House,** home of Bishop William White, rector of Christ Church, first Episcopal bishop of Pennsylvania, and spiritual leader of Philadelphia for 60 years. Built in 1786, this upper-class house has been restored to Colonial elegance. White, who was chaplain to the Continental Congress, entertained many members of the first families of the country, including Washington, Franklin, and Robert Morris (the bishop's brother-in-law). The second-floor study contains much of the bishop's own library. Unlike most houses of the period, the bishop's house had an early form of flush toilet. The house tour is not recommended for children (they get bored). *309 Walnut St., tel. 215/597–8974. Open daily 9:30–4:30; obtain tickets at the Visitor Center for a free 1-hr tour that includes the Bishop White House and the Todd House.*

31 On the same block, the simply furnished **Todd House** stands in direct contrast to the lavish Bishop White House. Built in 1775, it has been restored to its appearance in the 1790s, when its best-known resident lived here. Dolley Payne Todd lost her husband, the lawyer John Todd, to the yellow-fever epidemic of 1793. She later married James Madison, who became the fourth president. *4th and Walnut Sts., tel. 215/597–8974. Open daily 9:30–4:30; obtain tickets at the Visitor Center for a free 1-hr tour that includes the Todd House and the Bishop White House.*

32 A few steps south on 4th Street is the nation's first fire-insurance company, the **Philadelphia Contributionship for the Insurance of Houses from Loss by Fire.** The contributionship was founded by Benjamin Franklin in 1752; the present building dates from 1836. The museum, upstairs room, and garden are open to the public. *212 S. 4th St., tel. 215/627–1752. Open weekdays 10–3.*

33 A block south on 4th Street is the 22-room **Hill-Physick-Keith House,** built in 1786. Philip Syng Physick, a leading physician in the days before anesthesia, is known as the "Father of American Surgery." He developed techniques and instruments that helped place American surgery at the forefront of the profession. While caring for victims of the yellow-fever epidemic of 1793, he contracted the disease himself. His most famous patient was Chief Justice John Marshall, who came from Washington and was successfully treated for bladder stones. This is the only free-standing house left in Society Hill. Surrounding it on three sides is a garden filled with plants common in the 19th century. *321 S. 4th St., tel. 215/925–7866. Admission: $2 adults, 50¢ children. Open Tues.–Sat. 10–4; Sun. 1–4.*

Take a pleasant walk east on Delancey Street and then turn right on 3rd Street to Pine Street. At the northwest corner is **34** the **Thaddeus Kosciuszko National Memorial.** A Polish general who later became a national hero in his homeland, Kosciuszko came to the United States in 1776 to help fight the Revolution. The first floor has a portrait gallery and a chronology of his life. The second floor displays many of the general's possessions. A six-minute film in English and Polish portrays his activities during the Revolution. *301 Pine St., tel. 215/597–8974. Open daily 9–5, July and Aug. 10–5.*

㉟ A block east is **Head House Square** (2nd and Pine Sts.), an open-air Colonial marketplace that extends from Pine Street to Lombard Street. It was established as New Market in 1745. George Washington shopped here. Built in 1804, the Head House was both the home of the market master and a firehouse. Today, on summer weekends, the square is used for craft fairs, food festivals, and other activities. A host of street performers, including jugglers, magicians, and mimes, draws crowds.

㊱ East of Head House Square is **New Market,** a once-thriving but currently vacant complex of boutiques and restaurants. It's still worth a walk-through, from the 18th-century homes on 2nd Street to the contemporary glass facade on Front Street.

Time Out You can find food and drink on both sides of 2nd Street between Pine and South streets.

Heading north on 2nd Street to Locust Street, note Society Hill Towers, three high-rise apartment buildings dating from 1964; and the Society Hill Townhouses at 3rd and Locust streets, designed in 1962 by I. M. Pei, who also designed the towers.

㊲ Cross Locust Street and turn right on 3rd Street to the **Powel House,** a brick Georgian house built in 1765 and purchased by Samuel Powel in 1769. Powel was the last mayor of Philadelphia under the Crown and the first in the new republic. The lavish house is furnished with 18th-century antiques and has such appointments as a mahogany staircase from Santo Domingo, a 1765 mahogany secretary, and a signed Gilbert Stuart portrait. Here the "Patriot Mayor" and his wife, Elizabeth, entertained such dignitaries as Washington, Lafayette, and foreign ministers. Next door lived John Penn, governor of Pennsylvania. The house, which has a ballroom on the second floor, can be rented for parties and other events ($1,000 a night). *244 S. 3rd St., tel. 215/627–0364. Admission: $2 adults; $1 students with ID; 50¢ children under 12. Open Tues.–Sat. 10–4, Sun. 1–4.*

Tour 3. City Hall and Environs

Numbers in the margin correspond with points of interest on the Tours 3 and 4 map.

For a visual introduction to the downtown, climb the few steps to the plaza in front of the **Municipal Services Building** at 15th Street and John F. Kennedy Boulevard. No spot on the ground provides a better up-close overview of the city. You'll feel surrounded by Philadelphia—City Hall; the PSFS Building; the Art Museum; the new skyscraper, One Liberty Place; the Clothespin statue; and other places we'll cover.

❶ One block west of the Municipal Services Building plaza is the **Philadelphia Visitors Center.** Here you can get brochures about the city and surroundings, lists of restaurants and hotels, and information about current events. Volunteers and staff members are on hand to answer your questions. What are the most common questions they hear? Where's the Liberty Bell? Where's Independence Hall? Where's the nearest bathroom?

In the gift shop—where the staff wears Colonial garb—you can buy a Philadelphia T-shirt, a necktie with a pattern of Liberty Bells, and a sticker showing a tombstone inscribed, "I would rather be in Philadelphia." *16th St. and John F. Kennedy Blvd., tel. 215/636-1666. Open daily 9-6.*

Located in the Visitors Center is the **Cultural Connection Tix-Stop,** which sells half-price tickets for music, theater, dance, gallery, and other special events. Tickets are on sale the day of the event. *Tel. 215/636-1666. Open Tues.-Thurs. 11:30-3:30, Fri. and Sat. 11:30-5. For a taped message listing tickets offered that day, call the Cultural Connection TixStop Hotline, 215/564-4414.*

Walk east on Kennedy Boulevard to 15th Street for an incomparable, unobstructed view of **City Hall.** Topped by a newly restored 37-foot bronze statue of William Penn, the city's founder, City Hall stands 548 feet high and until 1987 was Philadelphia's tallest building. With 642 rooms, it is the largest city hall in the country and the tallest masonry-bearing building in the world: No steel structure supports it. It took 30 years to build (1871 to 1900) and cost the taxpayers more than $23 million. Scattered about the exterior are hundreds of statues by Alexander Milne Calder, who also designed the Penn statue at the top. You won't get to see all the statues or the tower—scaffolding used in restoration work has shrouded it since 1985 and will probably remain through 1990. The observation deck —closed until further notice as part of the restoration—affords a 30-mile view of the city and surroundings. Even the clock, 16 feet in diameter, is visible for miles (when no scaffolding covers it).

Not only the geographic center of Penn's original city, City Hall is also the governmental center. Start at the northeast corner and ascend one flight to the mayor's ornate reception room (Room 202), and the recently restored Conversation Hall (Room 201). Take a look, too, at the City Council Chambers (Room 400) and the Supreme Court of Pennsylvania. Municipal court sessions are open to the public. "Art in City Hall" has changing exhibits of local artists; you'll find it on the second floor outside the mayor's office and on the fourth floor outside City Council chambers. *Broad and Market Sts., tel. 215/686-1776; Mayor's Office of Information, Room 121, tel. 215/686-2250; 1-hr tours of City Hall weekdays at 12:30, tel. 215/567-4476 for taped message.*

Leave City Hall by the northern exit and cross Kennedy Boulevard to the **Masonic Temple.** Philadelphia is the mother city of American Masonry, and the temple is home to the Grand Lodge of Free and Accepted Masons of Pennsylvania. The gavel used at the laying of the cornerstone in 1868 was the one that Brother George Washington used to lay the cornerstone of the U.S. Capitol. Designed by Brother James H. Windrim and built by Masons, the ornate interior consists of seven Lodge Halls built to represent seven styles of architecture: Corinthian, Ionic, Italian Renaissance, Norman, Gothic, Oriental, and Egyptian. The collection of Masonry items includes handwritten letters from Washington to brothers of the Grand Lodge and Benjamin Franklin's printing of the first book on Freemasonry published in America. *1 N. Broad St., tel. 215/988-1917. Free 45-min tours weekdays 10, 11, 1, 2, and 3; Sat. 10 and 11. Closed Sat. July and Aug.*

Tours 3 and 4

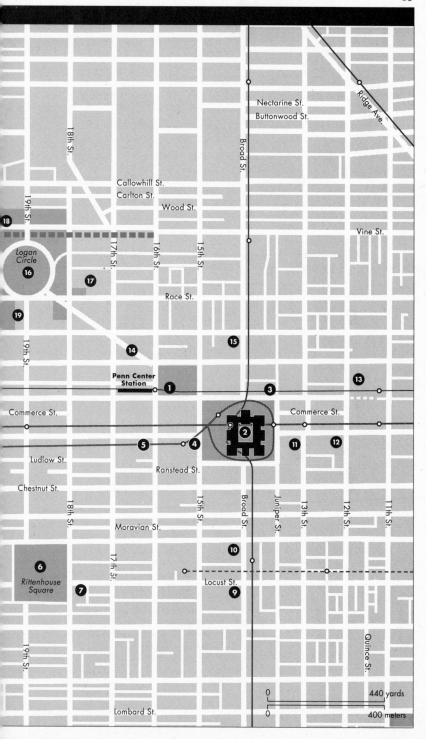

Nectarine St.

Buttonwood St.

Ridge Ave.

Callowhill St.

Carlton St.

Wood St.

Vine St.

18th St.

19th St.

18

Logan
Circle
16

17

17th St.

16th St.

15th St.

Race St.

19

19th St.

15

14

Penn Center
Station **1**

3

13

Commerce St.

Commerce St.

2

5

4

11

12

Ludlow St.

Ranstead St.

Chestnut St.

18th St.

15th St.

Broad St.

Juniper St.

13th St.

12th St.

11th St.

Moravian St.

10

17th St.

6

Rittenhouse
Square

7

Locust St.

9

Quince St.

0   440 yards

0   400 meters

Lombard St.

4 Walk to 15th and Market streets and you'll see Claes Oldenburg's 45-foot-high, 10-ton steel *Clothespin* in front of the Center Square Building. Lauded by some and scorned by others, this pop art piece contrasts with the traditional statuary so common in Philadelphia.

Time Out For a refreshing pause with a nearly eye-to-eye view of the statue of Billy Penn, enter the Center Square Building behind the *Clothespin* and take the elevator to the 41st-floor restaurant, **Top of Center Square** (tel. 215/563–9494). It's the highest restaurant in Philadelphia.

5 Two blocks west, **One Liberty Place** (1650 Market St.) is the 945-foot, 63-story office building that propelled Philadelphia into the "ultra-high" skyscraper era. Built in 1987 at a cost of $225 million, it became the tallest structure in Philadelphia, breaking an unwritten law against buildings higher than the William Penn statue atop City Hall. The Art Deco structure, reminiscent of New York's Chrysler Building, is visible from almost everywhere in the city.

6 Walk to 18th Street, head south, and you soon come upon **Rittenhouse Square** (between 18th and 19th Sts. at Walnut St.). Once grazing ground for cows and sheep, this is now Philadelphia's classiest park. At lunchtime, workers from surrounding office buildings picnic on the grass and feed the squirrels. Until 1950 town houses bordered the square, but they have now been replaced on three sides by swank apartment buildings and hotels. The square is also the scene of annual events such as the Rittenhouse Square Flower Market, the Easter Parade, the Fine Arts Annual, the Clothesline Art Exhibit, and the Mozart on the Square Festival.

7 East of the square are the Barclay Hotel; the Philadelphia Art Alliance, a gay-'90s mansion with galleries open to the public; and the **Curtis Institute of Music** (1726 Locust St., tel. 215/893–5261), a tuition-free school for outstanding students whose graduates include Leonard Bernstein, Samuel Barber, Ned Rorem, and Anna Moffo. You may recognize the exterior of the Curtis Institute from the Eddie Murphy film *Trading Places*. Free student and faculty concerts are given from October through May at 8 PM, almost every Monday, Wednesday, and Friday.

West of the square are Holy Trinity Episcopal Church, a branch of the Free Library of Philadelphia, and the brand new Rittenhouse Hotel.

8 Leave the square on the southern side, continue south on 19th Street to Delancey Place, and turn right. A block west is the **Rosenbach Museum and Library**, which has more than 130,000 manuscripts and 30,000 rare books. This 1863 three-floor town house is furnished with Persian rugs and 18th-century British, French, and American antiques such as Chippendale, Adam, and Hepplewhite furniture. Amassed by Philadelphia collectors Philip H. and A.S.W. Rosenbach, the collection includes paintings by Canaletto, Sully, and Lawrence; drawings by Daumier, Fragonard, and Blake; book illustrations ranging from medieval illumination to Maurice Sendak; the first edition of Benjamin Franklin's *Poor Richard's Almanac;* and manuscripts of Chaucer's *Canterbury Tales* and James Joyce's *Ulysses. 2010 Delancey Pl., tel. 215/732–1600. Admission:*

$2.50, $1.50 senior citizens and students. Open Tues.–Sun. 11–4. Guided 1-hr tour (come no later than 2:45). Closed Aug. and national holidays.

On your way back to Rittenhouse Square, you may want to wander through the neighborhood west of the square. Cypress Street just north of Delancey Place, and Panama Street just south, are two of the many intimate streets lined with trees and town houses characteristic of the area.

From Rittenhouse Square, walk east on Locust Street four blocks to the **Academy of Music** (Broad and Locust Sts., tel. 215/893–1900 or 215/893–1930 for the box office). Modeled after Milan's La Scala opera house, it opened with a lavish ball in 1857. Home of the Philadelphia Orchestra, the academy attracts not only music lovers and students but also many members of Philadelphia's elite. Friday afternoon concerts are legendary for their audience of "Main Line matrons." Tickets are available at the box office; if you're willing to wait in line and sit in the cramped amphitheater four levels above the stage, you can take advantage of one of the cultural world's great bargains, the $2 "nosebleed" seats. The academy is also home to the Opera Company of Philadelphia and the Luciano Pavarotti International Voice Competition, and the site of the Pennsylvania and Milwaukee Ballet's annual Christmas production of *The Nutcracker*.

A block north of the academy is the second "Grande Dame of South Broad Street," the **Bellevue Stratford Hotel** (Broad and Walnut Sts., tel. 215/893–1776). The epitome of the thirst for opulence characteristic of the early 1900s, it was the city's leading hotel for decades. It closed after the 1976 outbreak of Legionnaire's disease, which spread through the building's air-conditioning system during an American Legion convention. Reopened as the Fairmont several years later, it failed to regain its luster and closed again in 1986. Recently renovated, this magnificent building has reopened as home to a number of shops and offices, as well as the luxurious Hotel Atop the Bellvue (*see* Chapter 7).

As you continue up Broad Street, you pass a French Renaissance–style building, the **Union League of Philadelphia** (140 S. Broad St.). A bastion of Philadelphia conservatism, the Union League is a social club founded during the Civil War to preserve the Union.

Just east of City Hall is the **John Wanamaker Store,** the grandest of Philadelphia's department stores. Wanamaker began with a clothing store in 1861 and became one of America's most innovative and prominent retailers. From 1889 to 1893 he was U.S. Postmaster General under President Benjamin Harrison. Designed by the Chicago firm of D. H. Burnham and Company, the building has a nine-story grand court with a 30,000-pipe organ—the largest ever built—and a 2,500-pound statue of an eagle, both remnants of the 1904 Louisiana Purchase Exposition in St. Louis. "Meet me at the Eagle" is a popular way for Philadelphians to arrange get-togethers. Organ performances are held at 11:15 and 5:15. The store is famous for its Christmas sound-and-light show. *13th and Market Sts., tel. 215/422–2000. Open Mon.–Sat. 10–7, Wed. 10–9, Sun. 11–6.*

Leave Wanamaker's at the Market Street exit, turn right, and go one block to 12th Street. Here is the **Philadelphia Saving**

Fund Society (PSFS) Building, one of the city's first skyscrapers. The 1930 structure still looks modern and was influential in the design of other American skyscrapers. Pay special attention to the enormous escalators and the main banking floor, two striking contrasts to the utilitarian approaches of architecture today. If you have any banking needs, here's a place to handle them and see an interesting sight at the same time. *12th and Market Sts., tel. 215/629–7000. Open Mon.–Thurs. 9–3, Fri. 9–6.*

⑬ A half-block north on 12th Street is the **Reading Terminal Market.** One floor beneath the defunct Reading Railroad's 1891 train shed, the sprawling market has 79 stores, stalls, and other places of business. Some 70 are food-related; the remainder include a flower shop, bookstores (one just for cookbooks), and a wine shop. Some stalls change daily, offering items from hooked rugs and handmade jewelry to Mexican and African crafts. No other place in the city offers a wider variety of eating places—a vegetarian restaurant, a gourmet ice cream store, a cookie shop, and a Philadelphia cheesesteak store. Most stalls have their own counters with seating; there's also a central eating area, where at lunchtime on the second Friday of each month a group of local politicians called the Reading Terminals play jazz. You can also buy a large variety of fresh food to cook from vegetable and fruit stands, butchers, fish stores, and Pennsylvania Dutch markets. The entire building is a National Historic Landmark and the train shed is a National Engineering Landmark. *12th and Filbert Sts., tel. 215/922–2317. Open Mon.–Sat. 8–6 PM. To arrange a tour, call the market office.*

Tour 4. Museum Area

⑭ The spine of this tour is the **Benjamin Franklin Parkway,** which angles across the city grid system from City Hall to Fairmount Park. It was not part of William Penn's original plan for Philadelphia. Lined with a distinguished assemblage of museums, institutions, hotels, and apartment buildings, this 250-foot-wide boulevard inspired by the Champs Élysées was designed by French architect Jacques Greber and built in the 1920s. Adorned by fountains, statues, trees, and flags of every country, the parkway is the route of most of the city's parades and the site of many festivals, including the Thanksgiving and Easter parades, the Big Apple Circus, and the CoreStates Pro Cycling championship.

Before heading out the parkway, we'll take a short detour to
⑮ the **Pennsylvania Academy of the Fine Arts.** Starting at the Visitors Center (16th St. and Kennedy Blvd.), walk east on Kennedy Boulevard and turn left on Broad Street; go two blocks to Cherry Street and you'll see a High Victorian Gothic building (1876) that's a work of art in itself. Designed by the noted, sometimes eccentric, Philadelphia architects Frank Furness and George Hewitt, the multicolored stone-and-brick exterior is an extravagant blend of columns, friezes, Art Deco, and Moorish flourishes. Inside, the oldest art institution in the United States (founded 1804) boasts a collection that ranges from Winslow Homer and Benjamin West to Andrew Wyeth and Red Grooms. The academy faculty has included Thomas Sully, Thomas Eakins, and Charles Willson Peale. The permanent collection is supplemented by constantly changing exhibits of sculpture, paintings, and mixed-media artwork.

Broad and Cherry Sts., tel. 215/972-7600. Admission: $5 adults, $3 senior citizens, $2 students. Free Sat. 10-1. Open Tues.-Sat. 10-5, Sun. 11-5.

Head west on Cherry Street past the American Friends Service Committee and the Race Street Friends Meeting House. At 17th Street, you'll find yourself on the Benjamin Franklin Parkway.

16 Walk northwest on the parkway one block to **Logan Circle.** Originally this was one of four squares Penn had built at the corners of a rectangle around Center Square, where City Hall now stands. (The others are Franklin Square to the northeast, Washington Square to the southeast, and Rittenhouse Square to the southwest.) The focal point of Logan Circle is the Swann Fountain of 1920, designed by Alexander Stirling Calder, son of Alexander Milne Calder, who did the William Penn statue atop City Hall. The main figures in the fountain symbolize Philadelphia's three leading waterways: the Delaware and Schuylkill rivers and Wissahickon Creek. In October 1979 Pope John Paul II celebrated mass on a platform over the fountain before 150,000 people.

17 The **Cathedral of Saints Peter and Paul** at 18th Street and the parkway is the basilica of the Archdiocese of Philadelphia and the spiritual center for the Philadelphia area's 1.4 million Roman Catholics. Topped by a huge copper dome, it was built between 1846 and 1864 in the Italian Renaissance style. Many interior decorations were done by Constantino Brumidi, who painted the dome of the United States Capitol. Six Philadelphia bishops and archbishops are buried beneath the altar. *18th and Race Sts., tel. 215/561-1313. Open 9-3:30.*

Walking counterclockwise around Logan Circle, you'll see twin marble Greek Revival buildings off to your right. The nearer is
18 the city's Family Court; the other is the **Free Library of Philadelphia.** Along with a collection of more than 2 million volumes (*see* Libraries in Exploring, *below*), the central unit of the public-library system presents concerts, movies, lectures, and historical displays. *19th St. and Benjamin Franklin Pkwy., tel. 215/686-5322. Open Mon.-Wed. 9-9, Thurs. and Fri. 9-6, Sat. 9-5, Sun. (Sept.-May) 1-5. Closed Sun. in summer.*

Time Out The rooftop cafeteria of the **Free Library** (19th St. and Benjamin Franklin Pkwy.) provides inexpensive meals at umbrellaed tables.

19 Cross Logan Circle to the **Academy of Natural Sciences,** America's first museum of natural history. Founded in 1812, the present building dates from 1868. The collection is famous for stuffed animals from around the world, displayed in 35 natural settings. The second-floor "Outside In" exhibit is a minimuseum where children handle fossils, dinosaur teeth, even live animals such as snakes and lizards. Since 1986 the main attraction has been "Discovering Dinosaurs": reconstructed skeletons of a tyrannosaurus and others, movies, computer videos, and a Cretaceous landscape complete with animals and plants. Step on a scale to compare your weight with a dinosaur's. *19th St. and Benjamin Franklin Pkwy., tel. 215/299-1020. Admission: $5 adults, $4 children. Open weekdays 10-4:30, weekends and holidays 10-5.*

From the Academy, walk west on Race Street to 20th Street
20 and the **Franklin Institute.** Founded to honor Benjamin Franklin, the institute is a science museum with an abundance of
hands-on exhibits. You can sit in the cockpit of a T-33 jet train-
er, trace the route of a corpuscle through the world's largest
artificial heart (15,000 times life-size), and ride to nowhere on a
350-ton Baldwin steam locomotive. The many exhibits cover en-
ergy, motion, sound, physics, astronomy, aviation, ships,
mechanics, electricity, time, and other scientific subjects.
You'll also find a working weather station, computers to operate, and the world's largest pinball machine. Lectures/
demonstrations illustrate scientific concepts—a rose immersed
in liquid nitrogen freezes and is then smashed on the floor. The
Fels Planetarium features shows about the stars, space exploration, comets, and other phenomena. The second-floor
Benjamin Franklin National Memorial has a 21-foot-high, 122-
ton statue by James Earle Fraser, the designer of the buffalo
nickel. *20th St. and Benjamin Franklin Pkwy., tel. 215/448-
1200. Admission: $5.50 adults, $4.50 children 4–11, $4 senior
citizens. Planetarium shows: $1.50 additional. Open Sept.–
June, weekdays 9:30–4:30; summers daily 10–5.*

Winter Street bounds the Franklin Institute to the north. Take
it west one block to 21st Street; cross it and turn left to the
21 **Please Touch Museum,** the only U.S. museum designed specifi-
cally for children seven and younger. (It also appeals to adults.)
The premise here is hands-on, feet-on, try-on: Perform in a circus ring; pet small animals in the "Animals as Pets" exhibit;
dress up in costumes, wigs, and masks. The museum also has
two special exhibits a year, theater programs, workshops, and
a resource center with computers, games, books, and other educational activities. *210 N. 21st St., tel. 215/963–0667.
Admission: $4. Open Tues.–Sun. 10–4:30.*

Cross to the north side of the parkway and walk northwest. On
your right is the Youth Study Center (a detention center for ju-
venile offenders) with two striking tableaux depicting families.

At the next corner, guarded by the statue of *The Thinker*, is the
22 **Rodin Museum,** the best collection of Auguste Rodin's works
outside France. Before entering, marvel at the *Gates of Hell*, a
21-foot-high sculpture with more than 100 human and animal
figures. Inside are 124 sculptures by the French master, including *The Kiss, The Burghers of Calais, Eternal Springtime*,
and hands and busts of his friends. One small room is devoted to
the French novelist Balzac. Photographs by Edward Steichen
show Rodin at work. *22nd St. and Benjamin Franklin Pkwy.,
tel. 215/787–5431. Donation requested. Open Tues.–Sun. 10–5.*

Atop Faire Mount, the plateau at the end of Franklin Parkway,
23 stands the **Philadelphia Museum of Art.** This mammoth building of Minnesota dolomite is modeled after ancient Greek
temples but on a grander scale. Covering 10 acres, it has 200
galleries and a collection of over 300,000 works. You can enter
the museum from the front or the rear; we recommend the
front, where you can run up the 98 steps made famous in the
movie *Rocky*. From the expansive terrace, look up to the pediment on your right at a group of 13 glazed, multicolored statues
of classical gods. After passing Jacques Lipchitz's statue *Prometheus Strangling the Vulture*, climb the last flight of steps,
and, before entering the museum, turn around to savor the
view down the parkway.

Once inside, you'll see the grand staircase and Saint-Gaudens's statue of *Diana*, which formerly graced New York's old Madison Square Garden. The John G. Johnson Collection covers Western art from the Renaissance to the 19th century. The Arensberg and A. E. Gallatin collections contain modern and contemporary works by artists such as Brancusi, Braque, Matisse, and Picasso. Famous paintings from among these collections include Van Eyck's *St. Francis Receiving the Stigmata*, Rubens's *Prometheus Bound*, Benjamin West's *Benjamin Franklin Drawing Electricity from the Sky*, Van Gogh's *Sunflowers*, Renoir's *The Bathers*, and Picasso's *Three Musicians*.

Marcel Duchamps is a specialty of the house; the museum has the world's most extensive collection of his works. Another specialty is reconstructions of entire buildings: a 12th-century French cloister, a 16th-century Indian temple hall, a 16th-century Japanese Buddhist temple, a 17th-century Chinese palace hall, and a Japanese ceremonial teahouse. Among the other collections: costumes, early-American furniture, and Amish and Shaker crafts. An unusual touch—and one that children especially like—is the Kienbusch Collection of Arms and Armor. Recent special exhibitions have spotlighted Marc Chagall, Van Gogh, 17th-century Dutch landscape painting, and the Annenberg collection of Impressionist and post-Impressionist paintings. Pick up a map of the museum at either of the two entrances and wander on your own; or choose from a variety of guided tours. *26th St. and Benjamin Franklin Pkwy., tel. 215/763–8100, 215/787–5488 for 24-hr taped message. Admission: $5 adults, $2.50 senior citizens, students, and children; free Sun. 10–1. Open Tues.–Sun. 10–5; closed on legal holidays. Warning: Budgetary constraints cause frequent and irregular gallery closings.*

Although the bulk of Philadelphia tourist attractions are located in and around Center City, other areas also merit your attention. Here we'll present a tour of one area and briefly describe two others.

Fairmount Park Tour

Numbers in the margin correspond with points of interest on the Fairmount Park map.

Stretching from the edge of downtown to the city's northwest corner, Fairmount Park is the largest city park in the world. The total park system, including other parks under the Fairmount Park Commissioner's jurisdiction, contains 8,900 acres. Fairmount Park itself covers about 4,500 acres.

The park encompasses beautiful natural areas—woodlands, meadows, rolling hills, two scenic waterways, and a forested 5½-mile gorge. It also contains tennis courts, ball fields, playgrounds, trails, exercise courses, several celebrated cultural institutions, and some fine early-American country houses.

Philadelphia has more works of outdoor art than any other city in North America. More than 200 of these works—including statues by Frederic Remington, Jacques Lipchitz, and Auguste Rodin—are scattered throughout Fairmount Park.

The park was established in 1812 when the city purchased 5 acres behind Faire Mount, the hill upon which the Philadelphia

Museum of Art now stands, for waterworks and public gardens. Through private bequests and public purchases (which continue today), it grew to its present size and stature.

The following tour highlights many of the park's treasures. Do it by car, starting near the art museum, or take a narrated tour on the Fairmount Park Trolley Bus. The trolley bus visits many of these sites, and you can get on and off all day (*see* Chapter 1).

Although some of the directions may sound complicated, signs help point the way. An excellent map of the park is available at Memorial Hall and most park mansions and sites for 25¢.

1 The park tour starts where the park began, at **Faire Mount,** now the site of the Philadelphia Museum of Art (*see* Tour 4, *above*). In 1812 a reservoir was built here to distribute water throughout the city.

2 Park behind the art museum and walk down to the **Waterworks.** Designed by Frederick Graff, this National Historic Engineering Landmark was the first steam pumping station of its kind in the country. The notable assemblage of Greek Revival buildings is undergoing extensive renovation.

3 A few steps north of the Waterworks, **Boathouse Row** begins. These 11 architecturally varied 19th-century buildings are home to the 13 rowing clubs that make up the "Schuylkill Navy." The view of the houses from the west side of the river is splendid—especially at night, when they're outlined with hundreds of small lights.

4 Continuing north along Kelly Drive, you soon reach the **Ellen Phillips Samuel Memorial Sculpture Garden.** Bronze and granite statues by 16 artists stand in a series of tableaux and groupings on riverside terraces. Portraying American themes and traits, they include *The Quaker* by Harry Rosen, *Birth of a Nation* by Henry Kreis, and *Spirit of Enterprise* by Jacques Lipchitz.

5 Drive north on Kelly Drive for about 200 yards. Take the second right (at the end of Boathouse Row) and go up to **Lemon Hill.** Built in 1800 on a 350-acre farm, this is a beautiful example of a Federal country house. *Poplar Dr., East Fairmount Park, tel. 215/232-4337. Admission: $1.50. Open Wed.–Sun. 10–4:30.*

6 Head back to Kelly Drive, turn right, and then right again at the equestrian statue of Ulysses S. Grant. The first left takes you to **Mt. Pleasant.** Built in 1761 by Captain John Macpherson, a pirate, the house was later purchased by the Revolutionary War traitor Benedict Arnold. John Adams called the Georgian mansion "the most elegant seat in Pennsylvania." *Mt. Pleasant Dr., East Fairmount Park, tel. 215/763-8100, ext. 333. Admission: $1.50. Open Tues.–Sun. 10–4:30.*

7 Double back to Reservoir Drive, pass Rockland and Ormiston (two other park mansions), and take the next left, Randolph Drive, to **Laurel Hill.** Built around 1767 on a laurel-covered hill overlooking the Schuylkill, the Georgian house was once owned by Dr. Philip Syng Physick (*see* Tour 2, *above*). On some Sunday evenings during the summer, Women for Greater Philadelphia sponsors candlelight chamber-music concerts here. *E. Edgely Dr., East Fairmount Park, tel. 215/235-1776. Admission: $1.50. Open Wed.–Sun. 10–4.*

Fairmount Park

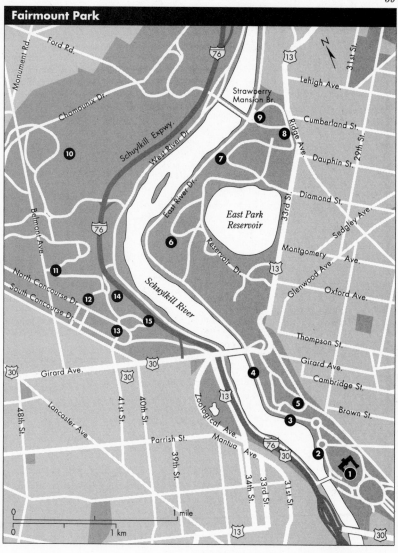

Belmont Plateau, **10**
Boathouse Row, **3**
Cedar Grove, **14**
Ellen Phillips Samuel
Memorial Sculpture
Garden, **4**
Faire Mount, **1**
Japanese House, **11**
Laurel Hill, **7**
Lemon Hill, **5**

Memorial Hall, **12**
Mt. Pleasant, **6**
Smith Civil War
Memorial, **13**
Strawberry Mansion, **9**
Sweetbriar, **15**
Waterworks, **2**
Woodford, **8**

Edgely Drive turns into Dauphin Street. Just before reaching 33rd Street, turn left on Strawberry Mansion Drive and you're **⑧** at **Woodford,** a fine Georgian mansion built about 1756. Inside is the Naomi Wood collection of household goods, including furniture, unusual clocks, and English Delftware. *Near 33rd and Dauphin Sts., East Fairmount Park, tel. 215/229-6115. Admission: $1.50. Open Tues.–Sun. 10–4.*

A few steps northwest of Woodford stands the house that gave **⑨** its name to the nearby section of Philadelphia, **Strawberry Mansion.** The largest mansion in Fairmount Park, it has furniture from the three main phases of its history: Federal, Regency, and Empire. In the parlor is a collection of rare Tucker porcelain; in the attic is a fine assortment of antique dolls. *Near 33rd and Dauphin Sts., East Fairmount Park, tel. 215/228–8364. Admission: $1.50. Open Tues.–Sun. 10–4.*

Go back to Strawberry Mansion Drive, turn left, and cross the Strawberry Mansion Bridge to West Fairmount Park. Looping through the park, you'll reach Chamounix Drive, a long **⑩** straightaway. Turn left on Belmont Mansion Drive to **Belmont Plateau.** Here are Playhouse in the Park and Belmont Mansion, but the main attraction is the view, from 243 feet above river level. In front of you lie the park, the Schuylkill River winding down to the Philadelphia Museum of Art, and—4 miles away— the Philadelphia skyline.

Follow Belmont Mansion Drive down the hill. Where it forks, stay to the left, cross Montgomery Drive, and turn left to reach the Horticulture Center (*see* Parks, Zoos, and Gardens, *below*). Loop all the way around the Horticulture Center to Shofu-So, **⑪** the **Japanese House,** a reconstructed 16th-century house and garden built in Japan, exhibited temporarily at the Museum of Modern Art in New York, and reassembled here in 1958. Enjoy the serenity of the architecture and the waterfall, gardens, Japanese trees, and the pond. *Lansdowne Dr. east of Belmont Ave., West Fairmount Park, tel. 215/686–0104 or 879–4062. Admission: $1.50. Open May–Aug. Wed.–Sun. 11–4; Sept. and Oct. weekends.*

Go back around the Horticulture Center and continue through the gates straight to Belmont Avenue. Turn left and then left again at the first light (North Concourse Drive). On your left is **⑫** **Memorial Hall,** the only major building remaining from the Philadelphia Centennial Exposition of 1876. This grand stone building with a glass dome and Palladian windows was the Centennial art museum. A 20-by-40-foot model of the exposition is the focus of an occasional 15-minute sound-and-light show. *N. Concourse Dr., West Fairmount Park, tel. 215/686–1776. Admission free. Open daily 8:30–5.*

The two towers to your left as you leave Memorial Hall are part **⑬** of the **Smith Civil War Memorial** (N. Concourse Dr., West Fairmount Park). Built from 1897 to 1912 with funds donated by wealthy foundry owner Richard Smith, the memorial honors Pennsylvania heroes of the Civil War. Among those immortalized in bronze are Generals Meade and Hancock—and Smith himself. At the base of each tower is a curved wall with a bench. If you sit at one end and listen to a person whispering at the other end, you'll understand why they're called the Whispering Benches. Unfortunately, the litter around the site reflects its location near a declining neighborhood.

⑭ To the east stands **Cedar Grove,** where five styles of furniture—Jacobean, William and Mary, Queen Anne, Chippendale, and Federal—reflect the accumulations of five generations of the Paschall-Morris family. The house stood in Frankford for 180 years before being moved to this location in 1927. *Lansdowne Dr. off N. Concourse Dr., West Fairmount Park, tel. 215/763–8100, ext. 332. Admission: $1.50. Open Tues.–Sun. 10–4:15.*

Just south of Cedar Grove atop a hill sloping gently down to the
⑮ Schuylkill is **Sweetbriar.** Built in 1797, it was the park's first year-round residence. *Lansdowne Dr. off N. Concourse Dr., West Fairmount Park, tel. 215/222–1333. Admission: $1.50. Open daily except Tues. 10–4. Call ahead.*

A trip farther down Lansdowne Drive takes you to the Philadelphia Zoological Gardens (*see* Parks, Zoos, and Gardens, *below*).

The northwest section of Fairmount Park is **the Wissahickon.** A gorge carved out by the Wissahickon Creek, it is 5½ miles of towering trees, cliffs, trails, and animals, and retains many traces of history.

Of the Philadelphia areas that William Penn founded, Wissahickon has changed the least. You can easily visualize the Lenni-Lenape Indians who lived there, beat its trails, and gave the creek its name. "Wissahickon" is an Anglicized version of the Lenni-Lenape words for yellow creek and catfish creek.

Forbidden Drive, a dirt-and-gravel pathway along the west side of the creek, is a haunt of joggers, bikers, horseback riders, fishermen, and nature lovers. For the more adventurous there are foot trails along the east side of the creek.

Many inns once stood along the banks of the Wissahickon; only one remains. The **Valley Green Inn,** built in 1850 on the site of an earlier inn, is today a restaurant filled with restored antiques and is the focal point of the Wissahickon.

The inn is nestled in one of the loveliest parts of the Wissahickon gorge. Sit on a bench alongside the creek, feed bread crumbs to the ducks, look at the stone bridge reflected in the water, and savor the beauty and the tranquillity. It's an experience you'll long remember.

Valley Green Inn is an excellent departure point for exploring the Wissahickon. You can saunter along one of the trails, enjoy the stream, lose yourself in the wilderness, and investigate some of the sights. To find the sights listed here, ask a mounted policeman or inquire at the inn; a map of the Wissahickon showing all the trails and sites is available ($3) at the inn's snack-booth window.

To reach Valley Green Inn, take the Schuylkill Expressway west to the Lincoln Drive–Wissahickon Park exit (Exit 32). Follow Lincoln Drive to Allen's Lane, then turn right. At Germantown Avenue turn left, go about a mile, turn left at Springfield Avenue, and follow it to the end.

South of
Valley Green Inn About a quarter mile south of Valley Green Inn on the east side of the creek, near where Cresheim Creek joins the Wissahickon, is a picturesque spot with an intriguing name—**Devil's Pool.** Neighborhood kids dive off the rocks into the pool, which local legend says is bottomless. (It's really about 10 feet deep.)

Along the path near the pool, look for **Shakespeare Rock,** with a quotation, appropriate to the setting, carved on its face:

The current that with gentle murmur glides
. . . makes sweet music with th' enamell'd stones,
Giving a gentle kiss to every sedge . . .
And so by many winding nooks he strays
With willing sport, to the wild ocean.

Fingerspan, the newest addition to the Wissahickon, is a steel sculpture of a bridge spanning a ravine. It was done by local artist Jody Pinto.

Toleration, a granite statue of William Penn erected in 1883, stands on Mom Rinker's Rock. This dramatic spot affords a magnificent view of the Wissahickon Valley.

Rittenhousetown, near where Forbidden Drive runs into Lincoln Drive, is a cluster of six small historic whitewashed Colonial buildings. One house, built in 1707, is the birthplace of David Rittenhouse, the clockmaker, astronomer, and patriot after whom Rittenhouse Square is named (*see* Tour 3, *above*). Built around 1683, the mill is the sole survivor of the 60 mills that once lined the Wissahickon. It was the first paper mill in America.

Hermit's Cave was a favorite hangout of the Wissahickon's most famous inhabitant, the German mystic Johannes Kelpius. In 1694, Kelpius and his followers, the Society of the Woman in the Wilderness, moved to the Wissahickon to await the millennium. Kelpius is buried in an unmarked grave near his cave. Look up and you'll see the graceful arch of the Henry Avenue Bridge and, nearby, the broad rock outcropping called **Lover's Leap**—for obvious reasons.

North of Valley Green Inn On the east side of the Rex Avenue Bridge (1 mile north of Valley Green Inn), a path through a stone arch leads up, up, up to **Indian Rock,** where the Lenni-Lenape held council until their disappearance from the valley around 1750. Atop the rock is a stone statue of a kneeling warrior, called Tedyuscung, after a local chief.

The red wooden **Covered Bridge** at the foot of Thomas Mill Road is 97 feet long and 14 feet wide. Built in 1855, it's the last covered bridge still standing within the boundaries of a major American city.

At the north end of Forbidden Drive (2½ miles north of Valley Green Inn) is the **Andorra Natural Area.** Its Tree House Visitors Center has exhibits, a reference library, self-guiding materials including trail maps, and a changing collection of local fauna—toads, rabbits, turtles, and snakes. Tree House hours vary, but the information center is always open (tel. 215/685–9285).

Selected Neighborhoods Worth a Visit

Chinatown Philadelphia's numerous ethnic groups lend their distinctive qualities to the fabric of the city. One prominent group, the Chinese, has been here since the 19th century.

Centered on 10th and Race streets just two blocks north of Market Street, Chinatown serves as the residential and the commercial hub of the Chinese community. Along with more than 50 restaurants (*see* Chapter 6), Chinatown attractions include grocery stores, souvenir and gift shops, martial-arts studios, a fortune-cookie store, bilingual street signs, and red-and-green pagoda-style telephone booths.

One striking Chinatown site is the **Chinese Friendship Gate** straddling 10th Street at Arch Street. This intricate and colorful 40-foot-tall arch—the largest authentic Chinese gate outside China—was created by Chinese artisans, who brought their own tools and construction materials. The citizens of Tianjin, Philadelphia's sister city in the People's Republic of China, donated the building materials, including the tile.

From February to May, you can celebrate Chinese New Year with a 10-course banquet at the **Chinese Cultural Center** (125 N. 10th St., tel. 215/923–6767). The center occupies an 1831 example of the Peking Mandarin palace style.

University City University City, in West Philadelphia directly west of Center City across the Schuylkill River, has three college campuses—the University of Pennsylvania, Drexel University, and the Philadelphia College of Pharmacy and Science. It also has the University City Science Center (a leading think tank), a large and impressive collection of houses, and a variety of restaurants, movie theaters, stores, and bars catering to students and other residents.

Prominent on your itinerary here should be the **University of Pennsylvania.** For a good look at the Ivy League campus stop at the **Information Center** at 34th and Walnut streets (tel. 215/898 –1000), then follow **Locust Walk** between 33rd Street and 40th Street.

Starting at 33rd Street, you see **Franklin Field,** the university football stadium and home of the Penn Relays (*see* Festivals, Seasonal Events, Chapter 1; and Sports and Fitness, Chapter 5). At 33rd and Spruce streets is the **University Museum** (*see* Libraries and Museums, below). And just north of Locust Walk along 33rd Street is the Moore School of Engineering, home of **ENIAC,** the world's first all-electronic general-purpose digital computer (*see* Off the Beaten Track, *below*).

At 34th Street and Locust Walk is the **Furness Building.** Formerly the university's main library and now the graduate-school fine-arts library, it is an architectural gem by the innovative Frank Furness.

You're now at the edge of **College Green** (Blanche Levy Park), the crossroads of the campus. In the middle stands a statue of Benjamin Franklin, who founded the university in 1740. To your right, the huge **Van Pelt Library** stretches from 34th Street to 36th Street. In front is Claes Oldenburg's *Broken Button* statue. To your left is **College Hall,** an administration building said to be the inspiration for the scary Addams House of the cartoonist Charles Addams.

Just west of 36th Street, the **Annenberg School of Communication** and the **Annenberg Center** (*see* Chapter 8) are to the right, and the famed **Wharton School of Economics** is to the left. As you pass the intersection of 37th Street, say hello to Ben Franklin sitting on a bench.

At 38th Street is the well-stocked **University Bookstore** (*see* Chapter 4). A footbridge takes you over 38th Street (turn around for a good view of Center City) to **Superblock,** three high-rise student dormitories. Locust Walk ends at 40th Street with the Dental School, a row of stores, restaurants, and two movie theaters.

Two other notable university sights a short distance from Locust Walk are the **Hospital of the University of Pennsylvania** at 34th and Spruce streets and the **Quad** near 37th and Spruce streets. The university's first dorm buildings, the Quad was designed by Cope and Stewardson in 1895 and became the prototype of the Collegiate Gothic style prevalent in campuses coast to coast.

Germantown and Chestnut Hill In the late 1600s, Francis Pastorius led 13 families out of Germany to seek religious freedom in the New World. They settled 6 miles northwest of Philadelphia in what is now Germantown.

The Germantown area is rich in history. It was the site of Philadelphia's first gristmill (1683) and America's first paper mill (1690). The American Colonies' first English-language Bible was printed here (1743). By the time of the Revolution, Germantown had become a bustling industrial town. In 1777, Colonial troops under George Washington attacked part of the British force here and fought the Battle of Germantown in various skirmishes.

Germantown was incorporated into the City of Philadelphia when the city was consolidated in 1854. Today, Germantown is a successfully integrated neighborhood with a wealth of still-occupied and exceptionally well-preserved architectural masterpieces.

You can reach Germantown from Center City via the no. 23 trolley, by the two Chestnut Hill SEPTA commuter trains, or by car. The best way to tour the area is by car. From City Hall, drive north on Broad Street for about 3½ miles to Pike Street (two blocks north of Erie Avenue). Turn left, go one block to Germantown Avenue, and turn right.

About a mile up Germantown Avenue on the left side is **Loudon,** an 1801 Greek Revival house filled with antique furniture, household goods, and paintings. *(4650 Germantown Ave., tel. 215/685–2067). Open Tues., Thurs., and Sat. 1–4.*

Six blocks farther north is the **Germantown Historical Society.** Occupying a complex of six late-18th- and early-19th-century houses, the society has a historical and genealogical library and collections of industrial and decorative arts. Nearby is **Grumblethorpe** (5267 Germantown Ave., tel. 215/843–4820). Built by John Wister in 1744, this Georgian house is one of Germantown's leading examples of early-18th-century architecture. *5214 Germantown Ave., tel. 215/844–0514. Open Tues., Thurs., and Sat. 1–4.*

Two blocks north is the **Deshler-Morris House,** where President Washington lived in 1793–94 while the yellow-fever epidemic plagued Philadelphia. It was known as the Germantown White House. *5442 Germantown Ave., tel. 215/596–1748. Open Thurs. and Sat. 1–4. Closed Dec.–March.*

One of the oldest buildings in Philadelphia is **Wyck** built in 1690. Both the house and the garden are notable examples of early-American lifestyle. The house remained in the ownership of the same Quaker family from 1690 to 1973. *(6026 Germantown Ave., tel. 215/848–1690). Open Tues., Thurs., and Sat. 1-4.*

To see fabulous Germantown architecture, wander the area west of Wyck, between Walnut Lane and Tulpehocken Street. Included here is the **Ebenezer Maxwell House.** Built in 1859, this Gothic extravaganza of elongated windows, arches, and a three-story tower is the incarnation of an old haunted house and Philadelphia's only mid-19th-century house-museum. *200 W. Tulpehocken St., tel. 215/438–1861. Open Wed.–Sun. 1-4*

If you have time for only one site in Germantown, make it **Cliveden.** Built in 1763 by Benjamin Chew, Germantown's most elaborate country house was occupied by the British during the Revolution. On October 4, 1777, Washington's unsuccessful attempt to dislodge the British resulted in his defeat at the Battle of Germantown. You can still see bullet marks on the outside walls. Today a museum, the house occupies a 6-acre plot with outbuildings and a barn converted into offices and a gift shop. It remained in the Chew family until 1972, when it was donated to the National Trust for Historic Preservation. *6401 Germantown Ave., tel. 215/848–1777. Open Tues.–Sat. 10–4, Sun. 1–4.*

Across the street from Cliveden is **Upsala,** built about 1755 and one of Germantown's best examples of Federal-style architecture. Continental troops set up their cannons on Upsala's front lawn and shelled the British at Cliveden. *6430 Germantown Ave., tel. 215/842–1798. Open Tues. and Thurs. 1–4. Closed Jan.–Mar.*

North of Germantown is the residential community of Mount Airy, and north of that is Chestnut Hill. One of Philadelphia's poshest neighborhoods, Chestnut Hill has numerous impressive mansions, more than 120 shops and restaurants, several art galleries, two train stations, and an arboretum.

Chestnut Hill sights include **Pastorius Park** at Lincoln Drive and Abington Avenue (one block west of the 8100 block of Germantown Ave.) and **Morris Arboretum** (*see* Parks, Zoos, and Gardens, *below*). The **Woodmere Art Museum** (9201 Germantown Ave., tel. 215/247–0476) displays paintings, tapestries, sculpture, porcelains, ivories, Japanese rugs, and works by contemporary local artists.

Historical Buildings and Sites

Many of Philadelphia's historic sites have been described in the Exploring section. Here are some that are not on the tours.

Andalusia. In the early 1800s, Philadelphia banker Nicholas Biddle toured Greece and returned determined to re-create its architecture in his backyard. He commissioned the prominent architect Thomas U. Walter to add a Doric colonnade and other alterations to his 18th-century farmhouse, Andalusia, which transformed it into one of the nation's first examples of Greek Revival architecture. Wander throughout the 220-acre estate to see the boxwood and rose gardens, various outbuildings, and the grotto. The house remains in the Biddle family; it is administered by the National Trust for Historic Preservation. *State Rd., Andalusia, Bucks County, tel. 215/848–1777. Cost: $7 per person, 5-person minimum. Open for guided tours Tues.–Sat. 10–2, by appointment only; 10 days' notice requested.*

Gloria Dei. One of the few remnants of the Swedes who settled Pennsylvania before William Penn is Gloria Dei (Old Swedes') Church. Organized in 1642, Gloria Dei is the oldest church in Pennsylvania. Built in 1698, the church has numerous religious artifacts, such as a 1608 Bible owned by the Swedish Queen Christiana, and carvings on the lectern and the balcony salvaged from the congregation's first church, which was destroyed by fire. Models of two of the ships that transported the first Swedish settlers hang from the ceiling—right in the center of the church. Grouped around the church are the parish hall, caretaker's house, rectory, guild house, and graveyard. *916 Swanson St., near Christian and Delaware Aves., tel. 215/ 389-1513. Open daily 9-5.*

Mikveh Israel Synagogue and Cemetery. Nathan Levy, a Colonial merchant whose ship, *The Myrtilla*, brought the Liberty Bell to America, organized the synagogue in 1740. It is the oldest synagogue in Philadelphia and the second-oldest in the United States. Originally located at 3rd and Cherry streets, it now occupies the same building as the National Museum of American Jewish History (*see* Libraries and Museums, *below*). The cemetery was organized in 1738. Levy acquired the land from William Penn as a family burial ground, and it was later expanded to accommodate the Jewish community. Buried there are Haym Salomon, financier of the American Revolution, and Rebecca Gratz, the inspiration for Rebecca in Sir Walter Scott's novel *Ivanhoe. Synagogue: 44 N. 4th St., tel. 215/922-5446. Open Mon.-Thurs. 10-5, Fri. 10-3, Sun. noon-5. Cemetery: Spruce St. between 8th and 9th Sts., tel. 215/922-5446. A guide is present in summer, weekdays 10-4. From Sept. to June, visiting arrangements can be made through the Park Service or the synagogue.*

Fort Mifflin. Because of its Quaker origins, Philadelphia had no defenses until 1772, when the British began building Fort Mifflin. It was completed in 1776 by Revolutionary forces under General Washington. In a 40-day battle in 1777, 300 Continental defenders held off British forces long enough for Washington's troops to flee to Valley Forge. The fort was almost totally destroyed and was rebuilt in 1798 from plans by Pierre Charles L'Enfant, who designed the plan for Washington, D.C. In use until 1962, the fort has served as a prisoner-of-war camp, an artillery battalion, and a munitions dump. On the 49-acre National Historic Landmark, you can see its cannons and carriages, officers' quarters, soldiers' barracks (which contain an exhibit called "Defense of the Delaware"), an artillery shed, a blacksmith shop, a bomb shelter, and a museum. *Island Rd. and Hog Island Rd. on the Delaware River near Philadelphia International Airport, tel. 215/365-9781. Admission: $2 adults, $1 children under 12. Open Wed.-Sun. 10-4. Closed mid-Dec.-early Mar.*

Pennsylvania Hospital. Another in the long list of "firsts" and institutions founded by Benjamin Franklin is Pennsylvania Hospital, the oldest hospital in the United States. Inside the fine 18th-century original buildings are the nation's first medical library and first surgical amphitheater, an 1804 innovation with a skylight, and the only one still in existence. It also has a portrait gallery, early medical instruments, art objects, and a rare-book library with items that date from 1762. The artwork includes the Benjamin West painting *Christ Healing the Sick in* *the Temple.* Today Pennsylvania Hospital is a full-service modern medical center. Pick up a copy of *Pennsylvania Hospital: A Walking Tour* in the marketing department on the second floor of the Pine Building. *8th and Spruce Sts., tel. 215/829–3971. Admission free. Open weekdays 9–5.*

Libraries and Museums

Libraries If you want to read or do research, Philadelphia is the place to be. In addition to the Free Library—the vast public-library system—the city also has some of the oldest, largest, and most comprehensive private collections in the country. All five libraries described below are located within the boundaries of our downtown Exploring tours, and all are open to the public.

Housed in a national landmark Italianate brownstone dating from the mid-1800s, the **Athenaeum of Philadelphia** is a research library specializing in 19th-century social and cultural history. Founded in 1814, the library contains significant materials on the French in America and early-American travel, exploration, and transportation. Its American Architecture Collection has close to a million items. Besides books, the Athenaeum houses notable paintings and period furniture. *219 S. 6th St., tel. 215/925–2688. Admission free; tours by appointment. Open weekdays 9–5.*

Free Library of Philadelphia. Philadelphia calls its public-library system the Fabulous Freebie. Founded in 1891, the central library has more than 1 million volumes. With its grand entrance hall, sweeping marble staircase, 30-foot ceilings, enormous reading rooms with long tables and spiral staircases leading to balconies, this Greek Revival building looks the way libraries ought to look. With more than 12,000 musical scores, the Edwin S. Fleischer Collection is the largest of its kind in the world. Tormented by a tune whose name you can't recall? Hum it to one of the Music Room's librarians and he'll track it down. The Social Science and History Department has nearly 100,000 charts, maps, and guidebooks. The Newspaper Room stocks papers from all major U.S. and foreign cities and back issues on microfilm, some going all the way back to Colonial times. The Rare Book Room is a beautiful suite that has first editions of Dickens, ancient Sumerian clay tablets, illuminated medieval manuscripts, and more-modern manuscripts, including Poe's *Murders in the Rue Morgue* and "The Raven." *19th St. and Benjamin Franklin Pkwy., tel. 215/686–5322. Open Mon.–Wed. 9–9, Thurs. and Fri. 9–6, Sat. 9–5, Sun. 1–5. Closed Sun. June–Aug. Tours of Rare Book Room Mon.–Fri. at 11.*

The **Historical Society of Pennsylvania** contains more than a half-million books and 14 million manuscripts—the largest privately owned manuscript collection in the United States. Founded in 1824 for the purpose of "elucidating the history of the state," the society has expanded its scope to cover the original 13 colonies. Notable items from the collection include Penn family archives, President Buchanan's papers, a printer's proof of the Declaration of Independence, and the first draft of the Constitution. The staff in the genealogical library will help you trace your roots. The first floor has changing exhibits from the permanent collection of portraits and artifacts. Paintings include the earliest portrait of Washington (1772) and the last of

Franklin (1789), both by Charles Willson Peale. *1300 Locust St., tel. 215/732–6200. Use of library $5; museum and exhibits free. Exhibits open Tues.–Fri. 9–5, Sat. 10–3. Library hours Tues., Thurs., Fri. 9–5, Wed. 1–9.*

The **Library of the American Philosophical Society** is one of the country's leading institutions for the study of science. Its collection includes first editions of Newton's *Principia Mathematica,* Franklin's *Experiments and Observations,* and Darwin's *On the Origin of Species.* The collection also covers American natural history, medical science, and American Indians. Here you'll find many of Franklin's original books and papers as well as journals from the Lewis and Clark expedition of 1803–1806. *105 S. 5th St., tel. 215/627–0706. Admission free. Open weekdays 9–4:45.*

Founded in 1731, the **Library Company of Philadelphia** is one of the oldest cultural institutions in the United States and the only major Colonial American library that has survived virtually intact. From 1774 to 1800, it functioned as the de facto Library of Congress, and until the late 19th century it was the city library. Its membership has included 10 signers of the Declaration of Independence, among them Robert Morris, Benjamin Rush, and Thomas McKean. The 400,000-volume collection includes 200,000 rare books. First editions—many of which were acquired when they were first published—include Melville's *Moby Dick* and Whitman's *Leaves of Grass.* The library is particularly rich in Americana up to 1880, black history to 1915, the history of science, and women's history. *1314 Locust St., tel. 215/546–3181. Admission free. Open weekdays 9–4:45.*

Museums Some of Philadelphia's most interesting museums fall outside the confines of our walking tours but are most certainly worth a visit. Here are a few:

Afro-American Historical and Cultural Museum. Opened in the Bicentennial year of 1976, this is the first museum of its kind funded and built by a city. Exhibits are dedicated to the history, arts, crafts, and culture of blacks in the United States— with a focus on blacks of Philadelphia and Pennsylvania. Exhibits in 1990 will include "The Great Migration" from the South to the North between the 1880s and World War I and "Black Photographers Bear Witness." Every year the museum presents a "Jazz and Music" series and a literary series with appearances by major black writers. Its bookshop offers the area's widest selection on black culture, history, fiction, poetry, and drama. The gift shop features carvings from Togo, Senegal, and Ghana, and hand-cut jewelry from Zaire. *7th and Arch Sts., tel. 215/574–0380. Admission: $3.50 adults, $1.75 senior citizens and children. Open Tues.–Sat. 10–5, Sun. noon–6.*

American-Swedish Historical Museum. The Swedes settled the Delaware Valley in the mid-1600s before William Penn but few traces remain other than Old Swedes' Church (*see* Historical Buildings and Sites, *above*) and the American-Swedish Historical Museum. Modeled after a 17th-century Swedish manor house and located on land settled by the Swedes, the museum's 14 galleries trace the history of Swedes in the United States. The newest exhibit is "Before Penn," the nation's only permanent exhibit on the New Sweden colony. The John Ericsson room honors the designer of the Civil War ironclad ship, the

Monitor; the Jenny Lind room contains memorabilia from the Swedish Nightingale's American tour of 1848 to 1851; other rooms display handmade, costumed Swedish peasant dolls; crafts; paintings; and drawings. *1900 Pattison Ave., tel. 215/389-1776. Admission: $2 adults, $1 students and senior citizens, children under 12 free. Open Tues.-Fri. 10-4, Sat. noon-4.*

Atwater Kent Museum. Founded in 1938 and housed in an elegant 1826 Greek Revival building, the museum portrays Philadelphia history from the beginning to the present day. It includes exhibits on municipal services such as police, fire, water, and gas; shipbuilding; model streets and railroads; and maps showing the city's development. One gallery, "The City Beneath Our Feet," has changing exhibits culled from the thousands of artifacts uncovered during 20th-century excavations. Temporary exhibits scheduled for 1990 include "Tune In—Philadelphia Radio, 1820-1950." *15 S. 7th St., tel. 215/922-3031. Admission free. Open Tues.-Sat. 9:30-4:45.*

Balch Institute for Ethnic Studies. More a research center than a museum, the Balch Institute has a 60,000-volume library on immigration history and ethnicity. The institute's permanent exhibit, "Freedom's Doors—Immigrant Points of Entry to the U.S.," focuses on immigration in port cities such as Philadelphia, Boston, and Baltimore. Temporary exhibits planned for 1990 include "Appalachian Quilts" and "Ethnic Images in Toys and Games." *18 S. 7th St., tel. 215/925-8090. Admission: $2 adults; $1 students, senior citizens, and children. Exhibits open Mon.-Sat. 10-4, library 9-5.*

Barnes Foundation. Located just over the city line in Merion (Montgomery County) is one of the Philadelphia area's better-kept secrets, one of its best attractions, and one of the great collections of paintings in the world. The Barnes Foundation contains more than 1,000 works—mostly French impressionists—hung one on top of another just as Dr. Albert C. Barnes left them. Barnes made millions from the invention of Argyrol, an eye disinfectant, and he spent it on art. The collection includes 175 Renoirs, 66 Cézannes, 65 Matisses, and numerous works by van Gogh, Rousseau, Degas, El Greco, and Tintoretto, among many others. The museum, which was Barnes's home, also has Pennsylvania Dutch bric-a-brac, Mayan ornaments, and 16th-century Chinese art. Interested in art for teaching's sake, Barnes wanted no part of the art establishment, critics, or the general public: Until a 1961 court order, the collection was open only to students. Barnes's public-be-damned attitude has been more or less perpetuated: Hours are limited; no catalogue of the works has even been published; there's no gift shop and no postcards for sale. Even the guards are surly. But forget these minor obstacles; don't miss it. *300 Latches La., Merion, tel. 215/667-0290. Admission: $1, children under 12 not admitted. Open Fri.-Sat. 9:30-4:30 (100 reserved, 100 unreserved), Sun. 1-4:30 (50 reserved, 50 unreserved). Closed July-Aug.*

Mummers Museum. Even if you aren't in Philadelphia on New Year's Day, here's a chance to see a unique local institution and a phenomenon. Famous for extravagant sequined-and-feathered costumes and string bands, the Mummers spend the entire year preparing for an all-day parade up Broad Street every January 1. The museum has costumes, photos of parades from as far back as the turn of the century, and audiovisual displays of Mummerabilia. You can push buttons to compose your own Mummers medley with banjos, saxophones, and xylophones, and dance the Mummers strut to the strains of "Oh, 'Dem Golden Slippers." A 45-inch screen shows filmed highlights of past parades. On most Tuesday evenings from May to September, the museum presents free outdoor concerts (weather permitting). *2nd St. and Washington Ave., tel. 215/336-3050. Admission: $2 adults, $1 children under 12 and senior citizens. Open Tues.-Sat., 9:30-5, Sun. noon-5.*

Mutter Museum. Skulls, antique microscopes, and a cancerous tumor removed from President Grover Cleveland's mouth in 1893 form just part of the medical collection in the Mutter Museum. The museum has hundreds of anatomical and pathological specimens, medical instruments, and organs removed from patients, including John Marshall's bladder stones and a piece of John Wilkes Booth's thorax. The collection contains 139 skulls plus items belonging to Madame Curie, Louis Pasteur, and Joseph Lister. Also included is a 7-foot-6-inch skeleton, the tallest on public exhibition in the United States. The autopsy of Chang and Eng (the original Siamese twins) was done here, and the museum displays their joined livers and a plaster cast of their "connection." *19 S. 22nd St., tel. 215/563-3737 ext. 241. Admission free; donations accepted. Open Tues.-Fri. 10-4.*

National Museum of American Jewish History. This is the only museum in the country devoted to Jewish participation in the growth and development of America. It opened on July 4, 1976. Its permanent exhibit, the "American Jewish Experience," documents American Jewish history from 1654 to the present. It also has changing exhibits, lectures, workshops, films, and theater; and a collection of art, artifacts, and archival material. *55 N. 5th St., tel. 215/923-3811. Admission: $1.75 adults, $1.50 senior citizens and students, $1.25 children under 12. Open Mon.-Thurs. 10-5; Fri. 10-3; Sun. noon-5.*

Poe House. Edgar Allan Poe lived here from 1843 to 1844. In this, the only one of his Philadelphia residences still standing, he penned some of his best-known short stories: "The Telltale Heart," "The Black Cat," and "The Gold Bug." You can tour the 19th-century three-story brick house; to evoke the spirit of Poe, the National Park Service deliberately keeps the house empty. Restoration is under way. The adjoining house has exhibits on Poe and his family, his work habits, his literary contemporaries, and his "statement of taste," an eight-minute slide show and a small Poe library; and a reading room. At night, a statue in the garden casts the eerie shadow of a raven across the side of the house. *532 N. 7th St., tel. 215/597-8780. Admission free. Open daily 9-5.*

Norman Rockwell Museum. The Curtis Publishing Company Building, where Rockwell delivered his paintings to the editors of the *Saturday Evening Post*, now has the world's largest collection of the artist's works. Displays include all 324 Rockwell *Post* cover illustrations; lithographs, prints, collotypes, and sketches; and a replica of his studio in Stockbridge, Massachusetts. A one-hour video illustrates Rockwell's life. *6th and Sansom Sts. (lower level), tel. 215/922-4345. Admission: $1.50 adults, children under 12 free when accompanied by an adult. Open daily 10-4.*

Shoe Collection. Housed in the lobby and on the sixth floor of the Pennsylvania College of Podiatric Medicine, this unusual museum displays 500 pairs of "Footwear Through the Ages." The collection includes burial sandals from ancient Egypt, Eskimo snowshoes, Moroccan two-heeled shoes, and shoes used in the footbinding of Chinese women. Celebrity items include basketball-player Julius Erving's huge sneakers, Joe Frazier's boxing shoes, Billie Jean King's tennis shoes, and Bernie Parent's hockey skates. *8th and Race Sts., tel. 215/629–0300 ext. 219. Open weekdays 9–4. Call to arrange a tour.*

University Museum. Indiana Jones, look out! Rare treasures from the deepest jungles and most ancient tombs make this one of the finest archaeological/anthropological museums in the world. The collection of more than a million objects, gathered largely during worldwide expeditions by University of Pennsylvania scholars, includes a 12-ton giant sphinx from Egypt, a crystal ball owned by China's dowager empress, the world's oldest writing—Sumerian cuneiform clay tablets—and the 4,500-year-old golden jewels from the royal tombs of Ur. Kids run to "The Egyptian Mummy: Secrets and Science" exhibit. Exhibits in 1990 will include "The Dayaks of Borneo" and "The World of Alaska's Native People." *33rd and Spruce Sts., tel. 215/898–4026. Admission: $3 adults, $1.50 children and senior citizens. Open Tues.–Sat. 10–4:30, Sun. 1–5. Closed Sun. in summer. 24-hr taped message for events: 215/898–3447.*

The War Library and Museum. This is one of the premier collections of Civil War memorabilia in the Union. Artifacts include two life masks of Abraham Lincoln, dress uniforms and swords of Generals Grant and Meade, plus many other weapons, uniforms, and personal effects of Civil War officers and enlisted men. The library has more than 12,000 volumes on the war. *1805 Pine St., tel. 215/735–8196. Admission: $3. Open Mon.–Sat. 10–4.*

Wagner Free Institute of Science. Located in one of Philadelphia's poorest inner-city neighborhoods, this museum consists of an 1865 building with one huge exhibition hall. It's like a museum of a museum—hardly anything has changed in 125 years. The 21,000-specimen collection includes mollusks, minerals, birds, fish, and dinosaur bones. The Discovery Room allows children to handle some items. *17th St. and Montgomery Ave., tel. 215/763–6529. Admission free; Discovery Room, 50¢. Open Tues.–Fri. 10–4, Sun. noon–3. Call ahead.*

Parks, Zoos, and Gardens

In addition to Fairmount Park (*see* Tour 4, *above*), Philadelphia boasts recreational areas that range from peaceful landscaped grounds to wilderness preserves.

Bartram's Garden is a 44-acre oasis tucked into a heavily industrialized and depressed corner of southwest Philadelphia. Begun in 1728 by John Bartram, America's oldest surviving botanic garden has remained relatively unchanged while the surrounding areas have altered dramatically. With stone columns and carvings by Bartram himself, the 18th-century farmhouse on the grounds reflects his peculiar vision of classical and Colonial architecture. The self-trained Bartram became botanist to King George III, traveling throughout the Colonies and returning with many unusual species. The house is a National Historic Landmark, and the trails extending to the Schuylkill River are part of the National Recreation Trails System. *54th St. and Lindbergh Blvd., tel. 215/729–5281. Garden open daily, admission free. House open noon–4 Tues.–Sun. May–Oct.; Wed.–Fri. Nov.–Apr. Admission: $2 adults, $1 children 6–18, under 6 free. No. 36 trolley from City Hall stops at the entrance.*

Horticulture Center. Standing on the site of the 1876 Centennial Exposition's Horticultural Hall, the Horticulture Center consists of 22 wooded acres, a display house, and a greenhouse where plants and flowers used on city property are grown. Don't miss the whimsical *Seaweed Girl* fountain in the display house. *N. Horticultural Dr., West Fairmount Park, tel. 215/879–4062. Donation ($1) requested. Open daily 9–3. Fairmount Park Trolley Bus stops at door.*

Morris Arboretum. In the very northwest corner of the city, you'll find 166 acres of romantic landscaped seclusion. Morris Arboretum of the University of Pennsylvania is an eclectic retreat with a formal rose garden, English garden, Japanese garden, meadows, and woodlands. Begun in 1887 by siblings John and Lydia Morris and bequeathed to the University of Pennsylvania in 1932, the arboretum typifies Victorian-era garden design, with winding paths, a hidden grotto, tropical ferns, and natural woodland. It has 3,500 trees and shrubs from around the world, including one of the finest collections of Asian plants outside Asia. *Hillcrest Ave. between Germantown and Stenton Aves., Chestnut Hill, tel. 215/242–3399. Admission: $2 adults, $1 children and senior citizens. Open daily 10–5 Apr.–Oct.; 10–4 Nov.–Mar.; Thurs. Jun.–Aug. 10–8. Guided tours weekends at 2. Chestnut Hill East or West commuter trains stop a half-mile away; L bus stops at corner of Hillcrest and Germantown Aves.*

Schuylkill Center for Environmental Studies consists of more than 500 acres of wildflowers, ferns, and thickets; ponds, streams, and woodlands; 6 miles of winding trails; and the 8-acre Pine Plantation. You may spot deer, hawks, Canada geese, red fox, and other animals. Hands-on exhibits in the Discovery Museum explain the flora and fauna you see outside. Nature programs on Saturday and Sunday. The bookstore and gift shop follow the nature theme. *8480 Hagy's Mill Rd., Roxborough, tel. 215/482–7300. Admission: $3 adults, $2 children. Open Mon.–Sat. 8:30–5, Sun. 1–5. Closed Sun. in Aug. No. 61 bus stops at Ridge Pike and Port Royal Ave. 1 mi away.*

Tinicum National Environmental Center hosts more than 280 species of ducks, herons, egrets, geese, gallinules, and other birds. Resident earthbound animals include turtles, foxes, muskrats, deer, raccoons, weasels, and snakes. Facilities in this 900-acre wetland, the largest remaining in Pennsylvania (it used to be 6,000 acres), include 8 miles of foot trails, an observation blind, an observation deck, boardwalks through the wet areas, and a canoe launch into the 4½-mile stretch of Darby Creek that runs through the preserve (the best way to see it). Bird-watchers can prepare for their visit by calling 215/567-BIRD for recent sightings. *86th St. and Lindbergh Blvd., tel. 215/365–3118 or 215/521–0662. Admission free. Open daily 8 AM–sunset; visitor center open daily 8:30–4. The U and no. 37 buses stop nearby.*

Philadelphia Zoological Gardens. Opened in 1874, America's first zoo displays 1,600 animals on 42 acres. Orangutans, gorillas, gibbons, mandrills, and lemurs romp in the World of Primates, a 1-acre outdoor jungle. The African Plain is the stomping ground of giraffes, zebras, and rhinoceroses. Bear Country offers up-close views of sloths, spectacled bears, and polar bears diving off 12-foot cliffs. The George D. Widener Memorial Treehouse provides an animal's-eye view of a four-story tropical tree. The Children's Zoo has pony rides, a petting area, and a sea lion show. *34th St. and Girard Ave., tel. 215/243–1100. Admission: $5 adults, $4 children 2–11, $3.50 senior citizens, children under two free. Additional charges for Children's Zoo and Treehouse. Open Mon.–Fri. 9:30–5, Sat. and Sun. 9:30–6.*

Philadelphia for Free

Philadelphia has myriad free events and attractions. Those listed elsewhere in this book include all sites mentioned in **Off the Beaten Track,** and all libraries cited in **Libraries.**

In Exploring:

All sites in Independence National Historical Park
Many of the sites in Fairmount Park
Betsy Ross House
Christ Church Burial Ground
City Hall
Curtis Institute of Music recitals
Fireman's Hall
Masonic Temple
Pennsylvania Academy of the Fine Arts (Sat. 10–1)
Philadelphia Museum of Art (Sun. 10–1)
Rodin Museum
U.S. Mint

In Seasonal Events:

All parades and many of the other events listed

In The Arts and Nightlife:

Philadelphia Orchestra Concerts at Mann Music Center

In What to See and Do with Children:

Smith Playground

In Parks, Zoos, and Gardens:

Tinicum Wildlife Preserve

In Museums:

Wagner Free Institute of Science

Others not covered elsewhere:

University of the Performing Arts. (250 S. Broad St., tel. 215/875–2200). You can attend student and faculty piano recitals, dance concerts, orchestra performances, and choral programs.

Fleisher Art Memorial (709 Catherine St., tel. 215/922–3456). This art school in a former house has a gallery of changing exhibits and the Sanctuary, an 18th-century Portuguese chapel.

Philadelphia Navy Base and Naval Shipyard (foot of Broad St., tel. 215/897–8775). Take a guided bus tour past the shipyard's battleships, destroyers, a 300-ton shipbuilding crane, submarines, cruisers, and the quarters of officers and enlisted men.

What to See and Do with Children

W. C. Fields may have disliked children, but children love his hometown. In addition to places and events that appeal to children and adults alike, Philadelphia has many special attractions just for kids. This section describes some of the best; others are covered in other sections.

Annenberg Center Theater for Children (37th and Walnut Sts., tel. 215/898–6791). Part of a distinguished full-scale theater program, the Annenberg Center Theater for Children schedules productions in November, February, and April. The annual Philadelphia International Theater Festival for Children, held for five days at the end of May, features professional theater companies from around the world specializing in music, magic, dance, and circus performances.

Free Library Children's Department. With 100,000 books for preschoolers to eighth-graders, the Children's Department houses the city's largest collection of children's books in a made-for-kids setting (the infant-toddler corner, for instance, has infant-toddler-size furniture). Historical collections include such series as the Hardy Boys and Nancy Drew over which adults wax nostalgic. The foreign-language collection has children's books in more than 50 languages. The department holds story hours and film festivals; the annual Spring Book Review features reading lists, displays, and reviews of the previous year's best children's books. *19th St. and Benjamin Franklin Pkwy., tel. 215/686–5372. Open weekdays 9–6, Sat. 9–5, Sun. 1–5.*

Philadelphia Marionette Theater schedules hour-long performances featuring puppets, music, and magic introduced by a lecture-demonstration. Reservations a must. *Playhouse in the Park, Belmont Mansion Ave., West Fairmount Park, tel. 215/ 879–1213. Admission: $4. Performances weekdays at 10:30, some Sun. at 2.*

Sesame Place. A one-hour drive from Center City, Sesame Place is an amusement park based on the popular public-television show. Children play and learn, just as they are encouraged to on the show. It has Muppet characters, animal shows, computer games, climbing tunnels, playgrounds, a water park (bring a bathing suit), and healthful food. It's geared to children ages 3 to 13. *100 Sesame Rd., Langhorne, tel. 215/ 757–1100. Admission: $12.95 adults 16 and older, $14.95 children 3–15. Open daily May–mid-Sept.; weekends only mid-Sept.–mid-Oct. Call for hours.*

Smith Playground. This mansion, built just for kids, was donated to the city in 1899 by Richard and Sarah Smith in memory of their son Stanfield. For kids five and under the mansion has playrooms, a nature den, and a mini-village with metal kiddie cars from the 1950s. The playground has picnic tables, grills,

Jungle Gyms, swings, and an enclosed wooden slide wide enough for 10 children. It also has a wading pool, swimming pool, and equipment for disabled children. Although located at the edge of a disadvantaged inner-city neighborhood, it's a wonderful place to take the children. *33rd and Oxford Sts., East Fairmount Park, tel. 215/765–4325. House open Mon.–Sat. 10–3:30; playground 9–4:45.*

The following children's activities are discussed in other sections, as noted.

Academy of Natural Sciences (*see* Tour 4, *above*).
Franklin Institute Science Museum and Fels Planetarium (*see* Tour 4, *above*).
Penn's Landing: sailing ships, battleships, submarine, pleasure boats (*see* Tour 2, *above*).
Philadelphia Zoological Garden—especially the Children's Zoo, treehouse, jungle bird walk, and wolf woods (*see* Parks, Zoos, and Gardens, *above*).
Please Touch Museum (*see* Tour 4, *above*).
University Museum of the University of Pennsylvania (*see* Museums, *above*).

Off the Beaten Track

Benjamin Franklin Bridge. Cars, trucks, and trains zoom past, and brisk winds make your face tingle as you cross the Delaware River (150 feet below) and get the best view of riverfront Philadelphia. Walking across the Benjamin Franklin Bridge is an adventure few people undertake. When it opened in 1926, its 1,750-foot main span made it the longest suspension bridge in the world. It was designed by Paul Cret, architect of the Rodin Museum. After a new blue paint job and a lighting system specially designed to show off its contours, the bridge is more beautiful than ever. Start the 1.8-mile walk from either the Philadelphia or the Camden side. Only the south walkway is open, but that's the best view anyway. *5th and Vine Sts., tel. 215/925–8780. Admission free. Open daily (except a few days in winter when it gets too icy) 6 AM until around 7 PM (closes earlier in winter).*

Bryn Athyn Cathedral. Located at one of the most beautiful spots in the Philadelphia area is a spectacular cathedral built in 12th-century Romanesque and 14th-century Gothic styles. Atop a hill overlooking the Pennypack Valley, the cathedral is the episcopal seat of the Church of the New Jerusalem, a sect based on the writings of the Swedish scientist and mystic Emanuel Swedenborg. The main patrons of the church are descendants of John Pitcairn, an industrialist who made his fortune in paint and plate glass. Construction of the cathedral began in 1914 and went on for decades. It was built according to the medieval guild system: All materials—wood, metal, glass, stone—were brought to craftsmen at the site, and everything was fashioned by hand. The stained glass includes two colors, striated ruby and cobalt blue, found nowhere else in the Americas. Also on the hill is the former home of Raymond and Mildred Pitcairn, Glencairn, a neo-Romanesque building that's now a museum. *Rte. 232 (Huntingdon Pike) and Paper Mill Rd., Bryn Athyn 19009, 15 mi north of Center City, tel. 215/ 947–0266. Admission free. Open weekdays 10–4. Visitors are welcome at services Sun. 8:30 and 12:30. Tours Sat. and Sun.*

1–4:30 PM. *Visiting hours sometimes pre-empted by special church events. Directions: Go north on Broad St. to Rte. 611, right on County Line Rd., south on Rte. 232 to the 2nd traffic light. It's the cathedral on your right.*

Philadelphia City Council. For drama, comedy, and adventure, nothing rivals the Philadelphia city government. Some of the 17-member legislative branch of municipal government are capable and dedicated, but lawmaking often takes a back seat to righteous indignation, playing to the crowd, outrage, and profanity. Fistfights between council members occasionally break out. In the past 18 years, a half-dozen council members (including one former council president) have been convicted of crimes. If luck is against you, you may even witness a political debate. *City Hall, Broad and Market Sts., Council Chamber, Room 400, tel. 215/686–3432. Admission free. Meets Thurs. 10 AM.*

ENIAC. Here's a chance for computer aficionados to see the place where the computer age dawned. During World War II, engineers at the Moore School of Engineering at the University of Pennsylvania undertook a secret project to develop the world's first all-electronic, large-scale, general-purpose digital computer. They called it ENIAC, an acronym for electronic numerical integrator and calculator. The largest electronic machine in the world, it weighed 30 tons and contained 18,000 vacuum tubes—one of which, in the beginning, burned out every few seconds. While most of ENIAC is now in the Smithsonian Institution, a small portion is still on view at the Moore School. Photos and informative signs tell ENIAC's story. *Moore School of Electrical Engineering, University of Pennsylvania, 200 S. 33rd St., tel. 215/898–8294. Enter on 33rd St. just below Walnut St. The room containing ENIAC, at the top of the steps on the right, is usually locked, but you can always see the exhibit through the glass wall. Admission free. Open weekdays 9–5.*

Laurel Hill Cemetery is beautiful and a great place for a stroll. John Notman, architect of the Athenaeum (*see* Libraries, *above*) and many other noted local buildings, designed Laurel Hill in 1836. It is an important example of an early rural burial ground and the first cemetery in America designed by an architect. Its rolling hills that overlook the Schuylkill River, its rare trees, and monuments and mausoleums sculpted by greats such as Notman, Alexander Milne Calder, Alexander Stirling Calder, William Strickland, and Thomas U. Walter made it a popular picnic spot in the 19th century. Those buried in this 99-acre necropolis include prominent Philadelphians and Declaration of Independence signers. Burials still take place. *3822 Ridge Ave., East Fairmount Park, tel. 215/228–8200. Open weekdays 8–4, Sat. 9–1, closed Sun. Friends of Laurel Hill Cemetery arranges tours (tel. 215/242–9437). Go north on East River Dr.; turn right on Ferry Rd. (the 1st street after the 1st traffic light); go 1 block to Ridge Ave.; turn right. The cemetery entrance is about a half-mile on your right.*

4 Shopping

Introduction

Philadelphia is a shopper's paradise. It has an upscale shopping district centered on 17th and Walnut streets, a jewelers' row, an antiques row, the first downtown indoor shopping mall in the United States, an outdoor food market that covers five city blocks, and numerous department stores including one of the oldest and most elegant in the country.

Bargains are available, too—from discount stores, street vendors, and factory outlets.

You can also buy items representative of Philadelphia: from $2 parchment copies of the Declaration of Independence to $500 reproductions of the inkwell used in the signing of the Declaration. One T-shirt store sells more than 40 designs featuring Philadelphia. Other stores sell posters of the art museum, Boathouse Row, and Independence Hall.

The leading shopping area is **Walnut Street** between Broad Street and Rittenhouse Square, and the intersecting streets just north and south. These blocks are filled with boutiques, art galleries, jewelers, fine clothing stores, and many other unusual shops. On 18th Street in the block north of Rittenhouse Square, for example, you'll find entrepreneurs both indoors and out: a state-of-the-Yuppie department store (Urban Outfitters), street-vendor Mary Grace Gardner who sells handmade Peruvian shawls, street-artist Joe Barker who paints watercolors of Philadelphia cityscapes, and a shop that sells more than 30 flavors of frozen yogurt (Scoop De Ville).

The **Chestnut Street Transitway,** another shopping street, has rare-book sellers, custom tailors, sporting-goods stores, pinball arcades, and discount drugstores.

A block north of Chestnut Street is Philadelphia's landmark effort at urban renewal cum shopping, the **Gallery at Market East** (tel. 215/925-7162), America's first enclosed downtown shopping mall. The four-level glass-roofed structure on Market Street from 8th Street to 11th Street contains 220 shops and restaurants and three department stores—Stern's (tel. 215/922-3399), Strawbridge and Clothier (tel. 215/629-6000), and J. C. Penney (tel. 215/238-9100).

Next to the Gallery on Market Street between 7th Street and 8th Street is a pricier urban mall, **Mellon Independence Center** (tel. 215/592-8905). Saved from the wrecker's ball at the eleventh hour, the former Lit Brothers Department Store went through a $75 million renovation to emerge in 1987 as an office building featuring a five-level atrium with space for 50 stores and restaurants.

Jewelers' Row, centered on Sansom Street between 7th Street and 8th Street, is one of the world's oldest and largest markets of precious stones: More than 350 retailers, wholesalers, and craftsmen operate here. The 700 block of Sansom Street is a brick-paved enclave occupied almost exclusively by jewelers.

Pine Street from 9th Street to 12th Street is Philadelphia's **Antiques Row.** The three-block area has dozens of antiques stores and curio shops, many specializing in period furniture and Colonial heirlooms.

Across the street from the Liberty Bell, the **Bourse** (5th St. between Market St. and Chestnut St., tel. 215/625–0300) has 50 stores and restaurants, including designer boutiques such as Howard Heartsfield and Forgotten Woman. Even if the specialty stores are beyond your budget, the elegantly restored 1895 commodities exchange is worth a visit.

South Street, one of Philadelphia's few entertainment strips, is also one of its major shopping areas. From Front Street to 8th Street you'll find more than 180 unusual stores—New Wave and high-fashion clothing, New Age books and health food, avant-garde art galleries—and 70 restaurants.

If you want local color, nothing compares with South Philadelphia's **Italian Market.** On both sides of 9th Street from Christian Street to Washington Street and spilling onto the surrounding streets, hundreds of outdoor stalls and indoor stores sell such food items as spices, cheese, pasta, fruits, vegetables, freshly slaughtered poultry and beef; household items; clothing; shoes; and other goods. It's crowded and smelly, and the vendors can be less than hospitable—but the food is fresh and the prices are reasonable.

Department stores are the cornerstones of Philadelphia shopping. The granddaddy of local department stores is **John Wanamaker** (tel. 215/422–2000), a landmark store (*see* Chapter 3) that occupies the entire city block from 13th Street to Juniper Street and from Market Street to Chestnut Street. The list of Wanamaker's departments takes up nearly three columns in the local White Pages. The store has fashion boutiques, designer shops for men, the Williamsburg and Baker furniture galleries, a bargain-basement budget store, a travel agency, a ticket office, a watch-repair desk, a beauty salon, and a post office.

Strawbridge and Clothier (tel. 215/629–6000), whose main store is at 8th Street and Market Street in the Gallery, is the other leading department store. It was founded in 1868 and is still owned by the Clothier and Strawbridge families. Once a month, Strawbridge's has Clover Day, with special sale prices on items throughout the store.

Shopping Notes

Local stores have sales throughout the year. If you're looking for a particular item, check the daily newspapers. Every Wednesday, the *Philadelphia Daily News* runs a "Sales and Bargains" column. Most stores accept traveler's checks and Visa, MasterCard, and American Express. Diners Club, Carte Blanche, and Discover are less widely accepted. Policies on personal checks vary. As in many big cities, it's unwise to carry much cash.

Pennsylvania's 6% sales tax does not apply to clothing, medicine, and food bought in stores. Restaurant food is taxed.

Downtown shopping hours are generally 9:30 or 10 AM to 5 or 6 PM. Many stores close at 9 PM on Wednesday. Most downtown stores are closed on Sunday, but the Bourse and the Gallery are open from 12 to 5.

Shopping

Cherry St.

Arch St.

20th St.

19th St.

18th St.

Suburban Station

J. F. Kennedy Blvd.

Market St.

Ludlow St.

Chestnut St.

SEE DETAIL MAP

Sansom St.

Walnut St.

Locust St.

Rittenhouse Square

Locust St.

Spruce St.

21st St.

20th St.

19th St.

18th St.

17th St.

16th St.

15th St.

Pine St.

Lombard St.

South St.

Bainbridge St.

Fitzwater St.

0   440 yards

0   400 meters

Catherine St.

Broad St.

Cherry St.

Arc

City Hall

12th St.

Juniper St.

13th St.

Camac St.

Watts St.

611

Barnes and Noble, **2**

Bauman Rare Books, **14**

Book Trader, **37**

Bourse Building, **33**

Boyd's, **5**

Chef's Market, **44**

Destination Philadelphia, **29**

Europine, **26**

Food Hall at Strawbridge and Clothier, **22**

Gallery at Market East, **21**

Gargoyles, **43**

Gilbert Luber Gallery, **13**

Harry Sable, **25**

Hibberd's, **11**

Howard Heartsfield, **28**

I. Goldberg, **17**

J.E. Caldwell, **6**

Jack Kelmer, **24**

Jansen Antiques, **18**

John Wanamaker, **4**

Le Jour d'Amour, **30**

Kamikaze Kids, **40**

The Key and Quill Shop, **34**

Kosmin's Camera Exchange, **16**

The Last Woundup, **35**

M. Finkel and Daughter, **20**

Mellon Independence Center, **23**

Mid-City Camera Exchange, **10**

Neo Deco, **38**

Le Parfumier, **32**

Shopping (Sansom and Walnut Streets)

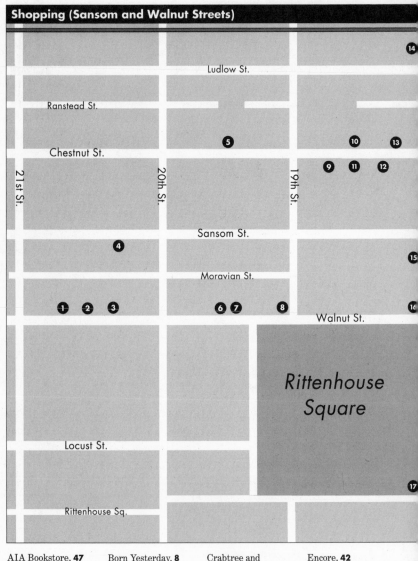

AIA Bookstore, **47**
Allure, **63**
Ambitions, **45**
B. Dalton Bookseller, **67**
Bailey, Banks, and Biddle, **57**
Banana Republic, **41**
Beige, **33**
Bernie Robbins, **52**
Bonwit Teller, **21**

Born Yesterday, **8**
Boyd's, **10**
Brooks Brothers, **66**
Burberry's Ltd., **34**
Calderwood Gallery, **40**
Cambridge Clothing Factory Outlet, **60**
Children's Boutique, **15**
The Compleat Strategist, **3**

Crabtree and Evelyn, **19**
Dandelion, **38**
David David Gallery, **17**
Deacon's Luggage, **56**
Descamps, **28**
Dimensions, **64**
Edward G. Wilson, **12**
Elder Craftsmen, **51**

Encore, **42**
Everyone's Racquet, **13**
Fat Jack's Comicrypt, **4**
Finish Line Sports, **6**
Frank S. Schwarz and Son, **11**
Freeman Fine Arts, **9**
Gross-McCleaf Gallery, **58**
Helen Drutt, **31**

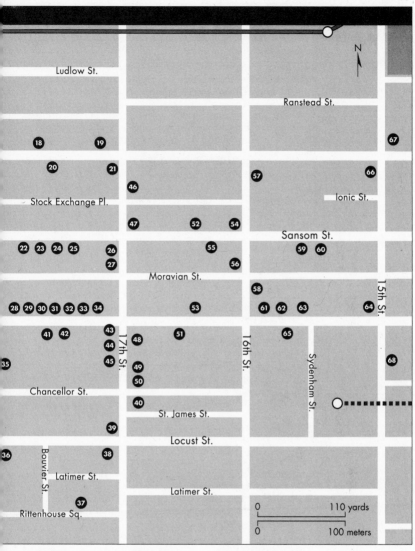

Ludlow St.

Ranstead St.

N

Stock Exchange Pl.

Ionic St.

Sansom St.

Moravian St.

15th St.

17th St.

16th St.

Sydenham St.

Chancellor St.

St. James St.

Locust St.

Bouvier St.

Latimer St.

Latimer St.

Rittenhouse Sq.

| 0 | | 110 yards |
| 0 | | 100 meters |

Holt's Tobacconist, **54**
How-to-Do-It Bookshop, **55**
I. Brewster, **22**
Intima, **25**
Jacob's, **20**
Jaeger International Sportswear, **32**
Janet Fleisher, **49**
Joseph Fox, **24**
Kitchen Kapers, **50**

Knit Wit, **44**
Laura Ashley, **30**
Love of Past, **48**
Marion Locks, **65**
Market at the Commissary, **27**
Muse Gallery, **7**
Nan Duskin, **29**
Newman Galleries, **53**
Paraphernalia, **18**

Past, Present, Future, **14**
Philadelphia Art Alliance, **36**
Philip Mendelsohn, **35**
Plage Tahiti, **26**
Pleasure Chest, **1**
Replique Fashion Jewelry, **39**
Richard Kenneth, **43**
Rittenhouse Bookstore, **37**

Sherman Brothers Shoes, **59**
Strega, **61**
Toby Lerner, **46**
Touches, **68**
Urban Objects, **23**
Urban Outfitters, **16**
Wayne Edwards Men's Loft, **62**
Whodunit, **5**
William H. Allen, **2**

Specialty Stores

Antiques Many dealers cluster on Antiques Row—Pine Street between 9th and 12th streets.

W. Graham Arader (1308 Walnut St., tel. 215/735–8811). The city's largest selection of antique prints and maps. Rare books and an extensive gallery of autographed documents and letters.

Architectural Antiques Exchange (715 N. 2nd St., tel. 215/922–3669). Victorian embellishments from saloons and apothecary shops, to stained and beveled glass, gargoyles, and advertising memorabilia.

Calderwood Gallery (221 S. 17th St., tel. 215/732–9444). Art Nouveau and Art Deco furniture, glass, bronzes, and rugs.

EuroPine (309 Arch St., tel. 215/238–0980). Country pine furniture crafted in the 19th and early 20th centuries by artisans from Northern Europe.

M. Finkel and Daughter (936 Pine St., tel. 215/627–7797). Late 18th- and early 19th-century American furniture, quilts, needlework, and folk art.

Freeman Fine Arts (1808 Chestnut St., tel. 215/563–9275). One of the city's leading auction houses. Examine furniture, china, prints, and paintings on Monday and Tuesday; bid for them on Wednesday. Freeman's auctioned one of the original flyers on which the Declaration of Independence was printed and posted throughout the city. It went for $400,000.

Gargoyles (512 S. 3rd St., tel. 215/629–1700) has 11,000 square feet of antiques and reproduction decorative and architectural pieces—archways, mantels, entranceways, carousel horses, stained-glass windows, and ornate mirrors.

Jansen Antiques (1036 Pine St., tel. 215/592–1670). Victorian and Art Deco jewelry.

Love of Past (205 S. 17th St., tel. 215/735–5565). Campaign buttons, baseball cards, collectibles, and memorabilia from the 1850s to the 1950s. Fun—rather than fine—antiques.

Schaffer Antiques (1014 Pine St., tel. 215/923–2263). 18th- , 19th- , and early 20th-century American furnishings, stained glass, silver, porcelain, paintings, and prints.

Vintage Instruments (1529 Pine St., tel. 215/545–1100). Antique strings and woodwinds.

Edward G. Wilson (1802 Chestnut St., tel. 215/563–7369). Small items such as antique coins, lamps, jewelry, silver, china, glass, and other collectibles. Founded in 1929.

Art For current shows in Philadelphia's numerous galleries, see listings in *Philadelphia Magazine* or the Weekend section of the Friday *Philadelphia Inquirer*. Many galleries are located near Rittenhouse Square; others are on South Street or scattered about downtown.

I. Brewster (1742 Sansom St., tel. 215/864–9222). Art Nouveau and Art Deco pieces; posters and paintings by Louis Icart, Erté, and Red Grooms.

David David Gallery (260 S. 18th St., tel. 215/735–2922). American and European paintings, drawings, and watercolors from the 16th to the 20th centuries.

Helen Drutt (1721 Walnut St., tel. 215/735–1625). Contemporary American and European artists, with a focus on ceramics and jewelry.

Janet Fleisher (211 S. 17th St., tel. 215/545–7562). Pre-Columbian, American Indian, and 20th-century American folk art.

Gross-McCleaf Gallery (127 S. 16th St., tel. 215/665–8138). Works by prominent and emerging artists, with emphasis on Philadelphia painters, printmakers, and sculptors.

Marian Locks (1524 Walnut St., tel. 215/546–0322). Contemporary regional, national, and international painters, sculptors, and mixed-media artists.

Gilbert Luber Gallery (1220 Walnut St., tel. 215/732–2996). Japanese and Chinese antique and contemporary prints.

Muse Gallery (1915 Walnut St., tel. 215/963–0959). Established in 1978 by the Muse Foundation for the Visual Arts, Muse Gallery is a women's cooperative committed to increasing the visibility of women's artwork.

Newman Galleries (1625 Walnut St., tel. 215/563–1779). A range of works, from 19th-century paintings to contemporary lithographs and sculpture. Strong on early 20th-century painters from the Bucks County area.

School Gallery of the Pennsylvania Academy of the Fine Arts (1301 Cherry St., tel. 215/569–2797). Rotating exhibits of works by faculty, alumni, and students.

Philadelphia Art Alliance (251 S. 18th St., tel. 215/545–4302). Mixed-media exhibits in a 1906 neo-classical Rittenhouse Square mansion. There are always two exhibits showing, one with works for sale. Also has a program of lectures and performances often related to the exhibit. Call for brochure and schedule.

University of the Arts' Rosenwald-Wolf Gallery (333 S. Broad St., tel. 215/875–1116). Works by faculty and local, national, and international artists. Student exhibits May through July.

Frank S. Schwarz and Son (1806 Chestnut St., tel. 215/563–4887). Nineteenth- and 20th-century American and European paintings, concentrating on Philadelphia artists of the past.

Snyderman Gallery (317 South St., tel. 215/238–9576). One-of-a-kind handmade furniture and glass by nationally known artists.

The Works (319 South St., tel. 215/922–7775). Avant-garde American crafts in wood, fiber, ceramics, metals, and glass.

Books   **AIA Bookstore** (17th and Sansom Sts., tel. 215/569–3188). Run by the American Institute of Architects, this shop specializes in architectural theory, building construction, interior design, furnishings, blueprint posters, international magazines, and unusual gifts.

William H. Allen (2031 Walnut St., tel. 215/563–3398). One of the city's best collections of used and scholarly books. Specializes in history, literature, and philosophy.

Barnes and Noble (1424 Chestnut St., tel. 215/972–8275). A full-scale bookstore in an elegant commercial space. Classical music in the background and strategically placed benches make browsing more comfortable.

Bauman Rare Books (1215 Locust St., tel. 215/564–4274). An antiquarian bookstore with volumes from the 19th century and earlier on law, science, English literature, travel, and exploration; print and map collection.

Book Trader (501 South St., tel. 215/925–0219). You'll find great browsing on the two floors of this eclectic used-book store. Prices on the high side. Open daily till midnight.

B. Dalton Bookseller (1431 Chestnut St., tel. 215/568–6590). One of the largest bookstores in the city, with more than 25,000 titles on two floors. Especially strong in cookbooks, sports, and fiction. Good travel section, including Philadelphia titles, tour books, and maps.

Encore (1712 Walnut St., tel. 215/735–8043). A discount chain with more than 20 locations, Encore offers 35% off *New York Times* best-sellers and up to 80% off closeouts and remainders.

Joseph Fox (1724 Sansom St., tel. 215/563–4184). A small, choice selection of fiction and nonfiction, gift books, and volumes on the arts.

Hibberd's (1310 Walnut St., tel. 215/546–8811). Rare and used books; art books a specialty. A fine selection of serious modern fiction that you won't find in chain stores.

How-to-Do-It Bookshop (1608 Sansom St., tel. 215/563–1516). Want to build a computer, grow rutabagas, groom your poodle? If there's a book telling you how to do something, chances are this unique place will have it.

Rittenhouse Bookstore (1706 Rittenhouse Sq., tel. 215/545–6072). The best medical bookstore in Philadelphia. If you can't find the book you want, they may be able to get it for you overnight.

Robin's Bookstore (108 S. 13th St., tel. 215/735–9600). Famous in the 1960s as the city's counterculture bookstore, Robin's has an exceptional variety of hard-to-find intellectual titles. Specializes in literature, poetry, and minority studies. A good children's section. Frequent poetry readings and book signings by local authors.

University of Pennsylvania Bookstore (3729 Locust St., tel. 215/898–7595). A huge selection of both popular and scholarly volumes. Especially strong in linguistics, anthropology, psychology, and sociology.

Whodunit (1931 Chestnut St., tel. 215/567–1478). A huge selection of mysteries, spy stories, and adventure books. It also stocks out-of-print mysteries. Owner Art Bourgeau has published six mystery books and a nonfiction book on mystery writing.

Women's Clothing **Ambitions** (212 S. 17th St., tel. 215/546–1133). Specializes in clothes for full-figured women sizes 14 to 24.

Bonwit Teller (1700 Chestnut St., tel. 215/563–7300). An upscale women's specialty department store, Bonwit's has classic fashions for career women, moderately priced sportswear for juniors, and the latest from hot designers. It also has a beauty salon, a shoe salon, and a small men's department.

Howard Heartsfield (Bourse Bldg., 21 S. 5th St., tel. 215/925–2070). Handmade sweaters, camisoles, and sequined evening wear—woven, knit, or crocheted by fiber artists.

Intima (1718 Sansom St., tel. 215/568–6644; 707 Walnut St., tel. 215/238–7727). Philadelphia's best selection of imported cotton and silk designer lingerie.

Jaeger International Sportswear (1719 Walnut St., tel. 215/751–9285). European collection of distinctive clothing, from classics to the latest silhouettes and proportions.

Knit Wit (208 S. 17th St., tel. 215/735–3642). Trendy high fashions from sportswear to cocktail clothes. Shoes and jewelry, too.

Toby Lerner (117 S. 17th St., tel. 215/568–5760). European high-fashion apparel with strong classic lines. Full line of shoes.

Philip Mendelsohn (229 S. 18th St., tel. 215/546–6333). Classic European and specialty clothing.

Paraphernalia (1729 Chestnut St., tel. 215/561–0279). Updated contemporary fashion with a European flair.

Plage Tahiti (128 S. 17th St., tel. 215/569–9139). Showcases promising young high-fashion designers. You'll also find swimwear.

Men's Clothing **Allure** (1509 Walnut St., tel. 215/561–4242). Classic and stylish Italian clothing and furnishings.

Boyd's (1217 Market St., 1818 Chestnut St. as of March 1990, tel. 215/564–9000). The largest men's store in the city and second largest (after Barneys in New York) in the country. Its nine shops feature the traditional English look, avant-garde Italian imports, and dozens of other styles and designers. Shops for extra tall, large, and short men; 65 tailors on the premises. Valet parking.

Brooks Brothers (1500 Chestnut St., tel. 215/564–4100). The oldest men's clothing store in America (founded in New York in 1818). Synonymous with Ivy League business clothing: conservative suits, button-down shirts, and striped ties.

Dimensions (15th and Walnut Sts., tel. 215/564–1132). European and updated traditional styles from socks to tuxedos. Also, Ralph Lauren's preppy look in the Polo Shop.

Wayne Edwards Men's Loft (1521 Walnut St., tel. 215/563–6801). Exclusive lines of classic contemporary designer clothing from Italy, Japan, France, and the United States.

Women's and Men's Clothing **Banana Republic** (1716 Walnut St., tel. 215/735–2247). A store —part of the national chain—with an African motif that features rugged travel and safari clothing plus a wide variety of travel bags.

Burberrys Ltd. (1705 Walnut St., tel. 215/557–7400). Named after Thomas Burberry, who designed the trench coat in the mid-1850s, this British-owned establishment features British raincoats, overcoats, sportcoats, and cashmere sweaters. High quality, high prices.

Destination Philadelphia (Bourse Bldg., 21 S. 5th St., tel. 215/440–0233). A clothing store where every item bears some form of Philadelphia logo or design—from a soft pretzel to a line drawing of Billy Penn. Sweatpants, sweatshirts, and more than 40 styles of T-shirts.

Nan Duskin (1729 Walnut St., tel. 215/567–1700). European and American designer clothes, sportswear, gold and costume jewelry, lingerie, shoes, millinery, and the Bottega Veneta leather line. Boutiques include Hermès, Chanel, and Valentino.

Neo Deco (414 South St., tel. 215/928–0627). European-style contemporary clothing: sportswear, shoes, and jewelry.

Urban Outfitters (1801 Walnut St., tel. 215/569–3131). This trend-setting store in a Beaux Arts mansion is a favorite of the collegiate crowd. Children's department, books, unusual toys, and apartment accessories.

Children's Clothing **Born Yesterday** (1901 Walnut St., tel. 215/568–6556). Unusual selection of clothing and toys for tots. Handmade goods, imported fashions, and styles you won't find elsewhere.

Children's Boutique (126 S. 18th St., tel. 215/563–3881). A look that falls between conservative and classic in infant to preteen clothes; complete wardrobes, specialty gifts, and handmade items.

Kamikaze Kids (520 S. 4th St., tel. 215/574–9800). Handmade fashions by local designers for infants to preteens. Also French lines.

Food **Chef's Market** (231 South St., tel. 215/925–8360). Philly's ultimate gourmet supermarket prepares 60 to 70 different entrées every day; also a fish market, meat market, goods from 20 bakeries. Packaged items include 150 varieties of imported jams, 40 olive oils, and 60 flavored vinegars.

Fante's (1006 S. 9th St., tel. 215/922–5557). One of the oldest gourmet supply stores in the country, it has the largest selection of coffee makers and equipment in the United States. It is located in the Italian Market. Family-owned since 1906, it is famous for oddball kitchen gadgets such as truffle shavers, pineapple peelers, and turbot cookers. Supplies restaurants and bakeries all over the country and overseas.

Food Hall at Strawbridge and Clothier (8th and Market Sts., tel. 215/629–6000). You can eat at the café, or take out breads, cheeses, salads, and ice cream. Daily cooking demonstrations with free samples. Also a large candy department and a charcuterie.

Kitchen Kapers (213 S. 17th St., tel. 215/546–8059). Fine cookware, cutlery, and special foods. Lots of French copper and porcelain.

Market at the Commissary (130 S. 17th St., tel. 215/568–8055). Ready-to-eat, ready-to-go gourmet food. Cheeses, pastas, and coffees. Food from the kitchen of the Commissary—Philadelphia's premier cafeteria—but a greater selection. Salad bar and dessert case. Opens 7:30 AM; sells food for breakfast, lunch, and dinner.

Pagano's Cheesery (1507 Walnut St., tel. 215/568–0891). Entrées, baked goods, and desserts to go. Coffee bar (with a varied selection, including coffee of the day) opens at 7 AM.

Gifts and Novelties **Laura Ashley** (1721 Walnut St., tel. 215/496–0492). Fabrics, traditional clothing, and home accessories from the British firm known for its floral prints.

The Country Sampler (1740 Sansom St., tel. 215/563–6602). Loads of country crafts—quilts, folk art, antiques, odds and ends—handmade by seven hundred American and European craftsmen.

Dandelion 2 (17th and Locust Sts., tel. 215/546–7655). Almost everything sold in this store is handmade: jewelry; clothing; ceramics; porcelains; glass; American handwoven batik pieces; and imported clothing, some from Indonesia, India, and Africa.

Descamps (1733 Walnut St., tel. 215/567–7886). Linens and domestics, sheets, and gift items from the popular French Primrose Bordier collection. This chain has 15 stores in Paris and many others around the world.

Elder Craftsmen (1628 Walnut St., tel. 215/545–7888). This nonprofit shop sells afghans, quilts, pillows, toys and dolls, household and nursery items, children's clothes, and other gifts handmade by senior citizens.

Holt's Tobacconist (114 S. 16th St., tel. 215/563–0763). The city's oldest (1898) and largest purveyor of pipes, tobacco, cigars, and lighters. Also the city's largest selection of writing instruments.

Le Jour d'Amor (Bourse Bldg., 21 S. 5th St., tel. 215/629–1179). High-fashion lingerie and unique gifts.

The Key and Quill Shop (129 S. 2nd St., tel. 215/923–8522). If you're looking for something distinctly Philadelphia, this is the place to find it. Selection includes fine reproductions of 18th-century furniture and objects found in Independence National

Historical Park, such as Thomas Jefferson's lap desk and the rising-sun chair in Independence Hall. Also available are reproductions of old maps, including Penn's first (1683) map of the city and "The East Prospect of the City of Philadelphia," a four-piece, seven-foot map of the city from 1759.

Popi (526 S. 4th St., tel. 215/922–4119). The most extensive selection of magazines in town—over 5,000 titles and expanding—and the largest assortment of imported cigarettes. One entire room is dedicated to back-issue magazines sold at half price.

Touches (225 S. 15th St., tel. 215/546–1221). Attractive shop with wall-to-wall upscale gifts: handmade shawls, handbags, belts, and unusual jewelry.

Urban Objects (1724 Sansom St., tel. 215/557–9474). Eclectic collection of contemporary gifts, home accessories, and antiques (both authentic and reproductions), lamps, and pictures. Many objects are imported from Europe and Asia but are reasonably priced.

Wine and Spirits Shoppe (Bourse Bldg., 21 S. 5th St., tel. 215/560–5504). The best you can find in a city where liquor stores are state run. For a better selection you have to go to New Jersey.

Jewelry **J. E. Caldwell** (Juniper and Chestnut Sts., tel. 215/864–8810). A local landmark since 1839, the store is adorned with antique, handblown crystal chandeliers by Baccarat, making it as elegant as the jewels it sells. Along with traditional and modern jewelry, Caldwell's has one of the city's largest selections of giftware and stationery, and a bridal registry.

Bailey, Banks, and Biddle (16th and Chestnut Sts., tel. 215/564–6200). Known for diamond and gold jewelry, fine china, silver, crystal, and stationery.

Bernie Robbins (1625 Sansom St., tel. 215/563–2380). Fine jewelry at discount prices.

Jack Kelmer (717 Chestnut St., tel. 215/627–8350). Diamonds, gold jewelry, and gifts at below retail price.

Harry Sable (8th and Sansom Sts., tel. 215/627–4014). The "king of the wedding bands" carries the largest selection in the Delaware Valley; it also sells engagement rings, diamond rings, gold jewelry, and watches.

Richard Kenneth (202 S. 17th St., tel. 215/545–3355). Jewelry from the late Georgian, Victorian, Art Nouveau, Art Deco, and retro periods. Specializes in antique and estate pieces, repairs, and appraisals.

Replique Fashion Jewelry (Warwick Hotel, 17th and Locust Sts., tel. 215/546–1170). Reproductions of fine gems and unique designs by local artisans.

Luggage and Leather Goods **Deacon's Luggage** (124 S. 16th St., tel. 215/567–5584). Luggage, briefcases, and accessories at discount prices.

Robinson Luggage Company (Broad and Walnut Sts., tel. 215/735–9859). Popular brands of luggage, leather, and travel accessories marked down at least 20%. The selection of briefcases and attaché cases is the largest in the Delaware Valley.

Records and Music **Jacob's** (1718 Chestnut St., tel. 215/568–7800). The best selection of sheet music in Center City. Specializes in classical, but also carries pop and will special-order anything.

Third Street Jazz and Rock (10 N. 3rd St., tel. 215/627–3366). Small shop specializing in hard-to-find jazz and soul records. Also rock, New Wave, reggae, Caribbean, and African music.

Salespeople are particularly knowledgeable, with at least one expert for each type of music. Good prices.

Tower Records (610 South St., tel. 215/574–9888). Open 9 AM to midnight 365 days a year. Stocks more than 250,000 records and tapes—the largest selection in the city. You can watch music videos on the 30 screens on three floors. Classical-music annex across the street.

Perfumes   **Crabtree and Evelyn** (1701A Chestnut St., tel. 215/665–9184; Bourse Bldg., 21 S. 5th St., tel. 215/625–9256). This British firm sells its own line of toiletries and soaps—perfumed with herbs, flowers, and fruit—plus specialty foods.

Le Parfumier (Bourse Bldg., 21 S. 5th St., tel. 215/922–7660). This "scent boutique" for men and women imports new fragrances, some not yet released elsewhere in the United States. Also carries cosmetics, perfume bottles, discontinued scents, and accessories.

Photography   **Kosmin's Camera Exchange** (927 Arch St., tel. 215/627–8231). Film, motion picture equipment, slide projectors, screens, darkroom supplies, and a half-dozen brands of camera.

Mid-City Camera Exchange (1316 Walnut St., tel. 215/735–2522; Bourse Bldg., 21 S. 5th St., tel. 215/627–3688). Sales, service, rentals. This major "stockhouse" has a large line of darkroom equipment and all major camera brands. It also buys and trades used cameras.

Roth Camera Repairs (1015 Chestnut St., tel. 215/922–2498). If you have camera trouble while you're in town, here's the place to have it fixed. Extra-quick service for tourists.

Sporting Goods   **Everyone's Racquet** (1809 Chestnut St., tel. 215/665–1221). Everything related to tennis and racket sports: tennis, racquetball, squash. Next-day racket-stringing service.

Finish Line Sports (1915 Walnut St., tel. 215/569–9957). Specialists in shoes and gear for triathlon sports: running, swimming, and cycling. Also aerobic and workout shoes and gear.

I. Goldberg (902 Chestnut St., tel. 215/925–9393). An army-navy-and-everything store. Not stylish but practical, with emphasis on sporting apparel and camping gear. Crammed with government-surplus, military-style clothing, jeans and work-clothes, and exclusive foreign imports. Huge stock of sizes. Rummaging here is a sport in itself.

Toys   **The Compleat Strategist** (2011 Walnut St., tel. 215/563–2960). Philadelphia's only store specializing in games, from board games and role-playing games like Dungeons and Dragons to military simulations such as the Battle of Waterloo. Also mystery games, military history books, and miniatures.

Fat Jack's Comicrypt (2006 Sansom St., tel. 215/963–0788). Old and new comics at catalogue prices. The largest selection in the Delaware Valley.

The Last Woundup (617 South St., tel.215/238–9440). Astounding collection of wind-up music boxes and toys: chattering teeth, somersaulting kangaroos, walking feet, an eight-legged walking camel, and a tin chicken that lays eggs. A new section features "antistress toys" for executives. All toys are on display, and customers (most are adults) are encouraged to "play, play, play."

Past, Present, Future (24 S. 18th St., tel. 215/854–0444). Distinctive toys, handcrafts, kaleidoscopes, and children's books.

Shoes   **Beige** (1715 Walnut St., tel. 215/564–2395). Women's Italian leather shoes in sizes 4–12, priced toward the high end.

Strega (1521 Walnut St., tel. 215/564–5932). A wide range of looks for men and women; exclusive footwear made for Strega primarily in Italy.

Sherman Brothers Shoes (1520 Sansom St., tel. 215/561–4550). An "off-price" retailer of men's shoes with name-brand merchandise, excellent service, and low prices. Extra-wide and extra-narrow widths, sizes to 14 and 15; 28 lines of shoes.

Bargain Shopping   **Cambridge Clothing Factory Outlet** (1520 Sansom St., second floor, tel. 215/568–8248). A manufacturers' outlet with a wide variety of better brands at 40% off retail. Immediate alterations for out-of-town buyers.

Fashion Direct (2313 Chestnut St., tel. 215/569–4101). Current first-quality overruns and cancellations from high-fashion designers. Up to 60% off retail on a wide range of men's wear, women's fashions, and accessories.

Night Dressing (724 S. 4th St., tel. 215/627–5244). Offers 50% off list prices on designer lingerie, 20% off hosiery.

5 Sports and Fitness

Participant Sports and Fitness

Bicycling Rentals are available at **Fairmount Park Bike Rental,** conveniently located in Fairmount Park on Kelly Drive. Rent a bike here and ride out on the east side of the Schuylkill River, cross Falls Bridge, and return on the west side of the river. The 8.2-mile loop takes about an hour of casually paced biking. *1 Boathouse Row, behind the Art Museum, tel. 215/236–4359. Cost: $6/hr ($10 deposit and picture ID required). Weekdays 10:30–8, weekends 9–8. Closed in winter.*

Boating and Canoeing Paddle or row through Fairmount Park along the scenic Schuylkill River, but yield the right of way to Olympic-caliber scullers speeding by. Rent canoes or rowboats at the **Public Canoe House.** *Kelly Dr., just south of Strawberry Mansion Bridge, tel. 215/225–3560. Cost for canoes or rowboats $10/hr with $10 deposit. Photo ID required. Open daily 10 AM–1 hour before dark, March–Nov.*

Bowling Bowling in Philadelphia seems to have lost some of its popularity. Alleys are no longer located downtown, but you can still bowl in other parts of the city. Two alleys worth trying are **Adams Lanes,** *Adams Ave. and Foulkrod St., tel. 215/533–1221, hours vary;* and **Oregon Bowling Lanes,** *24th St. and Oregon Ave., tel. 215/389–2200, open daily 9 AM–11:30 PM.*

Fishing and Hunting On the banks of Wissahickon Creek and Pennypack Creek, the catch varies but fishing is always good. Both creeks are stocked for the mid-April through December season. You'll need a license ($12.50): get one at most local sporting-goods stores.

Hunting is a popular activity in Pennsylvania, but not in Philadelphia proper. You have to go at least as far out as the suburban counties. For information about hunting regulations, contact the **Pennsylvania Game Commission** *(8600 Verree Rd., 19115, tel. 800/228–0791).*

Golf **Cobbs Creek,** 18-hole course. The most difficult course listed. *7800 Lansdowne Ave., tel. 215/877–8707. Greens fees: $11 weekdays, $13 weekends and holidays.*
J. F. Byrne, 18-hole course. *9500 Leon St., tel. 215/632–8666. Greens fees: $11 weekdays, $13 weekends.*
Juniata, 18-hole course. *L and Cayuga Sts., tel. 215/743–4060. Greens fees: $11 weekdays, $13 weekends.*
Walnut Lane, 18-hole course. *Walnut La. and Henry Ave., tel. 215/482–3370. Greens fees: $10 weekdays, $12 weekends.*
Franklin D. Roosevelt, 18-hole course. *20th St. and Pattison Ave., tel. 215/462–8997. Greens fees: $11 weekdays, $13 weekends.*

Hiking and Jogging Fairmount Park—especially along the river drives and Wissahickon Creek—is a natural for hikers and joggers. Starting in front of the Philadelphia Museum of Art, an 8.2-mile loop runs up one side of the Schuylkill, across Falls Bridge, and down the other side of the river back to the museum. Forbidden Drive along the Wissahickon offers more than 5 miles of scenic hiking or jogging on a dirt surface with no automobile traffic.

For organized hiking, check with the following organizations:

American Youth Hostels (tel. 215/925–6004).

Batona Hiking Club (tel. 215/635–0933). These organized hikes tend to be a little more strenuous than those of the other clubs.

The Department of Recreation **Wanderlust Hiking Club** (tel. 215/686–0152).

Horseback Riding Of the numerous bridle paths coursing through Philadelphia, the most popular are the trails of the Wissahickon in the northwest, in Pennypack Park in the northeast, and in Cobbs Creek Park in the southwest. Riding academies that offer instruction and rentals include **Cobbs Creek Academy**, *63rd and Catharine Sts., tel. 215/747–2300. Cost: $15/hr., weekends only; book ahead.* **Ashford Farms**, *River Rd., Miquon, tel. 215/825–9838. Cost: $18/hr.*

Tennis Fairmount Park has more than 100 free public courts but at many, players must bring their own nets. Call the **Department of Recreation** (tel. 215/686–0152) for information.

Many indoor courts are located in the surrounding areas. The only one close to Center City, the **Robert P. Levy Tennis Pavilion**, has eight courts open weekdays 7 AM–midnight, weekends 8 AM–midnight (closed weekends July and Aug.). *3130 Walnut St., tel. 215/898–4741. One-time membership fee $35. Cost: $20–$23/hr.*

Spectator Sports

Philadelphians are avid sports fans who support both professional and collegiate teams. The major-league sports teams play their home games in the sports complex at Broad Street and Pattison Avenue—the Phillies (baseball) and the Eagles (football) at Veterans Stadium, the 76ers (basketball) and the Flyers (hockey) at the Spectrum. Some collegiate games are played there too; others are played on the campuses of the various colleges and universities.

Tickets to professional baseball, basketball, football, and hockey games are available at Veterans Stadium or the Spectrum, at Ticketron outlets, at ticket agencies, and by mail and phone from the respective teams.

Baseball **Philadelphia Phillies**, *Box 7575, 19101, tel. 215/463–1000. Apr.–Oct.*

Basketball **Philadelphia 76ers**, *Box 25050, 19147, tel. 215/339–7676. Oct.–Apr.*

Bicycling One of the world's top four bicycling events, the **CoreStates Pro Cycling Championship**, is held each June. The 156-mile race starts and finishes at Benjamin Franklin Parkway, with 10 loops including the infamous Manayunk "Wall."

Football **Philadelphia Eagles**, *Veterans Stadium, 19148, tel. 215/463–5500. Aug.–Dec.*

Hockey **Philadelphia Flyers**, *The Spectrum, Broad St., and Pattison Ave., 19148, tel. 215/755–9700. Oct.–Apr.*

Horse Racing Thoroughbred racing takes place at **Philadelphia Park**, *Street Rd., Bensalem 19020, tel. 215/639–9000. Post time: 1 PM daily except Mon. and Thurs., mid-June to mid-Feb.* **Garden State Park**, *Rte. 70, Cherry Hill, NJ 08034, tel. 609/488–8400. Post*

*time: 7:30 PM daily except Sun. Thoroughbred racing Feb.–
Jun., harness racing Wed.–Sat., Sept.–Dec.*

Track and Field The **Penn Relays,** the world's largest and oldest amateur track
meet, held the last week of April at the University of Pennsyl-
vania's Franklin Field, features world-class performers in
track and field. The **Philadelphia Distance Run,** the nation's top
half marathon, takes place in September. The **Philadelphia Independence Marathon** is held each November. For more
information on these events, call 215/686–0053. The **Broad
Street Run** (tel. 215/686–0152), a 10-miler down Broad Street,
is held in May.

Tennis The **Ebel U.S. Pro Indoor Tennis Championships** are held at the
Spectrum (tel. 215/947–2530), usually in February. More than
60 of the world's top pros compete.

6 Dining

Introduction

Selected and edited by Sam Gugino

Sam Gugino has held a variety of positions in the food business since 1975. He has been chef and manager at two critically successful Philadelphia restaurants, and food and service director for two major hotels. The former restaurant critic for the Philadelphia Daily News, *he is now the food editor of the* San Jose Mercury News.

Since the "restaurant renaissance" of the early 1970s, Philadelphia has become a first-class restaurant city. There's no specific Philadelphia cuisine (unless you count soft pretzels, cheesesteaks, hoagies, and Tastykakes). The city does, however, have exemplary American and Continental cooking, and ethnic restaurants of almost all descriptions—Greek, Japanese, Middle Eastern, and Thai, among many others. Chinatown alone has more than 50 restaurants.

Dining experiences range from street-corner pretzel vendors and open-air cheesesteak shops to world-class French haute cuisine.

Meal times vary widely but, as a rule, breakfast is served from 7 to 11 AM; lunch from 11:30 AM to 2:30 PM; dinner from 5 to 10:30 PM.

Reservations are always advised, especially in the spring and fall, when Philadelphia has many conventions.

Only the fanciest restaurants require a jacket and tie for men. Most places have a liberal dress policy: Anything dressier than jeans and T-shirts is acceptable.

From the hundreds of restaurants in the city, we have provided a representative selection of the better ones. They are listed alphabetically according to cuisine.

To help you find restaurants downtown, we've identified their locations as within the following geographic areas: **Center City, Old City, Society Hill,** and **Chinatown.** Center City is bounded roughly by the Schuylkill River to the west, 6th Street to the east, Lombard Street to the south, and Race Street to the north. Old City is bounded by 6th Street, the Delaware River, and Race and Sansom streets. Society Hill is bounded by 6th Street, the Delaware River, Bainbridge Street, and Walnut Street. Chinatown lies between 9th and 11th streets, and Vine and Arch streets.

We also include several restaurants in **West Philadelphia** (the part of the city west of the Schuylkill River), **South Philadelphia** (south of Bainbridge Street), and **Chestnut Hill** (in the northwest part of the city).

The most highly recommended restaurants in each price category are indicated by a star ★ .

Category	Cost*
Very Expensive	over $35
Expensive	$25–$35
Moderate	$15–$25
Inexpensive	under $15

*per person excluding drinks, service, and sales tax (6%).

The following credit card abbreviations are used: AE, American Express; CB, Carte Blanche; DC, Diners Club; MC, MasterCard; V, Visa.

American-International

Very Expensive **The Fountain.** Nestled in the lavish yet dignified lobby of the
★ Four Seasons, the Fountain has the city's most varied and
freshest selection of meals. Cream of celery soup, fresh seafood
ravioli, and sautéed foie gras over asparagus are three enticing
appetizers. Entrées are predominantly local and American
dishes such as sautéed salmon fillet and roasted Pennsylvania
pheasant with bacon-flavored cabbage. A special health menu
offers foods low in cholesterol, calories, and sodium. Breads are
superb but desserts are a trifle disappointing. Service is atten-
tive and efficient yet relaxing. *1 Logan Sq., Center City, tel.
215/963–1500. Reservations necessary. Dress: informal. AE,
CB, DC, MC, V.*

Expensive **Bogart's.** Not your typical hotel restaurant, Bogart's is an excellent eatery that happens to be in a hotel (the Latham).
Humphrey would feel right at home with the Casablanca motif
—low ceiling fans, lights creating slatted shadowy patterns,
huge terra-cotta pots filled with ostrich plumes. The cuisine is
modern American and Continental. Steak tartare, Caesar salad, and flambé desserts are prepared at tableside. Appetizers
include wild mushrooms on spinach fettuccini. Recommended
entrées are veal Bogart and tender rack of lamb. Desserts,
such as double chocolate cake, come in portions large enough to
stuff Sidney Greenstreet. *1700 Walnut St., Center City, tel.
215/563–9444. Reservations recommended. Dress: informal.
AE, CB, DC, MC, V.*

The Chart House. People come here less for the food than the
atmosphere: dramatic views of the Delaware River; a nautical
theme combining ultramodern paintings, sculpture, and striking architecture; and a waterfall descending from the lobby to
the lounge. The spacious dining area and lounge seats 250, yet
afford a measure of intimacy lacking in many other large restaurants. For appetizers, try the oysters Rockefeller. Among
the recommended entrées are Hawaiian fish such as *onaga*
(red-tailed snapper), which are flown in daily and baked or
grilled in a champagne butter sauce. Mud pie, the house dessert, is coffee ice cream in a chocolate wafer crust topped with
fudge, fresh whipped cream, and diced almonds. Free valet
parking is available. *555 S. Delaware Ave., Society Hill, tel.
215/625–8383. No reservations accepted. Dress: informal. AE,
CB, DC, MC, V.*

The Garden. A classic Philadelphia dining experience, this
town house–turned–restaurant has dining inside and out—on
a canopied deck and at umbrella-covered tables in the garden
(hence the name). The specialty of the house is grilled Dover
sole. Desserts are all homemade, including ice cream, sorbet,
and the house favorite, white chocolate mousse. Two cruvinets
(devices for keeping opened bottles of wine fresh) dispense
glasses of various red and white wines. Some customers
complain about an occasionally irritable staff. *1617 Spruce St.,
Center City, tel. 215/546–4455. Reservations requested. Dress:
informal for oyster bar and outdoor areas; jacket and tie for
dining rooms. AE, CB, DC, MC, V. Closed Sun.; closed Sat. in
July and Aug.*

The Marker. Located in the Adam's Mark hotel, the Marker
combines traditional hotel fare (shrimp cocktail, Caesar salad,
tableside beef tenderloin) with more adventurous cuisine
(sweetbread sausage with wild mushroom sauce, cold black-

ened filet Mignon with country mustard). The three dining rooms include intimate areas, a walk-in wine closet, and The Library, which has a fireplace and built-in bookshelves. *City Line and Monument Rds., City Line area, tel. 215/581-5000. Reservations suggested. Jackets requested. AE, CB, DC, MC, V.*

Moderate **Apropos.** An innovative, trendy place, Apropos typifies the cui-
★ sine that's setting new standards in Philadelphia. The eclectic, frequently changing menu features California-cuisine staples such as sun-dried tomatoes, goat cheese, quail, rabbit, smoked breast of pheasant, distinctive salads, homemade pasta, wood-burning-oven pizza. The mauve-and-charcoal decor of the main dining room is as modern as the menu. You can also eat in the enclosed sidewalk dining area. *211 S. Broad St., Center City, tel. 215/546-4424. Reservations recommended. Dress: informal. AE, CB, DC, MC, V.*

Carolina's. Located a block from Rittenhouse Square, Carolina's opened in 1986 and quickly became a Center City hot spot. The dining room seats 60 at vinyl-covered tables and bentwood chairs under a stamped tin ceiling. The large menu of sandwiches, pastas, salads, a dozen appetizers, and more than a dozen entrées changes daily. Most popular are veal loaf with mashed potatoes and cob salad (a deep-fried tortilla shell stuffed with chicken, avocado, blue cheese, black olives, tomato, and romaine). The pastry chef's specialties are chocolate peanut butter pie and banana cream pie. *261 S. 20th St., Center City, tel. 215/545-1000. Reservations suggested. Dress: informal. AE, CB, DC, MC, V. No lunch weekends.*

City Tavern. For a taste of Olde Philadelphia, stop at the City Tavern, a haunt of the framers of the Constitution and the site of their 1787 post-Constitutional bash. It was rebuilt in 1975 in the exact location and to the exact specifications of the original; and nothing modern such as phones and smoke detectors—is visible. The staff is clad in period garb and much of the fare recalls Colonial times—pheasant, Cornish hen, rabbit, and a Tavern Pasty made of herbs, meats, and spices. The food won't bowl you over, though the sauces are fairly good. This is a nice place to take the family. In good weather you can enjoy the garden behind the restaurant, and there is live harpsichord music on Friday and Saturday nights. *2nd and Walnut Sts., Society Hill, tel. 215/923-6059. Reservations recommended. Dress: informal. AE, MC, V.*

Downey's. The mahogany bar was salvaged from a Dublin bank, artwork and memorabilia cover the walls, and owner Jack Downey's antique radio collection is on display. The upstairs bar has jazz Friday and Saturday nights; a Dixieland band plays downstairs on Sunday nights. Although the food is routine Irish fare, a lively crowd is always on hand. Irish stew and Irish whiskey cake are favorites. Downey's is popular with local athletes, especially baseball and hockey players. It has an oyster bar and outdoor tables. *Front and South Sts., Society Hill, tel. 215/629-0525. Reservations suggested. Dress: informal. AE, CB, DC, MC, V.*

Ecco. A tiny jewel box of a restaurant seating only 31, Ecco offers a distinctive and varied menu. One outstanding entrée is the duck breast, blackened on the outside and pink on the inside, set off by a not-too-sweet plum sauce. Extraordinary, too, is the syrupy Marsala that seasons the veal scallops. Desserts, such as the fruity strawberry tart atop a bed of cream cheese

Dining

Alouette, **38**	The Commissary, **16**	The Garden, **8**	Marrakesh, **39**
Apropos, **29**	Corned Beef Academy, **17**	Hoffman House, **27**	Melrose Diner, **33**
Boccie Pizza, **3**		Il Gallo Nero, **10**	The Middle East, **48**
Bogart's, **15**	DiLullo Centro, **30**	Imperial Inn, **23**	Monte Carlo Living Room, **42**
Bookbinder's Seafood House, **11**	Downey's, **43**	Joe's Peking Duck House, **22**	Morton's of Chicago, **18**
Carolina's, **5**	Ecco, **7**	La Truffe, **50**	
Chart House, **52**	The Famous Delicatessen, **37**	Le Bec-Fin, **13**	*Moshulu*, **51**
Chef Theodore, **45**	The Fountain, **19**	Lickety Split, **40**	Odeon, **26**
City Tavern, **46**	Friday, Saturday, Sunday, **4**	The Marker, **20**	Old Original Bookbinder's, **47**
			Osteria Romana, **34**

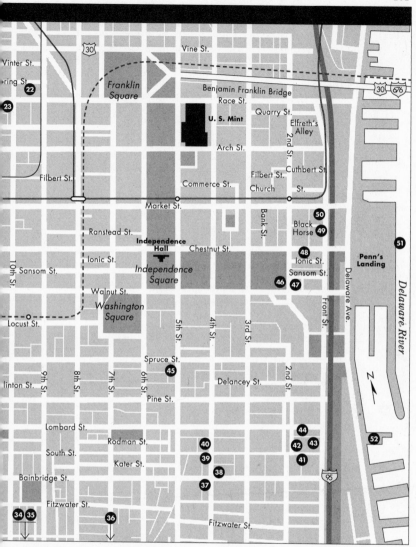

and sprinkled with chocolate, are made on the premises. The wines are varied and reasonably priced. The open kitchen is barely a nose-length away. One wall is covered with aqua, sunset pink, and yellow swatches of an abstract mural painted by local artist Michael Webb. *1700 Lombard St., Center City, tel. 215/735–8070. Reservations advised weeknights, essential weekends. Dress: informal. DC, MC, V.*

Friday, Saturday, Sunday. Fifteen years ago this place was considered daring and innovative, but today it's pretty tame—almost frozen in time. Plaid fabrics drape from the ceiling; mirrors and pinlights line the walls; classical and jazz music plays in the background. The blackboard menu changes frequently. Popular entrées include rack of lamb, chicken Dijon, and hot poached salmon with sorrel sauce. All desserts are made on the premises; chocolate marble cheesecake is the most popular. The wine list is extensive. *261 S. 21st St., Center City, tel. 215/546–4232. Reservations accepted for parties of 5 or more. Dress casual. AE, CB, DC, MC, V.*

Hoffman House. The only German restaurant in Center City, the Hoffman House has been in business since 1923. The dark curved wood, leaded glass windows, boars' heads, and old-fashioned steins are reminiscent of a Bavarian inn. (The upstairs dining room is less attractive.) German music plays in the background. The best appetizer is the Swiss cheese salad. No entrée is outstanding, but the *Schlacht Platte* (a mix of roast pork, pork chops, and frankfurters) and *Rehrucken auf Hoffman Art* (venison with ginger, gin, and green peppercorns) are worth trying. Wild boar and lion are occasionally served. Desserts, including *Sacher torte* (chocolate layer cake with an apricot glaze), an Austrian classic, are surprisingly good. Service could be better. *1214 Sansom St., Center City, tel. 215/925–2772. Reservations advised. Dress: informal. AE, CB, DC, MC, V. Closed Sun.; closed weekends in summer.*

Lickety Split. A charter member of the '70s "restaurant renaissance," Lickety Split has hardly changed in 15 years. It still has a plethora of plants, exposed brick walls, and pinlights; and a waterfall flows in the upstairs lounge. Much of the original menu also remains—stir-fried vegetables, avocado stuffed with crabmeat, and rack of lamb with mustard crumbed coating. Newer offerings include the squid salad appetizer, and entrées such as langostino-stuffed shrimp. Recommended for dessert are bourbon pecan pie and midnight chocolate cake. *4th and South Sts., Society Hill, tel. 215/922–1173. Weekend reservations advised. Dress: informal. AE, CB, DC, MC, V.*

Moshulu. The only restaurant in Philadelphia affected by the tides. The *Moshulu* is a 332-foot-long square-rigger sailing ship that spent 35 years hauling cargo before going into the restaurant business. The food—largely seafood and salads—is competently prepared, but the real attraction is the place itself. A gangplank leads from the pier to the front door. You can sit in two-person nooks in the restored Victorian interior, or outside on the deck looking out over the Delaware River. *Chestnut Mall Waterfront, Society Hill, tel. 215/925–3237. Reservations advised. Dress: informal. AE, MC, V.*

★ **Roller's.** A small, bustling, brightly lit place with floor-to-ceiling windows, Roller's is the best restaurant in Chestnut Hill. Sit near the open kitchen and watch master chef (and owner) Paul Roller prepare Vietnamese duck in *nuoc mam* (fish sauce); buffalo steak with cloves, green peppercorns, and zinfandel wine; and Norwegian salmon in hollandaise with fresh sorrel. First-rate desserts include linzer torte and pearl almond tart. The wine list is varied. Outdoor dining is available during the summer. *Top of the Hill Plaza, Chestnut Hill, tel. 215/242–1771. Dress: informal. Reservations advised. No credit cards. Closed Mon.*

White Dog Cafe. Canine memorabilia abounds; the back of the menu explains why, telling the story of the 19th-century mystic Madame Blavatsky and how this restaurant got its name. Gingham and flea-market furniture give the White Dog a country-inn atmosphere. Owner Judy Wicks joins chef Kevin Von Klaus in making the White Dog *the* restaurant in University City. Excellent regional cuisine uses the finest available local products, such as Bucks County broccoli, served the day it is picked. Try the whole-grain breads and the extra-tasty country terrine. Also recommended is the leg of lamb seasoned with a mixture of crushed black peppercorns, fennel, and mustard seeds. Entrées are served with an eclectic mix of vegetables. The small, lively bar serves 21 varieties of American boutique beer; the wine list is all-American. *3420 Sansom St., West Philadelphia, tel. 215/386–9224. Reservations advised. Dress: informal. AE, DC, MC, V.*

Inexpensive **The Commissary.** This gourmet cafeteria is the flagship of prominent Philadelphia restaurateur Steve Poses. To accompany omelets, soups, pastas, salads, and pastries, it offers a wide selection of coffees and wines. Browse through the library of international cookbooks along one of the mahogany counters. Upstairs is the full-service USA Cafe; alongside is a piano bar for cocktails and light meals. The paintings by local artists are all for sale. Food is available for takeout. *1710 Sansom St., Center City, tel. 215/569–2240. Dress: informal. AE, DC, MC, V.*

The Restaurant School. Here's the only place in Philadelphia where you can get haute cuisine and European service at a fraction of the normal price: A fixed price of $13.50 buys an appetizer and entrée. It is managed and staffed entirely by students attending the Restaurant School, an institution that has produced the chefs and owners of many Philadelphia restaurants. Although the menu includes some Continental (Italian and Hungarian) dishes, it is mainly French traditional, with a focus on sauces. Entrées change regularly, and may include sole Véronique garnished with white sauce and green grapes; or turkey rolled and stuffed with mushrooms and seasonings, and cut into medallions. Located in a 125-year-old restored Victorian brownstone, the dining area has high ceilings and two fireplaces with marble mantels. *2129 Walnut St., Center City, tel. 215/561–3649. Jacket and tie preferred. No pipes or cigars. AE, DC, MC, V. Closed Sun. and Mon.*

Silveri's. This Center City neighborhood bar is one of the few that serve restaurant-quality food. Glass-block windows and pastel colors make it open and airy. Owner Ken Silveri greets you at the door; his wife and sister are the cooks. Silveri is locally famous for introducing award-winning "Buffalo wings" (chicken wings cooked in butter, vinegar, and Louisiana hot sauce) to Philadelphia. Complementing the standard menu of omelets, pastas, sauces, and casseroles, a fancier tableside menu offers entrées such as baked ocean bass. *315 S. 13th St., Center City, tel. 215/545–5115. Dress: informal. MC, V:*

Cafés and Delis

Inexpensive **Corned Beef Academy.** This is *the* place to go for corned beef. ★ The chain of three boisterous modern delis has outstanding brisket and great pickles. Onion rings and french fries are popular. Beer is served at the 18th Street location only. *121 S. 16th St., Center City, tel. 215/665–0460; 18th St. and J. F. Kennedy Blvd., Center City, tel. 215/568–9696; 400 Market St., Old City, tel. 215/922–2111. No credit cards. Closed Sat. and Sun.*

The Famous Delicatessen. The closest thing in Philadelphia to a classic New York deli, the Famous is famous for corned beef, pastrami, and cookies. Other favorites include carp, sable, Nova Scotia salmon, herring, salami, and tongue. The bickering behind the counter is a show in itself, and the waitresses have been known to sit down and schmooze with the customers. Beer is available. *4th and Bainbridge Sts., Society Hill, tel. 215/922–3274. Dress: informal. AE.*

★ **Melrose Diner.** A classic Philadelphia diner and more, the Melrose serves nothing elaborate but offers fresh, top-quality ingredients at diner prices. Entrées cost $5 to $9. You can get breakfast 24 hours a day, including the house specialty, creamed chipped beef. Popular entrées include deviled crab cutlet made from backfin crabmeat, and fried 1620 shrimp (16–20 shrimps per pound), heavily breaded. The on-premises bake shop has eight bakers. Favorite desserts are cheesecake and buttercream layer cake. Waitresses know the names and usual order of all the regular customers. *1501 Snyder Ave., South Philadelphia, tel. 215/467–6644. Dress: informal. No credit cards. Open 24 hours.*

★ **Reading Terminal Market.** A Philadelphia treasure, the Reading Terminal Market is a potpourri of 70 stalls, shops, lunch counters, and food emporiums in a one-square-block indoor farmers market. You can choose from numerous cuisines— Chinese, Greek, Mexican, Japanese, Middle Eastern, Italian, and Pennsylvania Dutch. Food options include Oriental salad bar, seafood, deli, five bake shops, specialty hoagie shop, sushi bar, local winery shop, and Bassett's ice cream store. Lunch early to beat the rush. The Down Home Diner serves Brunswick stew with rabbit and chicken, and occasionally possum and raccoon. *12th and Arch Sts., Center City, tel. 215/922–2317. Closed Sun.*

Chinese

Expensive **Susanna Foo.** Susanna's is the most expensive Chinese restaurant ★ in Philadelphia, and one of the best. Owners Susanna Foo and E. Hsin used to own Hunan, another top-ranked Chinese restaurant. In a decidedly un-Chinese atmosphere—Tchaikovsky playing in the background and remnants from the steakhouse that used to occupy the building—Chef Foo presents an imaginative and varied menu. Entrées include steamed bass with scallion and ginger sauce, and shrimp with tomato, leek, and hot garlic. The bar has a full wine list and imported beers. Skip the Western-style desserts in favor of the chocolate-dipped fortune cookies. *1512 Walnut St., Center City, tel. 215/545–2666. Reservations required. Dress: informal. AE, MC, V. Closed Sun.*

Inexpensive **Imperial Inn.** This is one of Philadelphia's larger and better-known traditional Chinese restaurants. The decor—with white linen, flowers, and chandeliers—is fancier than that of most other restaurants in Chinatown. The menu offers Cantonese, Szechuan, and Mandarin selections. The Imperial is known for its lunchtime dim sum—"finger-food" appetizers that you choose from a cart wheeled to your table. *142 N. 10th St., Chinatown, tel. 215/627–2299. Dress: informal. AE, DC, MC, V.*

★ **Joe's Peking Duck House.** Not the best Chinese restaurant in Philadelphia but the best in Chinatown. With its friendly atmosphere and plain environment, it's like many of the other 50 or so Chinese restaurants around 10th and Race streets, but the quality is better. Joe's is known for Peking duck and barbecued pork. The Cantonese wonton soup is excellent. *925 Race St., Chinatown, tel. 215/922–3277. Reservations advised. Dress: informal. No credit cards.*

French

Very Expensive **Le Bec-Fin.** The most prestigious—and the most expensive—
★ restaurant in Philadelphia. The mise-en-scène is fit for a French king: apricot silk walls, crystal chandeliers, and gilt-framed mirrors. Craig Claiborne called it "the finest French restaurant in the East," but at about $100 per meal it doesn't always measure up to expectations. Chef-owner Georges Perrier's five-course prix fixe dinner includes choice of appetizer, fish course, main course, sorbet and cheese, and dessert cart. A sample meal: *ravioli de crevettes dans son coulis de tomates* (ravioli of shrimps); *feuillet de St. Jacques* (Napoleon pastry with scallops in butter sauce); and *rable de lapin* (roast breast of rabbit with a rosemary sauce); it also has a *charrette de dessert*, a cart with 40 desserts. Characteristic of the restaurant is the plethora of desserts: They're included in the fixed price, and patrons pile them on their plates. A more reasonably priced alternative at Le Bec-Fin is the $27 prix fixe lunch. *1523 Walnut St., Center City, tel. 215/567–1000. Reservations required. Jacket and tie required. AE, CB, DC, MC, V. Closed Sun.*

★ **La Truffe.** La Truffe serves both rich classic and lighter modern French cuisine in a French country-inn atmosphere. Specialties include appetizer—*mille-feuille de pleurotte* (wild mushrooms in a puff pastry); entrée—*carré d'agneau au thym* (rack of lamb with thyme sauce); dessert—white chocolate mousse with fresh raspberry sauce. The prix fixe dinner is $50 or $60. *10 S. Front St., Old City, tel. 215/925–5062. Reservations advised. Jacket and tie required. AE, CB, DC, MC, V. Closed Sun.*

Expensive **Alouette.** Alouette serves French cuisine with an Asian accent. Owner Kamol Phutlek, one of the better chefs in town, is famous for his sauces—tamarind, lime and pineapple, Thai curry, and raspberry lemon. A favorite appetizer is snails in puff pastry with white wine butter sauce. The elegant decor includes fresh flowers, candlelit tables, and a Victorian bar. The French flower-garden courtyard seats 20 people in summer. *4th and Bainbridge Sts., Society Hill, tel. 215/629–1126. Reservations advised weekdays, required weekends. Dress: informal. MC, V.*

Moderate **Odeon.** Among the trendiest new eateries in the city, Odeon is a posh restoration of a former flower shop, with large mirrors, green marble columns, and Art Deco sconces. The sautéed fresh goose liver in a syrupy glaze with a chestnut garnish makes a memorable first course. Recommended for dinner is the Szechuan-peppercorn–encrusted duck breast in star anise and tamari sauce. Desserts include hazelnut meringue layered with buttercream. At the bar a cruvinet serves 16 different wines by the glass. Try to sit at the balcony tables above the sweeping stairway or at the table by the window. *114 S. 12th St., Center City, tel. 215/922–5875. Reservations required on weekends. Dress: informal. AE, MC, V. Closed Sun.*

Indian

Moderate **Siva's.** Most Indian restaurants give you interesting food and good value but rarely much more. Siva's is different. It is fancier than most Indian restaurants, with saffron-colored linen, fresh flowers, and candlelight. The glass-enclosed kitchen with a 4½-foot-deep charcoal-burning tandoor oven produces tandoori specialties such as chicken *tikka*, pieces of boneless chicken marinated in yogurt sauce, cooked with onions and green peppers, and served sizzling in the skillet. The northern Indian cuisine includes vegetarian dishes and stuffed breads. *34 S. Front St., Old City, tel. 215/925–2700. Reservations suggested. Jacket and tie required. AE, MC, V. Closed Mon.*

Italian

Very Expensive **Monte Carlo Living Room.** Here Italian haute cuisine is served amid crystal chandeliers and imported furniture in two mirrored, candlelit dining rooms. Homemade pastas, pastries, and gelati are all recommended. Fish dishes are a specialty. Milk-fed veal stuffed with mozzarella and prosciutto, served with a Dijon mustard sauce, is a popular entrée. Dancing in a private club upstairs is free to diners. *2nd and South Sts., Society Hill, tel. 215/925–2220. Reservations required on weekends. Jacket required. AE, DC, MC, V.*

Expensive **DiLullo Centro.** Occupying the former Locust Theater, DiLullo Centro may be the most striking restaurant in Philadelphia. The two dining areas—one dark, one better lit—have murals, etched glass, dark wood, and brass and glass partitions. Food is good to excellent, but some dishes are overpriced. Recommended pasta dishes are *raviolini* (spinach pasta in a cream sauce) and *tonnarelli* (mushroom pasta in a fragrant sauce). *Bisteccalai ferri* (T-bone steak Florentine style) and whole *aragosta* (lobster) in white wine sauce with ginger are among the best entrées. The best dessert is orange and persimmon sorbet. The excellent wine list has some hard-to-find Italian selections, including Arneis Montebertotto Bianco. *1407 Locust St., Center City, tel. 215/546–2000. Reservations required on weekends. Jacket and tie advised. AE, CB, DC, MC, V. Closed Sun.*

Il Gallo Nero. This is the favorite restaurant of Philadelphia Orchestra conductor Riccardo Muti. You can order *rigatoni del Maestro Muti* (pasta with tomato and basil) and may even be seated next to him—he has a permanent table here. Four balcony tables overlook a fancy ebony–and–brass-rail bar; gracing one wall is a mural of a Renaissance town scene. The seasonal menu is strictly northern Italian. *Chicche della nonna* (grandmother's candy) is a tricolored pasta stuffed with ricotta cheese, two sauces, and a touch of mint. All desserts are homemade by owner Enzo Fusaro. His wife, Carla, is the chef. A pianist plays jazz and sings opera nightly. *254 S. 15th St., Center City, tel. 215/546–8065. Reservations advised. Dress: casual. AE, CB, DC, MC, V. Closed Sun. and Mon.*

★ **Osteria Romana.** You'll pay more than you're used to for Italian food, but Osteria Romana is worth it. It's the finest Italian restaurant in Philadelphia. The stucco walls are trimmed in dark wood and the white tile floors are styled after a Roman *ristorante.* The friendly staff makes you feel at home. Pastas are ample enough for a relatively inexpensive entrée: Don't pass up the gnocchi. Top entrées include suckling pig; *fritto misto* (a mixture of squid, scallops, and shrimp in a delicate batter); and saltimbocca (veal, sage, and prosciutto in white wine with a dash of cream). Sicilian chocolate cake is the star dessert. The excellent wine list includes a Cabreo and a Tunina. *935 Ellsworth St., South Philadelphia, tel. 215/271–9191. Reservations advised. Dress: informal. AE, DC, MC, V. Closed Mon.*

Moderate **Ristorante Primavera.** Get here early: This popular Italian bistro seats only 34 and takes no reservations. Cozy touches include soft track lighting, exposed brick walls, pink table linens, and wall-to-wall carpeting. *Insalata di frutti di mare* with lemon juice, olive oil, and parsley is a huge but inexpensive seafood appetizer. If your appetite is smaller, go with the Caesar salad. Some entrées, such as the *osso buco* (braised veal shank), are good, but pastas and appetizers are the strong suits. Saltimbocca (veal, prosciutto, sage, and white wine) is delicious. For dessert, try the *tiramisu*, a sweet from the recipe book of the manager's grandmother. The wine list is small; service is friendly. *146 South St., Society Hill, tel. 215/925–7832. Dress: informal. No credit cards. Closed Mon.*

★ **Victor Cafe.** Looking for your waiter? He may be on the stairway singing a Verdi aria. At the Victor Cafe the waiters are opera singers and the kitchen plays second fiddle to the music. The northern Italian cuisine has improved now that the third generation of the Di Stefano family has taken charge, but people still come here more for the music and the atmosphere. Busts of classical music composers adorn the shelves, and framed photos of opera singers line the walls. The family's record collection consists of 25,000 78 RPMs. *1303 Dickinson St., South Philadelphia, tel. 215/468–3040. Dress: informal. Packed weeknights; weekends booked weeks in advance. AE, CB, DC. Closed Mon.*

Inexpensive **Boccie Pizza.** Two sparkling wood-burning ovens in a refurbished warehouse turn out both traditional and "nouveau" pizzas. Design your own from 22 ingredients. Or choose one from the menu, such as the Moroccan (topped with lamb strips, scallions, and garlic). Non-pizza entrées are also available. After the meal, you can play a game of boccie on the court right in the middle of the restaurant. *4040 Locust St., University City, tel. 215/386–5500. Dress: informal. MC, V.*

Triangle Tavern. One of the many South Philadelphia neighborhood Italian bar-restaurants—only cheaper. The Triangle has lots of local color. Mussels are the specialty of the house; *calamari* (squid) with red sauce ("Italian gravy" to Philadelphia Italians) is also popular. Dusty's Trio has been providing live entertainment on Friday and Saturday nights here for 35 years. *10th and Reed Sts., South Philadelphia, tel. 215/467–8683. Dress: casual. No credit cards.*

Japanese

Moderate
★

Tokio. Decor here is Japanese minimalist: A toy Godzilla guards the sushi bar; Japanese rock plays in the background. Sushi and sashimi, which are attractively presented at most Japanese restaurants, are even more attractive here. Try the combination dish, which includes octopus, yellowtail, eel, and a ring of rice and is adorned with flying-fish eggs. If you can't fathom raw fish, consider the sukiyaki or the yosenabe—they're cooked on your table and you decide when they're done. No desserts. *124 Lombard St., Society Hill, tel. 215/922-7181. Dress: informal. BYOB. AE, MC, V. Closed Mon.*

Ziggy's. So much is happening here that dining may seem incidental. The sleek black interior with its geometric neon shapes, floor-to-ceiling video screen, and—at the mahogany bar—personal TV sets, has a mysterious ambience. Your waiter may be wearing theatrical makeup. Food is served under a spotlight at your table. The menu is mostly Japanese—sashimi, sushi, and maki sushi. *Chirashi sushi* is an assortment of *surimi*, salmon roe, giant clam, and squid garnished with vegetables atop vinegared rice. *1210 Walnut St., Center City, tel. 215/985-1838. Reservations advised on weekends. Dress: informal. AE, CB, DC, MC, V.*

Mexican

Moderate
★

Tequila's. The place to go for Mexican food in Philadelphia. For appetizers, skip the *nachitos obligatorios* and try one of the citric seviches (such as lobster stuffed in pineapple). The best entrée is the Mayan red snapper *filetina*. Others to sample are *chiles en nogada*—peppers filled with raisins, nuts, and ground beef, and topped with a cream cheese sauce—and the defatted duck baked in a ground squash seed sauce. The full bar serves wines and a variety of Mexican beers. The walls have photos of Pancho Villa and Emiliano Zapata and alcoves contain Mexican glassware and ceramics. For dessert, many favor the Chihuahua crepes with goat's-milk syrup. *1511 Locust St., Center City, tel. 215/546-0181. Dress: informal. AE, CB, DC, MC, V.*

Middle Eastern

Expensive

The Middle East. More than just a restaurant, the Middle East is a show. It has mirrors, Oriental rugs on the walls, and gilded portraits worthy of a sultan's harem. You might see a hula dancer or a fire-eater, but the Middle East is famous for its belly dancers. (Join them if you feel adventurous.) The owner, city Councilman James Tayoun, fills the menu with dishes from his ancestral Lebanon and other Middle Eastern countries. Lamb is the staple—on the shank, braised with tomatoes; in moussaka; on kebabs; and ground raw in *kibbie nayee* (raw lamb and wheat germ), the national dish of Lebanon. American food, including meatless Pritikin dishes, is also available. *126 Chestnut St., Old City, tel. 215/922-1003. Reservations required. Dress: informal. AE, CB, DC, MC, V.*

Moderate
★

Marrakesh. People who don't like eating with their hands—well, they'll survive. There are no utensils here, and diners sit on low cushioned benches at hammered-brass tables. After you wash your hands with warm water and dry them on towels, you're served a $20 prix fixe seven-course banquet: salads, *bastilla* (meat pie with chicken, almonds, and scrambled eggs), chicken and lamb with honey and almonds, couscous with vegetables, fresh fruit, baklava, and sweet mint tea. A fun dining experience. *517 S. Leithgow St., Society Hill, tel. 215/925–5929. Reservations required. Dress: informal. No credit cards. Dinner only.*

Inexpensive **Chef Theodore.** A narrow storefront with modest prices, Chef Theodore is a cut above the other Delaware Valley Greek restaurants. The beige walls are adorned with tasteful prints and posters, and accented with nut-brown wainscoting. The bargain-priced *meze* combination platter includes *baba cunush* (roast eggplant dip), *humus* (ground chick-peas with sesame paste), *taramosalata* (salty caviar spread), *tzatziki* (whipped yogurt with cucumbers and lemon), marinated octopus, stuffed grape leaves, calamata olives, and feta cheese. Among a dozen nightly specials are braised lamb with *avgolimono* (lemon) and dill sauce, served with artichoke hearts. You can end your meal with good Greek coffee and sweet but not overly rich desserts. *316 S. 5th St., Society Hill, tel. 215/592–1555. Dress: informal. BYOB (liquor store next door). DC, MC, V. Closed Mon.*

Seafood

Very Expensive **Old Original Bookbinder's.** This is a favorite haunt of celebrities, politicians, and athletes—many of whom appear in photos on the walls. The seafood is well prepared but not necessarily the best you'll ever eat. "Bookie's" is often criticized for being overpriced (entrées range from $25 to $30) and touristy (it runs a gift shop with Bookbinder souvenirs). You can select a lobster from a tank and have it cooked to order. This was the site of the Bookbinder family's first restaurant, opened in 1865. *125 Walnut St., Society Hill, tel. 215/925–7027. Reservations suggested. Dress: informal. AE, CB, DC, MC, V.*

Expensive **Bookbinder's Seafood House.** Bookbinder's, the most famous name in Philadelphia restaurants, is actually two separate restaurants with different owners in different parts of town. This one is owned by the original family; the other, Old Original Bookbinder's, stands on the site of the Bookbinder family's first restaurant. Seafood House, a tad less expensive than Old Original, has typical seafood restaurant decor like stuffed swordfish mounted on the walls and fishermen's nets dangling from the ceiling. The menu features lobster Coleman (chunks of lobster baked in a Newburg sauce), crab imperial, fresh stone crabs, snapper soup, and baked crabs. *215 S. 15th St., Center City, tel. 215/545–1137. Reservations required. Dress: informal. AE, CB, DC, MC, V.*

Moderate **Sansom Street Oyster House.** This Philadelphia favorite serves
★ first-rate raw oysters plus clams, fish, shellfish, and grilled and blackened dishes. It's an unpretentious place with dark wood paneling and uncovered tables. The family collection of over 200 oyster plates covers the walls. In 1988 they expanded both the space and the menu, adding a bar, more seating, and non-seafood items like steaks and chicken. The menu changes daily. For dessert, try the peanut butter pie with chocolate. *1516 Sansom St., Center City, tel. 215/567–7683. Reservations accepted only for parties of 5 or more. Dress: informal. AE, CB, DC, MC, V. Closed Sun.*

Steaks

Expensive **Morton's of Chicago.** With a tuxedoed maître d' and the atmosphere of a private club, Morton's is a steakhouse catering largely to businessmen on expense accounts. The balcony-level dining area overlooks the main dining room, which has an Art Deco bar and walls lined with bottles of wine. Choose your cut of meat or fish from raw items on a cart wheeled to your table; it will be cooked to your specifications. The house specialty, a 24-ounce porterhouse, should fill you up. *1 Logan Sq. (on 19th St.), Center City, tel. 215/557-0724. Reservations accepted for 5:30–7 PM only. Jacket and tie required. AE, CB, DC, MC, V. Closed Sun.*

The Saloon. Here's a steakhouse with Italian specialties. Everything it does is big: big pieces of meat, big drinks, big prices. Big money went into the antique turn-of-the-century decor—mahogany paneling, mirrors, and stained glass. For an appetizer, try the salad of radicchio with shiitake mushrooms, served warm. For an entrée, order the risotto with abundant porcini mushrooms, or cannelloni filled with veal in one of the excellent tomato sauces. Desserts include lemon and berry tarts. *750 S. 7th St., South Philadelphia, tel. 215/627–1811. Reservations required. Dress: informal. AE. Closed Sun.*

Thai

Inexpensive **Thai Garden.** A former dishwasher opened Thai Garden in
★ spring 1988 and it quickly became the foremost Thai restaurant in the city. Occupying the ground floor of a stately old apartment building, the elegant dining room has blocked mirrors, golden bamboo flatware, and traditional Thai flowers on white linen. The *miena cum* appetizer—toasted peanuts, coconut chips, and lime piled on spinach leaves spiced with chopped chili and a Thai plum sauce—is delectable. *Chu chee* (curried duck) and Thai-style barbecued chicken with sweet-and-sour sauce are among the excellent entrées. *47th St. between Spruce and Pine Sts., West Philadelphia, tel. 215/471–3663. Dress: informal. BYOB. MC, V.*

Vietnamese

Inexpensive **Van's Garden.** Van's is probably the least expensive Oriental
★ restaurant in Philadelphia, yet it's first rate. Hodgepodge decor includes flocked red and black wallpaper, linoleum floors, and blond wood wainscoting. A superb appetizer is grilled meatballs wrapped in rice paper, with carrots, radishes, cucumbers, noodles, and a thick brown bean sauce for dipping—a sort of Vietnamese hoagie. Among entrées, you can get 10 sweet-and-sour shrimp in a tempura-like batter; lobster salad at $6.95 is the most expensive item on the menu. Dinner here is a superb value. *121 N. 11th St., Chinatown, tel. 215/923–2439. Dress: informal. BYOB. No credit cards.*

Brunch

Sunday brunch is a Philadelphia tradition. Scores of local establishments open their doors on Sunday mornings, serving everything from traditional bagels and lox at the Famous Deli to the more unusual rock shrimp and grits baked in cream with pepper jack cheese and roasted peppers found at the White Dog Cafe.

Brunch connoisseurs will not want to miss the Sunday-morning spread at the Four Seasons Hotel, where for $21.50, diners can feast on one of two sumptuous buffets amid crystal, linen, and massive floral arrangements. The hearty buffet at the Swann Lounge Cafe features cooked-to-order omelets and waffles, as well as vegetable stir-fries, pasta, and a broccoli-and-cheese soufflé. In the adjacent, more elegant, Fountain Restaurant, diners can choose from either the menu or the buffet, which specializes in fish, including an occasional caviar dish. The menu features the "Melody of Pancakes," which includes corn-bread, whole wheat, regular, and bran—the fanciest stack of flapjacks in Philly.

All the restaurants listed below offer Sunday brunch. Descriptions, addresses, and phone numbers appear in the Dining section above: *Alouette, Apropos, Bogart's, Carolina's, Chart House, Commissary, Downey's, Ecco, Famous Deli, The Marker*, Moshulu, *Roller's, White Dog Cafe.*

7 Lodging

Introduction

Philadelphia hotels run the gamut from commonplace to world class, from a five-star hotel with every luxury to a 12-room country inn. While many are basic utilitarian hotels or national chains, others are experiences in themselves.

Although the number of rooms—11,000—is small for a city of nearly a million and half, it usually isn't difficult to find a place to stay. The only times you're likely to encounter problems are the weekend of the Army-Navy football game (usually the weekend after Thanksgiving weekend) and during occasional large conventions. Nevertheless, reservations are advised. The city has no central reservation office.

Hotels are listed geographically. Most hotels are downtown, grouped in three areas: the shopping/theater district, the Benjamin Franklin Parkway/museum area, and the historic district. A half-dozen hotels are clustered near Philadelphia International Airport. Several are on the campus of the University of Pennsylvania in West Philadelphia. Two are in the City Line area. One is in Chestnut Hill in the northwest part of the city.

Aside from a youth hostel and bed-and-breakfasts, the city has only a few moderately priced hotels; most are expensive.

Within geographic groupings, hotels are listed alphabetically according to the following price categories.

Unless otherwise noted, all rooms have private bath.

Highly recommended lodgings in each price category are indicated by a star ★.

Category	Cost*
Very Expensive	over $120
Expensive	$90–$120
Moderate	$50–$90
Inexpensive	under $50

All prices are for a standard double room; excluding 11% tax.

The following credit card abbreviations are used: AE, American Express; CB, Carte Blanche; DC, Diners Club; MC, MasterCard; V, Visa.

Philadelphia has no off-season rates, but most hotels offer discount packages for weekends when demand from business people and groups subsides. Besides substantially reduced rates, these packages often include an assortment of free features, such as breakfast, parking, cocktails, champagne, and the use of exercise facilities.

Aside from such packages, most downtown hotels charge around $13 a day for parking.

Center City

Hotels downtown are located in three areas. The shopping/theater district encompasses a few blocks on either side of

Lodging

Adam's Mark, **3**

Airport Hilton Inn, **20**

The Barclay, **10**

Chamounix Mansion, **2**

Chestnut Hill Hotel, **5**

Comfort Inn at Penn's Landing, **28**

Days Inn, **22**

Four Seasons, **8**

Guest Quarters, **18**

Hershey Philadelphia Hotel, **15**

Holiday Inn Airport, **23**

Holiday Inn Center City, **9**

Holiday Inn City Line, **4**

Holiday Inn Independence Mall, **27**

Holiday Inn Midtown, **16**

Hotel Atop the Bellvue, **14**

International House, **6**

Latham, **12**

Penn Tower, **7**

Philadelphia Marriott Hotel Airport, **19**

Quality Inn Airport, **21**

Quality Inn Center City, **1**

Quality Inn Downtown Historic Suites, **17**

Sheraton Society Hill, **24**

Society Hill Hotel, **26**

The Warwick, **11**

Thomas Bond House, **25**

Wyndham Franklin Plaza, **13**

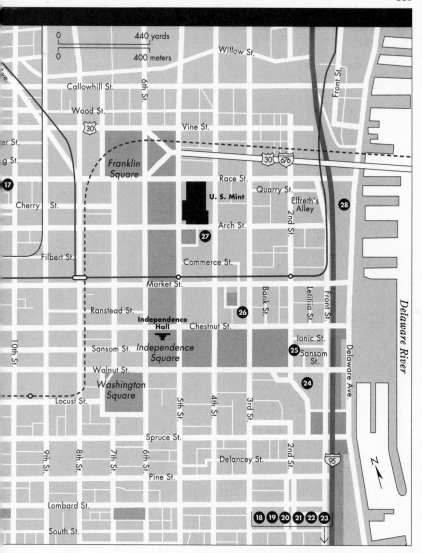

Broad Street, near Walnut Street. The Parkway/museum area
runs along the Benjamin Franklin Parkway from 16th Street to
the Philadelphia Museum of Art. The historic district on the
east side of downtown centers on Independence Hall and extends to the Delaware River.

Since all three areas have hotels in similar price ranges, make
your choice according to other factors, such as your individual
interests or the availability of rooms.

Very Expensive **The Barclay.** There's something special about having Rittenhouse Square right outside your front door *(see* Tour 3, Chapter
3). The elegant, dark-paneled lobby leads to a registration area
sparkling with a half-dozen crystal chandeliers and matching
wall fixtures. The hotel was built in 1929 and renovated in 1981.
The halls have hardwood floors and Oriental rugs. Half the
rooms have four-poster beds—and many of those have cano-
pies. Furniture is antique style throughout and in most rooms
TV sets are concealed in classic armoires. *Rittenhouse Sq. E.,
19103, tel. 215/545–0300 or 800/421–6662. 240 rooms. Facilities: concierge service, restaurant, lobby lounge with jazz
pianist. AE, DC, MC, V.*

★ **Four Seasons.** If a director wanted a location for a romantic
hotel-room view in Philadelphia, he would choose a room here,
overlooking the fountains in Logan Circle and the Benjamin
Franklin Parkway. Built in 1983, the eight-story U-shaped hotel has block-long hallways that some guests don't like. Guest-
room furniture is Federal style, dark and stately. Philadelphia's most expensive hotel provides terry robes and a
complimentary shoeshine—hang your shoes in the bag on your
doorknob and they come back shined the next morning. Bidets,
formerly in all the bathrooms, are now available only upon request. *1 Logan Sq. (near major museums), 19103, tel. 215/963–
1500 or 800/332–3442. 371 rooms. Facilities: 24-hr room service, 24-hr concierge service, 3 nonsmoking floors, exercise
room, dry sauna, massage, aerobics classes, indoor pool, restaurant, indoor/outdoor cafe (health menu available from
room service and in the restaurant). Weekend rates. AE, DC,
MC, V.*

Hershey Philadelphia Hotel. You can sit in the four-story atrium
lobby and behold one of the busiest corners of Philadelphia's
shopping and theater district. Rooms are decorated in earth-
tones, with modern furnishings. Opened in 1983, the hotel's
sawtooth design gives each room a peaked bay window with a
180-degree view. East-side rooms get a panoramic view of the
city, the Delaware River, and New Jersey. Eight baseball
teams stay here when they play the Phillies. At check-in, you
get a room key and a Hershey chocolate bar. *Broad and Locust
Sts., 19107, tel. 215/893–1600 or 800/533–3131. 428 rooms. Facilities: health club with indoor pool, saunas, tanning salon,
whirlpool, weight room, snack bar, racquetball courts, gift
shop, lobby lounge with live entertainment, restaurant in atrium area. AE, DC, MC, V.*

★ **Hotel Atop the Bellevue.** A Philadelphia institution for 80 years,
the elegant Bellevue hotel was reopened in 1989 on seven floors
in its original building. A three-year, $150 million renovation
transformed the lower floors into office and shop space, while
the 12th through 19th floors were redesigned to accommodate
the hotel. The Barrymore Room, topped by a stained-glass 30-
foot dome, and the seven-story Palm Court atrium are just two

of the hotel's lavish public areas. From the champagne tour available at registration, to the telephones and TVs in the bathrooms, the Bellevue has more luxurious amenities than any other hotel in town. Rooms are large and each has an entertainment center with color TV, stereo, and VCR (choose from the concierge's library of 50 cassettes); magazine rack with current periodicals; minibar; and computer modem data port. *Broad and Walnut Sts., 19102, tel. 215/893–1776 or 800/221–0833. 170 rooms. Facilities: 24-hr room service, 24-hr concierge, gourmet restaurant, atrium restaurant, lounge, wine bar, health club, three floors of shops. AE, DC, MC, V.*

Latham. This is a small, elegant hotel with a European accent and an emphasis on personal service. Doormen clad in vests and riding boots welcome you to the lobby. A concierge is on duty daily from 9 to 5. All rooms have marble-topped bureaus and French writing desks, full-wall mirrors, hair dryers, and makeup mirrors; most have minibars. The weekend package includes a deluxe room, valet parking, and gourmet breakfast. *17th St. at Walnut St. (one block from Rittenhouse Sq.), 19103, tel. 215/563–7474 or 800/528–4261. 139 rooms. Facilities: executive floor; Bogart's restaurant; piano lounge; business center with fax machine, copier, and secretarial service. AE, DC, MC, V.*

Sheraton Society Hill. Conveniently located for visits to the historic district, this red-brick, neo-Colonial building is two blocks from Penn's Landing, three blocks from Head House Square, and three blocks from Independence Hall (*see* Tour 1 in Chapter 3). Opened in 1986, its four-story atrium lobby is framed by archways and balconies, filled with trees and plants, and lit by wrought-iron lanterns. Rooms are furnished traditionally but have modern conveniences such as a bar and a remote-control TV. Fourth-floor rooms facing east toward the Delaware River have the best view. *1 Dock St., 19106, tel. 215/238–6000 or 800/325–3535. 365 rooms, 17 suites. Facilities: 24-hr room service, indoor pool, fitness center with whirlpool, sauna, and exercise room. AE, DC, MC, V.*

The Warwick. The lobby, brightened by mirrors and 18-foot Palladian windows, hosts a constant stream of activity. The 400 rooms are partly hotel rooms and partly apartments. It makes for an interesting mix of guests in business suits and residents in shorts and sneakers. The spacious rooms were totally redecorated in 1988 in "English country style." Bathrooms are flowery and bright, each adorned with commissioned watercolor by local artist Joe Barker. A complimentary shoeshine is available. Guests get free admission to posh Polo Bay Club, a nightclub. You'll find the current issue of *Philadelphia* magazine in your room. *17th and Locust Sts., 19103, tel. 215/735–6000 or 800/523–4210. 200 rooms. Facilities: restaurant/bar, business center. Weekend theater package. AE, DC, MC, V.*

Wyndham Franklin Plaza. "Please Wait for Next Available Receptionist" read the signs in the lobby of Philadelphia's biggest and busiest hotel. The 70-foot atrium lobby encompasses three restaurants, a bar, and numerous handsome sitting areas. Hallways show the wear and tear of being the city's main convention hotel, but rooms are well cared for. Decor is modern, in gray and silver with chrome tubular purple chairs, full-length mirrors, and cable TV. *16th and Vine Sts., 19103, tel. 215/448–2000 or 800/822–4200. 758 rooms, including 38 suites. Facilities: room service; access to health club with 3 racquetball* courts, *3 squash courts, 2 tennis courts, masseuse, exercise equipment, aerobics center, pool; beauty shop; barber shop; florist; travel service; gift shop. Weekend packages. AE, DC, MC, V.*

Expensive **Holiday Inn Center City.** Centrally located between Benjamin Franklin Parkway, Rittenhouse Square, and City Hall, this is an above-average Holiday Inn with an excellent location. The 25-floor hotel opened in 1971 and was completely renovated in 1986. All rooms have a mauve color scheme and contemporary decor. More than half have minibars. *1800 Market St., 19103, tel. 215/561–7500 or 800/HOLIDAY. 450 rooms. Facilities: 2 nonsmoking floors; 2 executive-level concierge floors; 8th-floor outdoor pool; weight room with Nautilus, rowing machines, exercise bikes; gift shop; restaurant; cocktail lounge. Weekend package. AE, DC, MC, V.*

Holiday Inn Independence Mall. "Independence Mall" in the name is no exaggeration: This is the hotel most convenient to the downtown historic area. To complement its location, all rooms are done in Colonial decor with Ethan Allen Georgetown furniture, including poster beds and wing chairs. *4th and Arch Sts., 19106, tel. 215/923–8660 or 800/HOLIDAY. 364 rooms, 7 suites. Facilities: outdoor pool, videogame room, gift shop, cocktail lounge, Benjamin's restaurant. Weekend package. AE, DC, MC, V.*

Holiday Inn Midtown. Rooms are more spacious than average here—perhaps because they're older (it opened in 1964). Rooms are decorated with prints of Philadelphia scenes or floral motifs. Rooms facing south to Walnut Street have the best views. Drive in off Walnut Street for valet parking. The location is excellent: one block from the Broad Street Subway, near the theater and shopping district, and two blocks from Jefferson Hospital. *1305 Walnut St., 19107, tel. 215/735–9300 or 800/HOLIDAY. 161 rooms. Facilities: nonsmoking rooms, outdoor pool, free parking, restaurant, wide-screen TV in lounge. Weekend package. AE, DC, MC, V.*

Moderate **Comfort Inn at Penn's Landing.** The price is the most noteworthy item here. The 10-story hotel, opened in 1987, provides basic rooms and service. Decor is contemporary, with oak furniture and a mauve color scheme. A bar enlivens the small, nondescript lobby. Tucked between the Benjamin Franklin Bridge, Delaware Avenue, and I–95, the location has more noise than charm. Rooms on upper floors facing the river have a good view of the Benjamin Franklin Bridge beautifully lit up at night. *100 N. Delaware Ave., 19106, tel. 215/627–7900. 185 rooms, including 9 suites with hot tubs. Facilities: lobby lounge, complimentary Continental breakfast, free parking. AE, DC, MC, V.*

Quality Inn Center City. If you're willing to stay a bit away from downtown but near the museums, you'll find a bargain here. The three-story, Y-shaped building underwent a $5 million renovation in 1984. Rooms are done in mauve and taupe with oak-finish furniture and individual climate control. The new security system uses electronic keycards. The best view faces south toward the Benjamin Franklin Parkway, the Rodin Museum, and the downtown skyline. *501 N. 22nd St., 19130, tel. 215/568–8300. 283 rooms, including 4 suites. Facilities: room service, restaurant, outdoor café, lounge with occasional entertainment, outdoor pool, free parking. Weekend rates (winter only). AE, DC, MC, V.*

★ **Quality Inn Historic Downtown Suites.** Because of the out-of-the-way location, you get suite accommodations at hotel-room prices. It opened late 1985 in a historically certified 1890 building that was once the Bentwood Rocker Factory. Much of the original building was incorporated into the present decor, including exposed brick walls and overhead beams which give rooms a rustic, homey atmosphere. Every suite has a kitchen. The environment is East meets West: Drexel Heritage furniture with Oriental prints and accent pieces. *1010 Race St., 19107, tel. 215/922–1730 or 800/228–5151. 96 suites. Facilities: lobby lounge, health club, sauna, limited free parking, free Continental breakfast. AE, DC, MC, V.*

Airport

Since the area has few attractions other than the airport and the hotels themselves, hotels here are less expensive than those downtown. For most attractions and entertainment, figure on heading into town, a 20-minute drive or taxi ride away. Three of the hotels are right at the airport and near a sewage-treatment plant; fortunately, their filtration systems effectively insulate guests from the noxious smells and loud noises.

Very Expensive **Guest Quarters.** This eight-story all-suite hotel has no corridors. A glass-walled elevator whisks you to your floor, where ★ suites front an ivy-covered balcony overlooking the light-flooded atrium lobby and restaurant. Suites are standard or deluxe: Deluxe have larger living rooms and better views. All suites have a king-size bed in the bedroom and a queen-size foldout in the living room; three telephones; two remote-control TV/clock-radios; honor bars; and coffee makers. Packages range from Bare Bones to Honeymoon (which includes breakfast, bubble bath, and champagne). *Gateway Center, 4101 Island Ave., 19153, 215/365–6600 or 800/424–2900. 251 suites. Facilities: atrium restaurant and lounge; free Continental breakfast; free hors d'oeuvres 5–7 PM; exercise room with Universal, bikes, rowing machines; indoor pool; whirlpool; steam room; free parking; free airport shuttle. AE, DC, MC, V.*

Philadelphia Marriott Hotel Airport. You can swim in the lobby of the Airport Marriott and walk across the street to the airport's Overseas Terminal. During the week, this is mostly a business travelers' hotel. Rooms have wood and wicker dressing tables and bureaus and cable TV. *4509 Island Ave., 19153, 215/365–4150 or 800/228–9290. 331 rooms. Facilities: concierge floor, nonsmoking floor, swimming pool in lobby; workout room with weights, machines, bikes, whirlpool, and saunas; 2 restaurants; nightclub; free parking; free airport shuttle. Weekend rates. AE, DC, MC, V.*

Expensive **Airport Hilton Inn.** Five miles from the airport, this could properly be called the Stadium Inn—the Veterans Stadium/Spectrum sports complex is across the street. Renovated in 1986, the 11-story structure features spacious rooms, bathrooms, and closets. Furniture is Spanish moss green, and an Oriental flower design marks wallpaper and bedspreads. The best view is north, to the city skyline 3 miles away. The sports bar, Cahoots, attracts both fans and athletes. *10th St. and Packer Ave., 19148, tel. 215/755–9500 or 800/HILTONS. 238* *rooms including 22 suites. Facilities: outdoor pool, restaurant, lounge, free parking, free airport shuttle. AE, DC, MC, V.*

Quality Inn Airport. The decor of this circular high rise— burgundy rugs with exaggeratedly curved brass light fixtures —is reminiscent of a casino. Rooms have cable TV with remote control. Upper floors have a good view of the city. The sports- theme lounge displays autographed photos of local heroes. *20th St. and Penrose Ave., 19145, 215/755–6500 or 800/221–2222. 228 rooms. Facilities: restaurant, lounge, free shuttle to air- port (8 min away). AE, DC, MC, V.*

Moderate **Days Inn.** Even though this new hotel is surrounded by high- ways and is across the street from the airport, special construction makes it quiet. The sunny, pastel-green corridors of the four-story L-shaped building lead to pleasant and spa- cious rooms. *2 Gateway Ctr., 4101 Island Ave., 19153, tel. 215/ 492–0400 or 800/325–2525. 177 rooms. Facilities: coin-operated launderette, Seasons Restaurant, 32 nonsmoking rooms, free airport shuttle. Special packages and senior-citizen rates, children under 18 free. AE, DC, MC, V.*

Holiday Inn Airport. White marble floors, rose floral arrange- ments, peach ceramic tile, and woven wall hangings in the lobby give this hotel what management calls a "Floridian" mo- tif. The slightly oversize rooms are pastel-colored with light- colored wood furniture. It's 3 miles west of the airport. *45 In- dustrial Hwy. (Rte. 291), Essington 19029, tel. 215/521–2400 or 800/HOLIDAY. 306 rooms. Facilities: Antonio's Restaurant (northern Italian cuisine), Angell's Lounge, gift shop, outdoor pool, free airport shuttle, weekend rates. AE, DC, MC, V.*

University City

Located in West Philadelphia, just across the Schuylkill River, this area is a five- to 10-minute drive from Center City. Slightly less expensive than downtown, the hotels are on the campus of the University of Pennsylvania, near Drexel University, and across the street from the Civic Center, the city's principal con- vention facility.

Expensive **Penn Tower.** The University of Pennsylvania purchased and renovated this 21-floor former Hilton in 1987. It is located on campus across the street from the university's hospital, the Children's Hospital of Philadelphia, and the Civic Center. Rooms have excellent views east to Center City and west across campus. All have live plants, Colonial decor, and a pastel color scheme. *34th St. and Civic Center Blvd., 19104, tel. 215/387– 8333 or 800/356–PENN. 216 rooms, including 10 suites. Facili- ties: concierge floor, 2 restaurants, lounge, free use of U. of Penn athletic facilities, including Olympic-size pool. AE, DC, MC, V.*

Inexpensive **International House.** This residence for students and profes- sors from around the world is located on the University of Pennsylvania campus. Rooms are available only from the end of May to the end of August, however, and guests must have an affiliation with an educational institution. The high-rise build- ing has an unusual poured-concrete, tiered design and an oddly barren atrium. Both the public areas and the rooms themselves have a rough-hewn, spartan feel. No children permitted. *3701 Chestnut St., 19104, tel. 215/387–5125. 379 rooms, but only a limited number are available for overnight guests. Single* *rooms share bath and living room; double rooms have 2 single beds and private bath. Facilities: cafeteria, bar. MC, V.*

City Line

If you prefer to stay outside the bustle of downtown and get free parking, you'll like the two hotels here. It's only a 10-minute ride on the Schuylkill Expressway to Center City under favorable conditions; however, the expressway is frequently under construction and often heavily congested.

Expensive **Adam's Mark.** This 23-story hotel is one of the tallest in Phil-
★ adelphia. Request a room on the upper floors facing south toward Fairmount Park and the downtown skyline. There's nothing special about the rooms, which are on the small side. The big attraction here is the nighttime activity: Quincy's, a turn-of-the-century nightclub; three restaurants; a popular lounge; and a sports bar. *City Ave. and Monument Rd., 19131, tel. 215/581–5000 or 800/231–5858. 515 rooms, including 56 suites. Facilities: indoor and outdoor swimming pools, whirlpool, exercise room, aerobics classes, hair salon, gift shop, travel agency. AE, DC, MC, V.*
Holiday Inn City Line. This eight-story Holiday Inn is perfectly ordinary, but it's a good value in a choice location. You could stay here to save money and just walk across the parking lot to the Adam's Mark nightclub, restaurants, and lounges. A five-minute walk takes you to four other restaurants. In the lobby you can sink into an overstuffed easy chair and watch swimmers in the glass-enclosed pool. *4100 Presidential Blvd., 19131, tel. 215/477–0200 or 800/HOLIDAY. 348 rooms. Facilities: restaurant, pool off lobby. AE, DC, MC, V.*

Chestnut Hill

Staying here puts you among some of Philadelphia's finest homes and shops. It has more than 120 shops—from Oriental-rug dealers to bookstores, clothing boutiques, crafts and music stores, and cheese shops. Nearby is the Wissahickon Valley of Fairmount Park.

Moderate **Chestnut Hill Hotel.** Here's a Colonial inn in the heart of Chestnut Hill. Built as a hotel in 1899, the four-story building was renovated in 1983. Ask to see the rooms first; they vary widely in size and ambience. Some have mahogany reproductions of 18th-century furniture, including four-poster beds. A packet of brochures in each room describes area shops and sights. *8229 Germantown Ave., 19118, tel. 215/242–5905. 28 rooms, including 3 suites. Facilities: 2 restaurants; adjacent to a farmers market and shopping complex. AE, MC, V.*

Bed-and-Breakfasts

Bed-and-breakfasts, which follow the European tradition of a room and meal in a private house or small hotel, are less expensive alternatives to hotels. Most operate under the auspices of central booking agencies that screen homes and match guests and hosts. Host homes offer considerable diversity in urban, suburban, and rural settings.

Services and policies vary. Some accept children and pets. Some provide free transportation from airports, and bus and train terminals. Some offer monthly rates. Breakfasts range from Continental to elegant.

Bed and Breakfast of Philadelphia. This reservation service books over 100 host homes in Philadelphia and surrounding counties. Options range from a Federal town house in the downtown historic area to a pre-Revolutionary farmhouse in Chester County and many suburban homes. Prices range from $25 to $110. *Box 252, Gradyville 19039, tel. 215/358–4747 or 800/733–4747. AE, MC, V.*

Bed and Breakfast, Center City. It represents a dozen homes in the city, from a posh high rise on Rittenhouse Square to a restored town house just off the square. Children permitted. Prices range from $45 to $75, 20% deposit required. *1804 Pine St., Philadelphia 19103, tel. 215/735–1137. No credit cards.*

Bed and Breakfast Connections. Its selection of more than 45 host homes includes a Colonial town house, an English Tudor mansion on Chestnut Hill, and an 18th-century farmhouse on the Main Line. Prices range from $35 to $110. *Box 21, Devon 19333, tel. 215/687–3565. AE, MC, V.*

Bed and Breakfast—The Manor. This service has various locations throughout Philadelphia and surrounding areas, including the New Jersey shore and the Amish country. Most hosts supply transportation free or for a nominal fee. Some accommodate the handicapped. Prices range from $35 to $65. *Box 656, Havertown 19083, tel. 215/642–1323. MC, V.*

Society Hill Hotel. This 1832 former longshoreman's house is one of the smallest hotels in the city. Renovated in 1988, all 12 rooms are uniquely furnished with antiques, brass beds, and lamps. Fresh flowers adorn all rooms and the breakfast tray is brought to your room with fresh-squeezed juice and hand-dipped chocolates. *301 Chestnut St., 19106, tel. 215/925–1394. 12 rooms, including 6 suites. Facilities: outdoor café (voted Philly's classiest by* Philadelphia *magazine), piano bar, restaurant. AE, DC, MC, V.*

Thomas Bond House. Spend the night in the heart of Olde City the way Philadelphians did 220 years ago. Built in 1769 by a prominent local physician, this four-story house recently underwent a faithful, meticulous restoration of everything from its molding and wall sconces to its millwork and flooring. All rooms have 18th-century features such as marble fireplaces and four-poster Thomasville beds. It doesn't get any more Colonial than this. *129 S. 2nd St., 19106, tel. 215/923–8523. 12 rooms, including 2 suites. Facilities: parlor, complimentary wet bar. AE, MC, V.*

Youth Hostel

Youth hostels provide dormitory-style accommodations for less than you'd pay to park your car at a downtown hotel. They also offer a sense of adventure and a chance to share living, eating, and sleeping quarters with travelers from all over the world.

Chamounix Mansion. Here's the cheapest place to stay in Philadelphia—$8 a night plus $3 American Youth Hostel membership. Located on a wooded bluff overlooking the Schuylkill River (and, unfortunately, the Schuylkill Expressway), the city's only youth hostel feels like it's out in the country. This restored 1802 Quaker country estate is loaded with character. The entrance hall is lined with flags; period rooms have antiques; walls display old maps, sketches, and paintings. Drawbacks: dormitory-style living, shared baths, hard to find. *Chamounix Dr., 19131, tel. 215/878–3676. 6 rooms for 45 people, shared baths and kitchen. Facilities: game room, outdoor sports. No credit cards. Closed Dec. 15–Jan. 15.*

8 The Arts and Nightlife

The Arts

For current productions and performances, check the "Guide to the Lively Arts" in the daily *Philadelphia Inquirer*, the "Weekend" section of the Friday *Inquirer*, the "Friday" section of the *Philadelphia Daily News*, and the Cultural Connection Information Hotline (tel. 215/564–4444). *Philadelphia Spotlite*, a free weekly guide listing plays, music, sports, and events, is available at the Visitors Center (16th St. and John F. Kennedy Blvd.).

Theater

Forrest Theater (1114 Walnut St., tel. 215/923–1515) has major Broadway productions, recently *Cats*, *La Cage Aux Folles*, *Les Misérables*, and *Phantom of the Opera*.

Annenberg Center (3680 Walnut St., tel. 215/898–6791) has four stages, from the 120-seat Studio to the 970-seat Zellerbach Theater. Something is going on almost all the time—with established stars like Liv Ullman and Jose Ferrer and oddball acts such as the Flying Karamazov Brothers and Avner the Eccentric.

Shubert Theater (250 S. Broad St., tel. 215/732–5446). Now part of the University of the Arts, the Shubert presents musicals and dramas occasionally performed by touring companies.

Walnut Street Theater (9th and Walnut Sts., tel. 215/574–3550). Founded in 1809, this is the oldest English-speaking theater in continuous use in the United States. The schedule includes musicals, comedy, and drama in a lovely auditorium where almost every seat is a good one.

Wilma Theater (2030 Sansom St., tel. 215/963–0345) has gained favorable critical notices for its innovative work since adopting a policy of hiring Equity actors. The season runs from October to June.

Philadelphia Theater Company (1714 Delancey St., tel. 215/592–8333) performs works by contemporary American playwrights, many of them off-Broadway hits. It also has Stages, a program of new plays by American playwrights.

Society Hill Playhouse (507 S. 8th St., tel. 215/923–0210). The main stage features contemporary works; the Second Space has more innovative productions.

Theater of the Living Arts (334 South St., tel. 215/922–1010) presents concerts of jazz, New Age music, rock, comedians, and off-Broadway fare.

American Theater Arts for Youth (Port of History Museum, Penn's Landing, tel. 215/563–3501) features morning and afternoon musicals and live productions of the National Theater for Children.

Riverfront Dinner Theater (Poplar St. and Delaware Ave., tel. 215/925–7000) and **Huntingdon Valley Dinner Theater** (2633 Philmont Ave., Huntingdon Valley, tel. 215/947–6000) specialize in Broadway musicals.

Philadelphia Festival Theater for New Plays (3680 Walnut St., tel. 215/222–5000) draws national attention with new works by new playwrights. It runs from October through June.

Freedom Theater (1346 N. Broad St., tel. 215/765–2793) is the oldest and most active black theater in Philadelphia. Its quartered in the Heritage House, the former residence of the great

American actor Edwin Forrest. Performances are held September through April.

Concerts

Philadelphia Orchestra. The world-renowned ensemble performs at the Academy of Music (Broad and Locust Sts., tel. 215/893–1900) from September to May and at the Mann Music Center (West Fairmount Park, tel. 215/878–7707) in summer. In its nearly 100-year history, the orchestra has been dominated by two conductors—Leopold Stokowski and Eugene Ormandy—and is now led by Riccardo Muti.

Concerto Soloists of Philadelphia (2136 Locust St., tel. 215/735–0202), directed by Marc Mostovoy, performs chamber music from September to June.

Music from Marlboro, a classical music series, is held at the Port of History Museum (Chestnut St. at the Delaware River, tel. 215/569–4690) throughout the year.

Robin Hood Dell East (Strawberry Mansion Dr., East Fairmount Park, tel. 215/477–8810) is the site for rhythm-and-blues and soul concerts each July and August.

Philly Pops (tel. 215/735–7506), conducted by Peter Nero, performs at the Academy of Music from October to May and, occasionally, at other local events.

All-Star Forum (tel. 215/735–7506). Presented by impresario Moe Septee, this 50-year-old organization features classical music superstars such as Itzhak Perlman and Isaac Stern.

Mellon Jazz Festival (tel. 215/636–1666) presents a series of concerts in June at the Academy of Music and locations around town. The top names in jazz perform, recently Sarah Vaughan, Wynton Marsalis, and Chick Corea.

Mozart on the Square (tel. 215/988–9830) takes place in May in or near Rittenhouse Square and features orchestral concerts, opera, chamber music, and recitals.

Philadelphia Folk Festival (Old Pool Farm, near Schwenksville, tel. 215/242–0150) is the oldest continuously running folk festival in the country. Renowned names in folk music perform, in recent seasons Doc Watson, Taj Mahal, Joan Baez, and Judy Collins.

Opera

Opera Company of Philadelphia (tel. 215/732–5811) productions at the Academy of Music between October and April feature such stars as Luciano Pavarotti—who also lends his name to an international voice competition and serves as one of the judges.

Pennsylvania Opera Theater (tel. 215/440–9797) performs operas in English and operas infrequently performed elsewhere.

Savoy Company (tel. 215/735–7161), the oldest amateur Gilbert and Sullivan company in the country, stages one G&S operetta each May at the Academy of Music.

Dance

Pennsylvania Ballet (tel. 215/551–7014) dances at the Academy of Music between September and June. The *Nutcracker* production at Christmastime is a perennial favorite.

South Street Dance Company (tel. 215/483–8482) presents modern dance at sites throughout the city.

Philadelphia Dance Company (Phildanco) (tel. 215/387–8200) performs modern dance in spring and fall at Annenberg Center and other locations.

Waves (tel. 215/563–1545). This internationally known company blends ballet with belly dancing, break-dancing, gymnastics, and other movement forms.

Film

Along with numerous first-run commercial movie theaters, Philadelphia has several art and repertory houses. Avoid the first-run theaters on Chestnut Street between Broad Street and 20th Street: They're frequented by rowdy urban youths.

Ritz Five (214 Walnut St., tel. 215/925–7900) is the finest movie theater in town. It has cushioned rocking-chair seats, clean surroundings, a first-rate sound system, and courteous audiences and staff. It shows avant-garde films and films from all over the world.

Roxy Screening Rooms (2021 Sansom St., tel. 215/561–0114) is an art house showing the intellectual and the esoteric. No Stallone or Schwarzenegger here.

Temple Cinematheque (1619 Walnut St., tel. 215/787–1529) is a favorite of film buffs who prefer old movies and foreign movies.

Nightlife

Nightlife in Philadelphia is far better than it used to be (when they supposedly rolled up the sidewalks at 8 o'clock). Today you can listen to a chanteuse in a chic basement nightclub; dance till 3 AM in a smoky bistro; and watch street jugglers, mimes, and magicians on a Society Hill corner.

For a quiet drink in a low-key setting, the hotel cocktail lounges will do nicely.

Bars and clubs can change hands or go out of business faster than a soft pretzel goes stale. For current information, check the entertainment pages of the *Philadelphia Inquirer*, the *Philadelphia Daily News*, and *Philadelphia* magazine. You can also call radio station WRTI's "Music Book," an extensive, up-to-the-minute listing of music in town, at 215/787–5277. For information about Penn's Landing events call 215/923–4992.

Bars, Lounges, and Cabarets

Apropos Bistro. Friday nights a Brazilian band plays sambas, bossa novas, and slow tunes for dancing in the middle of a chic restaurant. On Saturday nights, enjoy the rhythms of live "Island" music. *211 S. Broad St., Downtown, tel. 215/546–4424. Open 11:30 AM–2 AM. AE, DC, MC, V.*

Bacchanal. Live rock, rhythm-and-blues, salsa, and reggae bands nightly. The house band, Philly Gumbo, performs on Saturday night. *1302 South St., Downtown, tel. 215/545–6983. Open daily 5 PM–2 AM, Sat. noon–2 AM. No credit cards.*

Beverly Hills Bar & Grill. This restaurant-club featuring oldies from the '50s to the '80s is fancified with Tiffany lamps, stained glass, and chandeliers. DJ from 4:30 on; occasional live music. *Bourse Bldg., 21 S. 5th St., Downtown, tel. 215/627–0778. Mon. live bands; Tues.–Fri. club music; Sat. oldies. Hours weekdays 11:30 AM–2 AM, Sat. 8 PM–2 AM. AE, MC, V.*

Chestnut Cabaret. Located near the University of Pennsylvania campus, this concert hall/dance club features New Wave music, rhythm-and-blues, reggae, alternative, heavy metal, and rock 'n' roll. Popular Friday-night dance party. Crowd mostly in their 20s and early 30s. *3801 Chestnut St., University City, tel. 215/382–1201. Open Tues.–Sat. 7 PM–1 AM. No credit cards.*

Flanigan's. This huge, glittery night spot is a popular place for young singles. Top-40 dance music and videos attract a mixed crowd to a large, modern, laser-lit dance floor. Wednesday night is the Midweek Madness party. *Abbott's Sq., 2nd and South Sts., Society Hill, tel. 215/928–9898. Open Tues.–Wed. 9 PM–2 AM, Thurs.–Fri. 5 PM–2 AM, Sat. 8 PM–2 AM. Sun. teenage dance party 6 PM–10 PM. Happy hour Tues.–Fri.: buffet and five drinks for $5. AE, DC, MC, V.*

Happy Rooster. Along with the best selection of after-dinner drinks and liqueurs in the city, this place has French, Russian, and Gypsy music on tape. *118 S. 16th St., Downtown, tel. 215/563–1481. Jackets required. Open daily 11:30 AM–2 AM. Closed Sun. AE, DC, MC, V.*

Key West. This popular gay bar and disco is a favorite of the under-30 crowd. *207 S. Juniper St., Downtown, tel. 215/545–1578. Open weekdays 4 PM–2 AM, weekends noon–2 AM. No credit cards.*

Piano Bar at the Commissary. A variety of pianists play music ranging from jazz to popular in this small, attractive lounge. *1710 Sansom St., Downtown, tel. 215/569–2240. Bar open Mon.–Thurs. 11:30 AM–11 PM; Fri. 11:30–1 AM; Sat. 7 PM–1 AM. Music Thurs.–Sat. AE, DC, MC, V.*

Strand. This after-hours club and cruise bar has eclectic back-to-the-past decor, Art Deco lighting, and big, circa 1950s TV sets. It's multileveled, and has an outdoor deck with barbecue, bar, and music; separate dance floor; video lounge with pool table. Sounds are contemporary, progressive, urban rhythm-and-blues. Happy hour Wednesday, Thursday, and Friday at 5 PM. *1215 Walnut St., Downtown, tel. 215/592–7650. Open Wed.–Sun. 10 PM–3 AM. AE.*

Swann Lounge. Dance to piano music and a trio in an elegant hotel lounge. *Four Seasons Hotel, 18th St. and Benjamin Franklin Pkwy., Downtown, tel. 215/963–1500. Piano music Mon.–Thurs. 5 PM–1 AM; Viennese buffet with trio and dancing, Fri. and Sat. 9 PM–1 AM. AE, CB, DC, MC, V.*

Top of Centre Square. The bar with the best view in town—41 stories high, right across from the statue of William Penn atop City Hall—is a popular spot with young, single professionals. *15th and Market Sts., Downtown, tel. 215/563–9494. Fri. and Sat. soft contemporary jazz. Open Mon. 11:30 AM–midnight; Tues.–Thurs. to 1 AM; Fri. and Sat. to 2 AM; Sun. to 9 PM. AE, CB, DC, MC, V.*

Trocadero. This spacious rock 'n' roll club occupies a former burlesque house where W. C. Fields and Mae West performed. A lot of the old decor remains: Mirrors, pillars, and balconies surround a dance floor. Under-30 crowd. Nationally known concert acts most Monday to Wednesday nights. Local DJs host dance parties Thursday, Friday, and Saturday. *1003 Arch St., Chinatown, tel. 215/592–0386. Open Thurs. 9 PM–2 AM, Fri. 4 PM–2 AM, Sat. 7 PM–2 AM. AE.*

Comedy Clubs

Comedy Factory Outlet. Comics who perform include local amateurs (open stage Thursday at 8) and headliners from New York and Los Angeles. *31 Bank St., Old City, tel. 215/386-6911. Shows Fri. 8:30 and 11 PM; Sat. 7, 9:15, and 11:30. No credit cards.*

Comedy Works. Philadelphia's biggest full-time comedy club (seats 300) features top young comedians from both coasts. Open stage Wednesday at 8:30. Thursday, Philly Comedy Showcase. *126 Chestnut St., Old City, tel. 215/922-5997. Shows Fri. 8:30 and 11, Sat. 8 and 11. No credit cards.*

Going Bananas. Local and New York comics. *613 S. 2nd St., Society Hill, tel. 215/226-2621. Shows Fri. 9 and 11:30 PM, Sat. 8 and 11 PM. No credit cards.*

Dancing and Discos

Memphis. This casual dance bar sports ancient-Egyptian decor —such as sphinxes—plus modern touches like an optic-kinetic machine that projects pink blobs. *2121 Arch St., Downtown, tel. 215/569-1123.*

Monte Carlo Living Room. The DJ at this sophisticated watering hole plays Top-40 hits, European sounds, and South American music. A quiet and intimate room where all the furnishings, from the tapestries to the paintings, are European. Customers are in their 30s to 50s. *2nd and South Sts., tel. 215/925-2220. Open Tues.-Sat. 5:30-2. Jackets required. AE, DC, MC, V.*

Phoenix. This large club furnished in brass and dark green has five bars surrounding the dance floor. Dance music is played most often; occasionally some oldies and Top 40s. Radio stations broadcast live dance parties from here. *718 Arch St., Downtown, tel. 215/625-2446. Open Wed.-Sun. 4PM-2 AM. AE, MC, V.*

Polo Bay. Philadelphia's premier upscale "meet market" is famous for its happy-hour buffet. Tropical decor, small dance floor. *Warwick Hotel, 17th and Locust Sts., tel. 215/546-8800. Open Mon.-Sat. 5 PM-2 AM. AE, CB, DC, MC, V.*

Pulsations. At the biggest, highest-tech disco in the area—20 miles from Downtown—a 28-foot starship glides over the dance floor and an alien robot emerges. Lots of neon, lots of lasers, and hydraulically lifted lights emerging from the dance floor. It has a 25,000-watt sound system and holds more than 2,000 people, most of them in their 20s and early 30s. *Rte. 1, Glen Mills, tel. 215/459-4140. Open Tues., Thurs., Fri., and Sat. 9:30 PM-2 AM; Sun. 7:30-11 PM for people under 21 only. AE, MC, V.*

Quincy's. Live rock 'n' roll or dance music programmed by a DJ in a re-created turn-of-the-century atmosphere. *Adam's Mark Hotel, City Ave. and Monument Rd., City Ave. area, tel. 215/581-5000. No jeans. Open 4 PM-2 AM.*

Revival. Along with New Wave and contemporary music, this late-night dance club has performance art, fashion shows, theme nights, and classic movies. Showcases new bands. *22 S. 3rd St., Old City, tel. 215/627-4825. Open Tues.-Sun. 9 PM-3 AM. AE, MC, V.*

Jazz

Cafe Borgia. Local singers perform ballads, blues, and old songs in the Billie Holliday style. *Esquire* rated it one of the 100 best bars in America two years in a row. *406 S. 2nd St. (downstairs at Lautrec restaurant), Society Hill, tel. 215/574–0414. Music from 9:30 PM–1:30 AM. Bar closes at 2. AE, MC, V.*

Liberties. Handsome restored Victorian pub features live jazz Wednesday–Saturday. *705 N. 2nd St., Northern Liberties, tel. 215/238–0660. Open daily 11 AM–2 AM. AE, CB, DC, MC, V.*

Ortlieb's Jazz Haus. Hear good jazz in a 100-year-old bar. The celebrated jazz organist Shirley Scott and her quartet perform Wednesday, Friday, and Saturday. Tuesday jam session for local musicians. *847 N. 3rd St., Northern Liberties, tel. 215/922–1035. Music 9:30 PM–1:30 AM. Closed Sun. AE, DC.*

Miscellaneous

Painted Bride Art Center. By day it's a contemporary art gallery showing bold, challenging works. By night it's a club featuring performance art; prose and poetry readings; folk, electronic, and new music; jazz, dance, and theater. In 1990 this nonprofit educational institution celebrates its 21st season, with programs including a festival of post-modern choreography and an international performance series entitled "Theater Like You Never Seen It Before." *230 Vine St., Old City, tel. 215/925–9914. Gallery open Wed.–Sun. noon–6 PM. Call for performance schedule. AE, MC, V.*

9 Bucks County

Introduction

by Joyce Eisenberg

A freelance writer and editor whose travel and feature articles have appeared in local and national publications, Joyce Eisenberg, a Philadelphia native, is editor of the Delaware Valley edition of Travelhost *magazine.*

Bucks County, about an hour's drive north of Philadelphia, could have remained 625 square miles of sleepy countryside full of old stone farmhouses, lush rolling hills, and quaint covered bridges if it hadn't been discovered in the '30s by New York's Beautiful Brainy People. Such luminaries as writers Dorothy Parker and S. J. Perelman and composer Oscar Hammerstein bought country homes here, a short drive from Manhattan. Pulitzer Prize- and Nobel Prize-winning author Pearl S. Buck chose to live in the area because it was "a region where the landscapes were varied, where farm and industry lived side by side, where the sea was near at hand, mountains not far away, and city and countryside were not enemies."

Over the years, Bucks County has become known for art colonies and antiques, summer theater, and country inns. And although parts of the county have fallen prey to urban sprawl and hyper-development, many areas of upper Bucks County remain as bucolic as ever.

Named after England's Buckinghamshire, Bucks County was opened by William Penn in 1681 under a land grant from Charles II. The county's most celebrated town, New Hope, was settled in the early 1700s as the industrial village of Coryell's Ferry. (One of the original gristmills is the home of the Bucks County Playhouse.) The town was the Pennsylvania terminal for stagecoach traffic and Delaware River ferry traffic. Barges hauled coal along the 60-mile Delaware Canal until 1930.

Commerce built up New Hope but art helped sustain it. The art colony took root in the late 19th century and was revitalized first in the 1930s by New York theater folk and more recently with the formation of the New Hope–Lambertville Gallery Association, a cooperative network of gallery owners, artists, and the community. Today New York artists are again relocating to the region.

New Hope is a hodgepodge of old stone houses, narrow streets and alleys, pretty courtyards, and charming restaurants. Summer weekends can be frantic here, with shoppers wandering through the tiny boutiques and galleries along Main Street. The Delaware Canal threads through town and you can glide lazily along it in a mule-pulled barge.

Doylestown is the county seat. An important coach stop in the 18th century, the town is best known as the home of Henry Chapman Mercer, curator of American and Prehistoric Archaeology at the University of Pennsylvania Museum, master potter, self-taught architect, and writer of gothic tales. When Dr. Mercer died in 1930 at the age of 74, along with a legacy of artistic creativity he left a bizarre mansion named Fonthill, a museum displaying 40,000 implements and tools, and a pottery and tile works that still makes Mercer tiles.

The county is also a treasure trove for Colonial history buffs. Among the most interesting sites is Pennsbury Manor, a careful reconstruction of the brick Georgian-style mansion William Penn built for himself in the late 1600s. On the banks of the Delaware, the 500-acre Washington Crossing Historic Park is situated where George Washington and his troops crossed the icy river on Christmas night 1776 to surprise the Hessian mercenaries at Trenton.

The Delaware River and the canal that follows its path offer opportunities for canoeing, kayaking, and fishing. Thousands float down the river each year in inner tubes or on rubber rafts. Joggers, hikers, bicyclists, cross-country skiers, and horseback riders enjoy the 60-mile canal towpath.

The town of Lahaska is the center of antiques shopping in Bucks County. The bargain-price American treasures that made the area an antique hunter's paradise are nowadays few and far between, but there is good prowling between New Hope and Doylestown on U.S. 202.

Although you can see all the major tourist attractions in a daylong whirlwind tour, plan to stay overnight in Bucks County. A number of houses and mills, some dating back to a half-century before the Revolution, are now quaint bed-and-breakfasts and excellent restaurants. A hearty meal, blissful sleep, and a day spent wandering along River Road are what make visits to Bucks County most enjoyable.

Essential Information

Getting Around

By Car Bucks County is a large area—40 miles long and up to 16 miles across—and is almost impossible to tour without a car. From Philadelphia, the most direct route is to follow I–95 north to the Yardley exit; then go north on Route 32 toward New Hope, about 40 miles from Philadelphia.

By Bus **Greyhound/Trailways** (tel. 215/931–4000) has three buses a day to Doylestown from Philadelphia. The trip takes 80 minutes.

By Train **SEPTA** (tel. 215/574–7800) provides frequent service from Philadelphia (Market Street East, Suburban, and 30th Street stations) to Doylestown on the R5 line. From Doylestown, you can reach New Hope and Lahaska via West Hunterdon Transit (tel. 800/852–2877).

Guided Tours

Nancy Neely (tel. 215/822–6692) will drive you around the county in your car. A longtime Bucks County tour guide, she will take you off the main roads, show you the covered bridges, and amuse you with local color. Reservations required.

Bucks County Carriages (tel. 215/862–5883) offers three 20-minute horse-drawn carriage rides. Tours of New Hope, Peddler's Village, and Lambertville, NJ, are available. There are daily rides in summer, only on weekends in spring and fall. Customized tours—perhaps from your B&B to dinner and back—are available by reservation.

Coryell's Ferry Ride and Historic Narrative (tel. 215/862–2050) is a half-hour sightseeing ride on the Delaware River in a 40-foot, 28-passenger pontoon boat.

Ghost Tours of New Hope (215/357–4558) offers a one-hour lantern-led walk which explores the haunting tales of the area. The tour was designed by psychic investigator Adi-Kent Thomas Jeffrey, author of *The Bermuda Triangle* and former Bucks County resident.

Important Addresses and Numbers

Tourist Information **Bucks County Tourist Commission** (152 Swamp Rd., Doylestown 18901, tel. 215/345–4552). *Open weekdays 9–4.*

Central Bucks Chamber of Commerce (379 N. Main St., Doylestown 18901, tel. 215/348–3913). *Open weekdays 8:30–5.*

New Hope Information Center (S. Main and Mechanic Sts., Box 141, New Hope 18938, tel. 215/862–5880). It is a convenient place to stop or contact in advance for information about New Hope and its surrounding attractions. *Open weekdays 9–5, Saturday and Sunday 10–6.*

Emergencies Dial 911 for assistance, or go to the emergency room, **Doylestown Hospital** (595 W. State St., Doylestown, tel. 215/345–2200).

Pharmacy **Brooks Drugs** (314 W. Bridge St., New Hope, tel. 215/862–5917). *Open Mon.–Sat. 9–9, Sunday 9–6.*

Exploring Bucks County

Numbers in the margin correspond with points of interest on the Bucks County map.

Many Bucks County attractions are contained within the triangle formed by the towns of New Hope, Doylestown, and Newtown. Other interesting sites are located along River Road (Rte. 32), from Pennsbury Manor north to charming river towns such as Erwinna. If you have just one day to visit Bucks County, begin at Fonthill in Doylestown, check out the antiques shops along U.S. 202, stroll through New Hope, and head north on River Road for dinner at one of the inns. For a longer stay, you can pick and choose among the attractions listed below. We begin in the southern part of the county, closest to Philadelphia, and work our way north.

① Situated on a gentle rise 150 yards from the Delaware River, **Pennsbury Manor** is the Georgian-style mansion and plantation where William Penn lived for only 18 months with his second wife and infant son. His wife didn't care for country life and compelled Penn to move back to the city. The rebuilt manor house and work buildings on 40 of the estate's original 8,400 acres provide a glimpse of everyday life in 17th-century America. Among the antique furnishings in the house are some fine William-and-Mary and Jacobean pieces as well as some of Penn's furniture. Formal gardens, vineyards and orchards, an icehouse, smokehouse, bake and brew house, and collections of tools attest to the self-sufficient nature of Penn's early community. They also hint that although history portrays Penn as a dour Quaker, as governor of the colony he enjoyed the good life by importing the finest provisions and keeping a vast retinue of servants and slaves. These extravagances led to the financial difficulties that resulted in a nine-month term in debtor's prison. The house can be seen only on the tour. *U.S. 13 off Tyburn Rd., Morrisville 19067, tel. 215/946–0400. Admission: $2.50 adults, $1.75 senior citizens, $1 children 6–17. Open Tues.–Sat. 9–5, Sun. noon–5. Last tour at 3:30.*

② Six miles north is **Fallsington**, the pre-Revolutionary village where William Penn attended Quaker meetings of worship. The village displays 300 years of American architecture, from a simple 17th-century log cabin to the Victorian excesses of the late 1800s. Four historic buildings, including the log cabin, have been restored and opened for group tours of five or more. Two dozen remaining 18th-century houses are occupied by descendants of the original settlers or by owners who enjoy being a living part of history. *South off U.S. 1 at Tyburn Rd., Fallsington 19054, tel. 215/295–6567. Open Wed. 1–5 PM only. Individuals can buy a map (25¢) for a self-guided tour. Houses are open to the public on the second Sat. in May and second Sat. in Oct.*

③ **Washington Crossing Historic Park** is where on Christmas night 1776 a desperate George Washington crossed the icy Delaware River to surprise the Hessian garrison at Trenton. Attractions are divided between the Lower and the Upper Park, which are about 5 miles apart.

In the Lower Park, the fieldstone **Memorial Building and Visitors Center** (Rte. 32, 8 mi south of New Hope) displays a reproduction of Emanuel Leutze's famous painting of the cross-

Bucks County

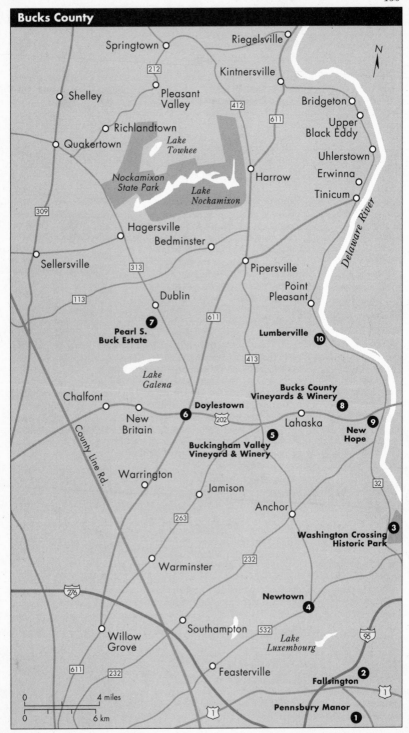

ing (the original hangs in the Metropolitan Museum of Art in New York). Even more realistic is the annual Christmas Day reenactment of the crossing when local businessmen don Colonial uniforms and brave the elements in small boats. The **McConkey Ferry Inn** where Washington and his staff had Christmas dinner while waiting to cross the river is nearby. Also open is **Taylor Mansion,** a completely restored 19th-century residence.

In the Upper Park, about 5 miles north on Route 32, stop at the landmark **Bowman's Hill Tower,** named after a surgeon who sailed with Captain Kidd. Washington used the hill as a lookout point. You can get a much better view of the countryside than he did by riding the elevator up the 110-foot-tall memorial tower. (A winding staircase leads to the top.) *Admission: $2 adults, $1.50 senior citizens and children 7–17, 50¢ children 2–6. Tower open daily 10–4:30; to 5:30 on summer weekends.*

Surrounding the tower, the 100-acre **Wildflower Preserve** has been planted with dozens of species of wildflowers, trees, shrubs, and ferns native to Pennsylvania. Take the guided tour or follow short trails clearly marked so as to bring you back to your starting point. At the same location, the **Platt Bird Collection** displays more than 1,300 stuffed birds, nests, eggs, and color photographs. Also in the Upper Park is the **Thompson–Neely House,** an 18th-century farmhouse furnished just as it was when the Colonial leaders planned the attack on Trenton in the kitchen. *Washington Crossing Historic Park, Rtes. 532 and 32, tel. 215/493–4076. Free admission to grounds. Ticket for 45-min walking tour of 5 historic park buildings: $1.50 adults, $1 senior citizens, 50¢ children 6–17, available at Visitors Center, Thompson-Neely House and Tower. Tours Mon.–Sat. 9:30, 11, 12:30, 2, 3:30; Sun. 12:30, 2, 3:30. Park open Mon.–Sat. 9–5, Sun. noon–5 year-round.*

❹ Newtown, founded by William Penn, was an important center during the American Revolution. The town takes pride in its many 18th- and 19th-century homes and inns; the downtown historic district is on the National Register of Historic Places. The Newtown Historic Association building (Court St. and Center Ave., tel. 215/968–4004) contains regional antiques and paintings by renowned local artist Edward Hicks. An association brochure provides a walking tour of the town, which is reminiscent of New Hope before all the tourists arrived. Most stores cater to the local community, although there are some gift and antiques shops such as Ren's Antiques (14 S. State St., tel. 215/968–5511), which specializes in one-of-a-kind china, glass, and antique silver.

❺ The **Buckingham Valley Vineyard & Winery** is a small family-owned winery that produces distinguished estate-bottled varietal wines. One of the state's first farm wineries, the vineyards and wine cellars are open to tours and tastings. *Rte. 413, 2 mi south of Buckingham, tel. 215/794–7188. Free self-guided tour. Open Tues.–Fri. noon–6, Sat. 10–6, Sun. noon–4.*

To sample other fruits of the earth, stop at **None Such Farms,** the Yerkes family's farm stand. Actually a full store, it is well stocked with fresh-picked corn, vegetables, fruits, flowers, and herbs. *Rte. 263, Buckingham, tel. 215/794–5201. Open daily.*

6 **Doylestown,** the county seat, is a showcase of American architecture. Although most buildings are in the early 19th-century Federal style, there are abundant reminders of the mid- to late 19th century. Examples of the Second Empire, Queen Anne, and Château styles can also be seen. But the most unusual are the buildings created by Henry Chapman Mercer. The three brilliantly eccentric structures on **Mercer Mile** are distinguished by virtue of the reinforced concrete used exclusively in their construction.

Fonthill, Henry Chapman Mercer's home, is modeled after a 13th-century Rhenish castle replete with turrets, towers, and balconies. Inside is a multilevel labyrinth of surprise passages, sudden stairways, and built-in concrete furniture. Fonthill's wealth of books, prints, and engravings is enhanced by the setting: the ceilings and walls is embedded with tiles from Mercer's own kilns and ancient tiles from around the world. *Swamp Rd. (Rte. 313) and E. Court St., Doylestown 18901, tel. 215/348 -9461. Admission: $4 adults, $3.50 senior citizens, $1.50 children and students. Open Mon.–Sat. 10–5, Sun. noon–5. Hour-long guided tours. Reservations suggested.*

The **Moravian Pottery and Tile Works** on the Fonthill grounds still make Mercer's unique picture tiles. As author and Bucks County resident James Michener described them, "Using scenes from the Bible, mythology, and history, Mercer produced wonderfully archaic tiles about 12 or 14 inches square in powerful earth colors that glowed with intensity and unforgettable imagery." Current editions can be bought in the Tile Works Shop. The factory, built in 1912, resembles a Spanish mission with an open-ended courtyard. *Swamp Rd. (Rte. 313) and E. Court St., Doylestown 18901, tel. 215/345–6722. Admission: $2 adults, $1.50 senior citizens and students, $1 children 7–17. Open daily 10–5, last tour at 4. 45-min tours.*

An archaeologist, Mercer worried that the rapid advance of progress would wipe out evidence of America's productivity before the Industrial Revolution. Consequently, from 1895 to 1915 he scoured the back roads of eastern Pennsylvania buying up implements, tools, and household items that might otherwise have been destroyed. His encyclopedic collection, representing every craft, ultimately included more than 40,000 objects from before the age of steam and are now displayed at the **Mercer Museum.** *Pine St., Doylestown 18901, tel. 215/345–0210. Admission: $4 adults, $3.50 senior citizens, $1.50 children and students. Open Mon.–Sat. 10–5, Sun. noon–5. Self-guided tours.*

From Doylestown, you can detour to Green Hills Farm, Pearl S. Buck's country home, where she wrote more than 100 novels, children's books, and works of nonfiction while raising seven adopted children and caring for many others. The stone house still bears the imprint of the girl who grew up in China and became the only woman to win both the Nobel and Pulitzer **7** prizes. She is best known for *The Good Earth.* The **Pearl S. Buck Estate** is filled with her collection of Asian and American antiques and personal belongings. The Pearl S. Buck Foundation, which supports Amerasian children in six Asian countries, operates out of an old barn on the property. *520 Maple Ave., Hilltown (mailing address: Box 181, Perkasie, PA 18944), tel. 215/249–0100 or 215/242–6779. Admission: $5 adults, $4 senior citizens and students, $2 children 6–17. One-*

hr tours weekdays 10:30 and 2, year-round; Sun. 1:30 and 2:30 May–Sept. only.

The road from Doylestown to New Hope (Rte. 202) is studded with antiques shops, especially around Lahaska. (*See* Chapter 4.)

8 On the road from Doylestown to New Hope you will see **Bucks County Vineyards & Winery,** which offers a tour of the winery and wine museum followed by a tasting of wine and cheeses made on the premises. It is also the home of the **Broadway Costume Museum,** where owner Arthur Gerold, a former theatrical costumer, displays his personal collection of originals worn by such Broadway stars as Ethel Merman, Mary Martin, Richard Burton, and Katharine Hepburn. *U.S. 202, 3 mi south of New Hope, tel. 800/523–2510 in PA, 800/362–0309 elsewhere. Self-guided tour free weekdays, $2 on weekends. Children free. Open weekdays 10:30–5, Sat. 10:30–6, Sun. noon–6.*

9 The cosmopolitan village of **New Hope** is a mecca for artists, shoppers, and lovers of old homes. Listed on the National Register of Historic Places, the town is easy to explore on foot; the most interesting sights and stores are clustered along four blocks of Main Street and on the cross streets—Mechanic, Ferry, and Bridge streets—which lead to the river. (Bridge St. leads to a bridge spanning the Delaware to the New Jersey village of Lambertville, another assemblage of shops and galleries.) For a good orientation to New Hope, take the Bucks County Carriages horse-drawn tour which starts by the cannon alongside the Logan Inn.

The **Parry Mansion** is a stone house built in 1784 by wealthy lumber-mill owner Benjamin Parry and occupied by five generations of his family. The furnishings reflect decorative changes from 1775 to the Victorian era—including candles, white-washed walls, oil lamps, and wallpaper. *S. Main and Ferry Sts., no phone. Admission: $2.50. Open May–Oct. Fri.–Sun. 1–5.*

Time Out Family-owned **Gerenser's Exotic Ice Cream** has been making ice cream—with 14% butterfat—since 1943. "Exotic" is no exaggeration: We recommend German peach brandy, Amaretto with roasted almonds, and peanut butter chocolate chip. *22 S. Main St., New Hope, tel. 215/862–2050.*

Beginning in 1840, coal barges plied the Delaware Canal. Today, the mules pull barges filled with relaxing tourists. The **Mule Barge Ride** is a one-hour narrated excursion past Revolutionary-era cottages, gardens, and artists' workshops. A barge historian/folk singer is often aboard. *New and S. Main Sts., New Hope, tel. 215/862–2842. Price: $6.50 adults, $6 seniors, $5 students 12 and over, $3.75 children under 12. Runs April, Wed., Sat., Sun. 1, 2, 3, 4:30; May 1–Oct. 15, daily 11:30, 1, 2, 3, 4:30, 6, Oct. 16–Nov. 15, Wed., Sat., Sun. 11:30, 1, 2, 3, 4:30.*

The **New Hope Steam Railway** makes a 9-mile, 90-minute scenic run from New Hope to Lahaska. The old steam train crosses a curved trestle familiar from the rescue scenes in the old "Perils of Pauline" movies. The New Hope depot is an 1891 Victorian gem embellished with a witch's hat on the roof. Also on site are a museum and a collection of old rolling stock—a caboose, railway post-office car, and 1911 steam locomotive. *32 W. Bridge St., tel. 215/862–2707. Admission: $5 adults, $3 children 12 and under. Open May–Oct., Sat. 1:30 and 3:30, Sun. 11:30, 1:30, 3:30.*

North of New Hope, the two-lane River Road (Rte. 32) winds scenically along the Delaware and the Delaware Canal is frequently in view. It is a lovely drive with charming old inns and ancient stone houses hidden around bends in the road. You'll pass through a series of tiny river towns along the way, many with a general store, inn, and restaurant. Stop for lunch at an inn or picnic along the river and take a walk or ride a bike along the towpath.

🔟 Open since 1770, the **Lumberville Store** in **Lumberville** is the focus of village life, the place to mail letters, buy groceries, and rent a bicycle. Across the street the **Black Bass Hotel** is a British-style pub with a stunning river view. Past Lumberville are the towns of Point Pleasant (*see* Chapter 5 for information on renting a canoe or inner tube), Erwinna, Upper Black Eddy, and Bridgeton. The *Homestead Store* in Bridgeton scoops out great big ice cream cones and makes hearty sandwiches.

What to See and Do with Children

Mule Barge (*see* Exploring, *above*).
New Hope Steam Railway (*see* Exploring, *above*).
Sesame Place. A recreation park designed for children aged from 3 to 13, Sesame Place is fun for older children and adults, too. Featured are Sesame Neighborhood, a replica of the street on the TV show; outdoor play and water activities (bring bathing suits); a computer gallery; the Count's Gallery, a room filled with 180,000 climb-through balls; and other activities named after Bert and Ernie, Big Bird, and all the *Sesame Street* favorites. *100 Sesame Rd., Langhorne, tel. 215/757–1100. Admission: $12.95 adults, $14.95 children 3–15, 2 and under, free. Parking $2.50. Open daily May–mid-Sept., weekends only to mid-Oct. Call for hours.*
Quarry Valley Farm. This Bucks County farm has a barnyard full of animals, two petting zoos, cow milking, a corn-shucking demonstration, a hayloft to jump in, and pony rides. The farm shop sells homegrown goodies. *Street Rd. near Peddler's Village, Lahaska, tel. 215/794–5882. Admission: $4 adults, $3.50 children 18 months–12. Open Apr.–Dec. daily 10–5.*

Off the Beaten Track

Twelve covered bridges are all that remain of the 36 originally built in Bucks County. Although the romantically inclined call them "kissing bridges" or "wishing bridges," the roofs were actually intended to protect the supporting beams from the ravages of the weather. The bridges are examples of the lattice-type construction of overlapping triangles, without arches or upright beams. They are delightful to stumble upon, but if you're serious about seeing them the Bucks County Tourist Commission (tel. 215/345–4552) and the New Hope Information Center (tel. 215/862–5880) distribute the *"Bucks County Covered Bridges Tour"* brochure which provides directions, driving distances, and a brief history of each bridge. The tour starts at the Memorial Building in Washington Crossing Historic Park, although it is set up so that you can start anywhere.

Trained as an architect, Bucks County woodworker **George Nakashima** has been crafting furniture from the souls of trees for more than 40 years. His work is distinguished by free-flowing natural contours that express his philosophy that trees are objects of "the highest artistic and spiritual worth." His furniture has been featured at the Metropolitan Museum of Art and the American Craft Museum in New York. *293 Aquetong Rd., tel. 215/862-2272. Showroom open to public Sat. 1-4:30.*

Shopping

Antiques

Bucks County has long been known for its antiques shops featuring everything from fine examples of early-American craftsmanship to fun kitsch. There are formal and country furnishings plus American, European, and Oriental antiques. Many shops are located along a 4-mile stretch of U.S. 202 between Lahaska and New Hope and on intersecting country roads. Shops are generally open on weekends with weekday hours by appointment: It's best to call first.

Sandors at Ingham Springs Antiques (6319 Old York Rd., tel. 215/862–9181), 18th-century American and European furniture; **Euro Pine II** (186 Old York Rd., tel. 215/862–3411), European country antiques; **Hobensack & Keller** (Bridge St., tel. 215/862–2406), old garden ornaments, cast-iron furniture, fencing and Oriental rugs; **Olde Hope Antiques** (U.S. 202 and Reeder Rd., tel. 215/862–5055), hooked rugs, Pennsylvania German textiles, furniture, and folk art; **Lahaska Antique Courte** (U.S. 202 opposite Peddler's Village, tel. 215/794–7884), 10 shops of American and European furniture and decorations.

Art Galleries

Many New York artists have relocated to Bucks County and more than 30 galleries in New Hope and neighboring Lambertville (across the river in New Jersey) showcase paintings, prints, and sculpture. The New Hope–Lambertville Gallery Association (12 W. Mechanic St., New Hope, tel. 215/862–9308) publishes the *Guide to the Galleries*.

Auctions

At **Brown Brothers** (Rte. 413 south of Rte. 263, Buckingham, tel. 215/794–7630), Saturday auctions start with box lots and move on to bigger and better things acquired at estate sales—jewelry, silver, linens, tools, books, frames, furniture, and other household items. Two auctioneers are in constant motion all day. It opens Saturdays at 8 AM September–May; auctions take place Thursday evenings June through August.

Flea Markets

Rice's Sale and Country Market (Green Hill Rd. near Peddler's Village, Solebury, tel. 215/297–5993) has been in operation for more than a century. It opens Tuesdays at 6 AM, when the local antiques dealers check out the goods, and closes at 1 PM. There are bargains on canned goods, clothing, linens, shoes, back-issue magazines, and plants.

Gift Ideas

New Hope's streets are lined with shops selling handmade crafts, art, and contemporary wares. **Peddler's Village** (U.S. 202 and Rte. 263, Lahaska, tel. 215/794–7055) began in the early '60s when Earl Jamison bought a 6-acre chicken farm, moved local 18th-century houses to the site, and opened a Carmel, California-inspired collection of 68 specialty shops and restaurants. Today, the 24-acre village peddles books, cookware, toys, leather goods, clothes, jewelry, dried wreaths, posters, candles, and a host of other decorative items. Crowd-drawing seasonal events include a Strawberry Festival in May and an All-American Teddy Bear's Picnic in July. On the grounds is the Golden Plough Inn (215/794–4004), a 40-room bed-and-breakfast decorated with early-American country furnishings.

Outdoor Activities and Participant Sports

Biking

From May to October, **Bucks County Bicycle Tours** (211H W. Callowhill Rd., Perkasie, tel. 215/257–6077) arranges two- to four-day inn-to-inn bicycling tours, supplying routes and a variety of rental bikes. Weekend tours are self-guided; weekday tours can be supported by vans bearing luggage and supplies. **Lumberville Store Bicycle Rental Co.** (River Rd., 8 mi north of New Hope, tel. 215/297–5388) rents mountain bikes with wide tires.

Camping

In the northern part of the county many of the parks have canoes for rent, well-marked trails for biking and hiking, and camping facilities. The largest and best-equipped is **Lake Nockamixon State Park** (Rte. 563, Quakertown) which has a 1,450-acre lake, boating and boat rental, swimming pool, bike path and bike rental, hiking trails, ice skating and sledding in winter, trap shooting, and picnic areas. Other fine parks include **Tohickon Valley Park** (Point Pleasant) and **Ralph Stover Park** (Pipersville), county and state parks respectively, joined along Tohickon Creek near Point Pleasant; and **Lake Towhee** east of Applebachsville. In the south, **Core Creek Park** (Langhorne) is a 1,200-acre facility with fishing and boating on Lake Luxembourg; and **Neshaminy State Park** is near Croydon. For information call the County Parks (tel. 215/757–0571) or State Parks (tel. 215/257–3646).

Canoeing/Tubing

More than half a million people a year—from toddlers to grandparents in their 80s—negotiate the Delaware River on inner tubes or canoes from **Bucks County River Country/Point Pleasant Canoe Outfitters.** It also rents rafts and kayaks. The Point Pleasant site on River Road (tel. 215/297–TUBE) is open weekends in April, May, September, and October, daily between Memorial Day and Labor Day. A bus transports people upriver to begin three- or four-hour tube or raft rides down to the base. Wear sneakers you don't mind getting wet and lots of sunscreen. Life jackets are available at no charge. Reservations are required.

Fishing

Fishermen are drawn to the Delaware River and Lake Nockamixon for small-mouth bass, trout, catfish, and carp. The most popular event is the annual shad run (early April to early June). The required fishing license can be purchased at any area sporting-goods shop; a seven-day tourist license costs $15.50. For a license and tips on where to fish, try the **Nockamixon Sports Shop** (Rte. 313 and 5th St., Perkasie, tel. 215/257–3133).

Glider Rides

Good thermals in the area make **Country Aviation** glider rides thrilling. Gliders seat one or two passengers plus the pilot. It costs $45 for a 3,000-foot tow (15-20 min ride) and $65 for a 5,000-foot tow (30-35 min ride). You can also ride in an open cockpit biplane; 10-minute rides are $45, 20-minute rides are $65. County Aviation even offers aerobatic flights. *Van Sant Airport, just off Rte. 611, Headquarters and Cafferty Rds., Ottsville, tel. 215/847–8401. Open year-round, daily 8:30– dusk. Call for reservations.*

Horseback Riding

West End Farm (River Rd. north of New Hope, tel. 215/862– 5883) offers one-hour escorted trail rides along the Delaware Canal. *Call ahead for reservations.*

Towpath

The 60-mile **Delaware Canal Towpath** is used for biking, hiking, jogging, and, in the winter, cross-country skiing. In winter the canal freezes over to form a great ice-skating rink. A recommended 6-mile route for hikers and bikers starts at Lumberville; from there cross the pedestrian bridge to Bull Island State Park; go south on the New Jersey side along the Delaware & Raritan Canal to Stockton. Cross the river again to Center Bridge, Pennsylvania, and head back up the towpath to Lumberville. Stop at Errico's Market on Bridge Street in Stockton for picnic supplies.

Dining and Lodging

Dining

Bucks County has no regional specialties to call its own. What makes dining here unique is the variety of food and settings in which diners can enjoy a fine meal: Continental, American, regional, nouvelle, and ethnic cuisine all served with a dollop of history in restored mills, pre-Revolutionary taverns, stage-coach stops, and elegant Victorian mansions.

Many area innkeepers keep menus from local restaurants on hand and are happy to offer dinner suggestions.

Category	Cost*
Very Expensive	over $30
Expensive	$20–$30
Moderate	$10–$20
Inexpensive	under $10

per person for a 3-course meal, without wine, tax (6%), or service

Lodging

Although Bucks County has limited lodging options for families, it offers numerous choices to couples. Accommodations ranging from modest to elegant can be found in historic inns, small hotels, and bed-and-breakfasts. Most hostelries include breakfast with their room rates. Plan and reserve early—as much as three months ahead for summer and fall weekends. Unless otherwise stated, all accommodations listed below require a two-night minimum stay on weekends and a three-night minimum stay on holiday weekends. Many inns prohibit or restrict smoking. Unless otherwise indicated, all rooms have private bath and hotels are open year-round. Since many inns are historic homes furnished with fine antiques, they often bar young children.

Category	Cost*
Very Expensive	over $105
Expensive	$85–$104
Moderate	$60–$84
Inexpensive	under $60

double occupancy, based on peak (summer) rates, not including room tax (6%)

The following credit card abbreviations are used: AE, American Express; CB, Carte Blanche; DC, Diners Club; MC, MasterCard; V, Visa.

Doylestown

Dining   **Cafe Arielle.** This "rotisserie" serves delicious grilled seafood
★   dishes (including tuna steak), prime meats, and duckling in an
open kitchen atmosphere amid country French furnishings and
striking artwork. *100 S. Main St. in the Doylestown Agricultural Works, tel. 215/345–5930. Reservations requested. Dress:
casual. Closed Mon. AE. Expensive.*

Lodging   **Highland Farms.** This Bucks County estate was the home of
★   lyricist Oscar Hammerstein from 1941–1960. The 1840s
federal-style country home is set on 5 acres and is elegantly furnished with antiques and Hammerstein family memorabilia.
The video library is stocked with Rogers and Hammerstein
films. A full country breakfast is served in the formal dining
room or on the brick patio overlooking the 60-foot pool. *70 East
Rd., 18901, tel. 215/340–1354. 4 rooms, 2 with bath. Facilities:
outdoor pool, tennis courts, badminton, croquet. Children over
12 welcome. MC, V. Moderate–Very Expensive.*

The Inn at Fordhook Farm. The Burpee family (of seed catalogue fame) country estate is now a B&B loaded with family
memorabilia and antiques. Built in 1760 and purchased in 1888
by W. Atlee Burpee, the house has high-ceilinged spacious bedrooms (two with Mercer tile fireplaces) brightened with floral
prints, a large Greek Revival parlor, and a dining room with
gorgeous Oriental rugs. The full country breakfast featuring
oatmeal buttermilk pancakes, cheese-filled French toast, and
homegrown berries is served in the dining room on a long mahogany table or in warmer weather on a verandah overlooking
carefully tended gardens. *105 New Britain Rd., 18901, tel. 215/
345–1766. 5 rooms, 3 with private bath in the main house, 2 in
carriage house. Facilities: lawn bowling, badminton, croquet.
Children over 12 allowed. AE, MC, V. Expensive–Very Expensive.*

Pine Tree Farm. A Colonial farmhouse dating from 1730 was redecorated with cheerful country antiques in light and airy
rooms. The glass-enclosed rear of the house, which includes the
dining room, library, and solarium, overlooks 16 acres of pine
trees, a pond, and the pool. Breakfast, served poolside in summer, features poached eggs Florentine and homemade apple
muffins. Room 1 is a favorite. *2155 Lower State Rd., 18901, tel.
215/348–0632. 4 rooms in main house, 2 in carriage house. Facilities: lighted tennis court, outdoor pool, pond. No children.
AE, MC, V. Expensive.*

Erwinna

Dining   **Evermay on the Delaware.** Ron Strouse, who has cooked at La
★   Varenne in Paris and with the late James Beard in New York,
serves an unforgettable prix fixe six-course dinner in an elegant Victorian mansion. The menu changes constantly, but
French and northern Italian dishes predominate; guests can
choose either of two entrées. Specialties include boned breast
of Muscovy duck served on a bed of onion marmalade with
lingonberry and cream sauce; and chicken Geneva, a boned
breast filled with cheddar cheese, wrapped with ham and
phyllo pastry, and baked in a light cream sauce. *River and
Headquarters Rds., 13 mi north of New Hope, tel. 215/294–
9100. Jackets required. Reservations required about a month*

in advance. Dinner Fri.–Sun. and holidays at 7:30. MC, V. Very Expensive.

Lodging
★ **Evermay on the Delaware.** A three-story Victorian mansion has been transformed into a small elegant hotel overlooking the Delaware River. The rooms in the cream-colored clapboard building and nearby carriage house are filled with antiques and fresh flowers. Guests take pre-dinner sherry and afternoon tea in a stately walnut wainscoted parlor furnished with camelback settees set by twin fireplaces. Breakfast of fresh fruit compote, croissants, juice, and coffee is served in the glassed-in conservatory overlooking great sweeps of lawn. Gardens feature resident peacocks and black-faced sheep. Request a room with a river view. *River and Headquarters Rds., 13 mi north of New Hope, 18920, tel. 215/294–9100. 11 rooms in main house, 5 in carriage house. No children. MC, V. Moderate–Very Expensive.*

Isaac Stover House. Talk-show host Sally Jesse Raphael's 1836 brick mansion is a delightful B&B full of personality. Theme rooms include: Shakespeare & Co., Cupid's Bower, Emerald City with Wizard of Oz memorabilia, the Amore Room adorned with watercolor prints of Italy, more. The opulent Victorian sitting room features pink swag curtains; innkeeper Susan Tettemer describes it as "reminiscent of a French brothel." Full breakfast is served on a sunny porch or in the breakfast room. The inn is set on 13 acres of woods and meadows overlooking the Delaware River. *Box 68, River Rd., 18920, tel. 215/294–8044. 8 rooms, 4 with private bath. Smoking only on first floor. Children over 12 welcome. AE, MC, V. Moderate–Expensive.*

Holicong

Lodging
★ **Barley Sheaf Farm.** At the end of a long, maple-fringed driveway is Barley Sheaf Farm, playwright George S. Kaufman's "Cherchez la Farm" from 1936–1953, Bucks County's theatrical heyday. A 1740 fieldstone mansion, the inn's 30-acre parklike setting includes a duck pond, a swimming pool, and a meadow full of sheep. The bedrooms are a medley of floral prints, brass, and white iron beds. A hearty breakfast is served on the glass-enclosed sun porch. *Box 10, U.S. 202, 18928, tel. 215/794–5104. 10 rooms. Facilities: outdoor pool, badminton, croquet. Children over 8 welcome. AE. Expensive–Very Expensive.*

Ash Mill Farm. A handsome 18th-century fieldstone manor house set on 10 acres is a country B&B. The parlor has high ceilings, ornate moldings, a walk-in fireplace, and deep-silled windows; rooms feature Irish and American antiques and thoughtful extras such as thick terry-cloth robes, hair dryers, and down comforters on canopy or four-poster beds. Full country breakfast is served. In season, afternoon tea and homebaked sweets are offered on a sunny porch with a view of resident sheep. *Box 202, U.S. 202, 18928, tel. 215/794–5373. 6 rooms with 1 suite, 4 with bath. Children over 14 welcome. MC, V. Moderate–Expensive.*

Lahaska

Dining
Jenny's. American regional cuisine is served in a dark, woodsy, hunt club setting. Lobster and crab sauté, and veal topped with mushrooms and Monterey Jack cheese are favorites. A DJ

plays dance tunes on Friday and Saturday nights. *U.S. 202, Peddler's Village, tel. 215/794–5605. Reservations recommended. Dress: casual. AE, CB, DC, MC, V. No dinner Mon. Expensive.*

Marcella's. Huge portions and homemade pastas and gravy ("Mama's secret recipes") distinguish this casual northern Italian restaurant furnished with wooden tables, bamboo chairs, and dried flowers. Its menu varies with the season; seafood Fra Diablo and ravioli dishes are specialties. *U.S. 202 opposite Peddler's Village, tel. 215/794–7216. Reservations required. Dress: casual. AE, MC, V. Closed Mon. Closed for lunch weekdays. Moderate.*

Lumberville

Dining   **Cuttalossa Inn.** The spectacular setting—a large porch overlooking a gurgling stream and a waterfall which once powered a lumber mill—is the main appeal of this 1750s former stagecoach stop. Cross a wooden bridge to the cocktail bar set amid the mill's ruins. American-international cuisine features such specialties as crab imperial and fresh fish. In warm weather, it's outdoor dining only. In winter, seating is in a casual room with pegged wooden floors and a stone hearth. *River Rd., 6 mi north of New Hope, tel. 215/297–5082. Reservations advised Oct. through April (indoors). No reservations for outdoor seating. Jackets suggested in winter. AE, MC, V. Closed Sun. Expensive.*

New Hope

Dining   **Hotel du Village.** Diners partake of country French fare in a converted private school. The chef-owner prepares tournedos Henri IV, fillet with bearnaise sauce; sweetbreads with mushrooms in madeira sauce; and fillet of sole in curried butter, topped off by extravagant desserts. Dinner is served in a Tudor-style room with working fireplaces or on the sun porch. *Phillips Mill and N. River Rds., tel. 215/862–5164. Reservations required. Jackets required. AE. Closed Mon. and Tues. Closed for lunch. AE. Expensive.*

Karla's. The atmosphere will remind you of a convivial European café; the menu is similarly international. Its specialties include moussaka à La Grecque and wild mushrooms in basil sauce. A light menu is also available. Late-night breakfast is served Friday and Saturday. A piano player entertains on Monday, Wednesday, Friday, Sunday, May–Nov. *5 W. Mechanic St., tel. 215/862–2612. Reservations recommended weekends. Dress: informal. AE, CB, DC, MC, V. Closed Mon. and Tues. nights Dec.–Apr. Expensive.*

Martine's. Reminiscent of a quaint English pub with a beamed ceiling, stone walls, and a walk-in fireplace, Martine's is more popular with locals than with visitors. The eclectic menu features filet Mignon au poivre, pasta, duckling, and fresh fish. Outdoor dining is on a small patio. *7 E. Ferry St., tel. 215/862–2966. Reservations recommended weekends. Dress: casual. DC, MC, V. Expensive.*

Mother's. One of New Hope's most popular dining spots, Mother's main claims to fame are sinful desserts representative of which are the chocolate mousse bombe and mocha Amazon. Homemade soups, stir-fries, pasta, and pizza stand out among the selections on the extensive menu. In summer, meals are also served in the garden. Expect to wait; it's always crowded here. *34 N. Main St., tel. 215/862–9354. Reservations recommended for dinner. Dress: informal. AE, DC, MC, V. Expensive.*

Odette's. In 1961, Parisian actress Odette Myrtil Logan converted a former canal lock house into a stylish restaurant. The atmosphere is French country bistro; the cuisine, American nouvelle with a menu that changes seasonally. Some of the dining rooms command a view of the canal and the river. Entertainment consists of a piano bar, cabarets, and art shows, frequently hosted by new owner Rocky Barbone. *S. River Rd., 4 mi south of New Hope, tel. 215/862–2432. Reservations advised; request a river view. Dress: informal. AE, DC, MC, V. Expensive.*

Havana Bar and Restaurant. The American regional and contemporary fare offered by the Havana is enhanced by its mesquite-grilled specialties. Dishes featured are Buffalo chicken wings, grilled shrimp, and stuffed mushrooms. The bar serves exotic elixirs enlivened by jazz bands Thursday through Sunday nights and jazz or rock and roll Monday through Wednesday. The view of Main Street is ideal for people-watching. *105 S. Main St. tel. 215/862–9897. No reservations. Dress: informal. AE, CB, DC, MC, V. Moderate.*

The Logan Inn. New Hope's oldest building (originally the Ferry Tavern) has a huge all-day-grazing menu offering everything from fettuccine Alfredo and artichoke cheese squares to barbecued spareribs and a macrobiotic peasant platter. Specialties include beef sauerbraten and duck à l'orange. *10 W. Ferry St., tel. 215/862–2300. Reservations advised. Dress: informal. AE, CB, DC, MC, V. Moderate.*

Lodging

★ **The Logan Inn.** A recent face-lift of the oldest inn in continuous operation in North America has restored its original Colonial charm. Built in 1727 as the Ferry Inn, it accommodated passengers who used the Delaware River ferry to Lambertville. George Washington stayed here at least five times. Rooms are decorated with original and reproduction Colonial furnishings, including canopy beds, plus original paintings by local artists. Some rooms have river views. Full breakfast from the restaurant downstairs is included. *10 W. Ferry St., 18938; tel. 215/862–2300. 16 rooms. Children welcome. AE, CB, DC, MC, V. Expensive.*

★ **The Whitehall Inn.** Guest rooms at the 18th-century manor house of what was once a gentleman's horse farm are furnished with period antiques, canopy beds, and patterned wallpaper. Guests get a bowl of fresh fruit and bottle of regional wine upon arrival. The spacious parlor has sofas facing a blazing fireplace. The four-course candlelit gourmet breakfast is served at tables set with white linen, English china, and heirloom silver; in the afternoon, high tea is served. *1370 Pineville Rd., 18938, 215/598–7945. 6 rooms, 4 with private baths. Facilities: outdoor pool, tennis, 12 secluded acres. Children over 12 welcome. No smoking. AE, CB, DC, MC, V. Expensive–Very Expensive.*

Holiday Inn. This comfortable motel is minutes from New Hope and 30 minutes from Sesame Place and is one of the few spots in Bucks County that welcomes children. *Box 419 (U.S. 202), 18938, tel. 215/862–5221 or 800/222–HOPE. 159 rooms. Facilities: restaurant, lounge with entertainment Tues.–Sat. nights, outdoor pool, tennis, playground. AE, CB, DC, MC, V. Moderate.*

Pineapple Hill. A 1780s farmhouse painted a sunny cream color is an inviting showcase for innkeepers Linda and Hal Chaize's collection of folk art and period antiques. The parlor has a brick hearth and comfy sofas; guest rooms are furnished with country and primitive antiques. A swimming pool is built into the picturesque ruins of an old stone barn. Continental-plus breakfast is included. *1324 River Rd., 18938, tel. 215/862-9608. 5 rooms, 3 with private bath. Facilities: outdoor pool, lawn games, close to canal and river. AE. Moderate-Expensive.*

★ **The Wedgwood Inn.** Three buildings comprise the Wedgwood Inn B&B lodgings: a white frame 1870 Victorian house with frilly woodwork, a gabled roof, wraparound porch, and a porte-cochere; a Classic Revival-style 1840 stone manor house; and a turn-of-the-century carriage house. Lively innkeepers oversee a homey atmosphere; Wedgwood pottery, antiques, and paintings add to its charm. Continental-plus breakfast and afternoon tea are served in the sun porch, gazebo, or guest room. *111 W. Bridge St., 18938, tel. 215/862-2570. 13 rooms, 11 with bath, including 2 suites and a carriage house. Facilities: pool and tennis club privileges; horse-drawn carriage rides that depart from the inn. 2 rooms accommodate children. Midweek discount. Pets allowed on a limited basis. No credit cards. Moderate-Very Expensive.*

New Hope Motel in the Woods. A clean, modern, one-story motel offers the lowest rates in the area and welcomes families. *400 W. Bridge St., 18938, tel. 215/862-2800. 28 rooms. Facility: outdoor pool. DC, MC, V. Inexpensive.*

Newtown

Dining **Jean Pierre's.** Owner/chef Jean-Pierre Tardy, formerly execu-
★ tive chef at Philadelphia's distinguished Le Bec-Fin, prepares classic French cuisine in a quaint country French setting. Specialties include a lobster in puff pastry, foie gras with sautéed apples, and rack of lamb. *101 S. State St., tel. 215/968-6201. Reservations required. Jackets recommended. AE, CB, DC, MC, V. Closed Mon.; dinner only weekends. Very Expensive.*

Ye Olde Temperance House. Continental cuisine is served in a meticulously restored circa 1770 inn. Homemade soup stocks and an in-house charcuterie ensure an appealing range of dishes featuring rack of lamb, roast Long Island smoked duck, and twice-cooked pork; beef, shrimp, and chicken preparations change each day. Request hearthside seating in the room adorned with artwork by Edward Hicks of "Peaceable Kingdom" fame. Listen to live blues in the tavern on Monday, live jazz Wednesday through Saturday nights, and enjoy a Cajun brunch accompanied by Dixieland jazz on Sunday. *5–11 S. State St., tel. 215/860-0474. Reservations required. Dress: casual. AE, DC, MC, V. Closed for lunch Sat. Expensive.*

Lodging **Ye Olde Temperance House.** A recent renovation of this 1770 inn included equipping each room with a variety of handsome furniture: the Benetz Suite has bent hickory and willow twig furniture; the Edward Hicks Suite has rich period mahogany and walls stenciled in a pattern derived from "Peaceable Kingdom" mosaic tile. Continental breakfast is served in bed or in the dining room. *5–11 S. State St., 18940, tel. 215/860-0474. 13 rooms and suites. Facilities: restaurant, access to Newtown Racquetball and Fitness Club. Children allowed. No minimum stay. AE, DC, MC, V. Expensive-Very Expensive.*

Upper Black Eddy

Lodging **Bridgeton House.** Wide, screened porches and a terrace provide close-up views of the Delaware River and the bridge to Milford, New Jersey. Guest rooms are furnished with country antiques, quilts, and many four-poster canopy beds. The informal sitting room has white- and plum-colored wood walls, Oriental rugs, intriguing books, and conversation-piece collectibles. Two-course gourmet country breakfast is served. Request a river view: In Room 4, you can see the river from your bed. *Box 167, 18972, tel. 215/982–5856. 11 rooms, including 3 suites. Children under 8 weekdays only. No credit cards. Moderate–Very Expensive.*

Washington Crossing

Lodging **Woodhill Farms.** Built in 1980, this is Bucks County's most contemporary B&B. The wide-open living room and dining room have the stone hearth and beamed ceiling of a country lodge. Rooms are equipped with television, hair dryers, air-conditioning, and individual thermostats. Though situated in a residential neighborhood, its quiet 10-acre grounds attract lots of deer. Continental-plus breakfast is served weekdays, full breakfast weekends, afternoon wine and cheese. *150 Glenwood Dr., 18977, tel. 215/493–1974. 5 rooms. Children over 6 or infants welcome. AE, MC, V. Expensive.*

The Arts

Theater

The **Bucks County Playhouse** (S. Main St., New Hope, tel. 215/862–2041) has long been considered one of the finest summer theaters on the East Coast. Its season runs from May through mid-December, with nine performances each week. Recent productions included such hits as *The Little Shop of Horrors*, *Annie Get Your Gun*, and *The Odd Couple*.

New on the scene is the **S. J. Gerenser Theater** (Bridge St. and Stockton Ave., New Hope, tel. 215/862–3777), where New Hope Showcase Productions stages professional off-Broadway fare such as *Leader of the Pack* and *Sister Mary Ignatius Explains It All for You* year-round.

10 Lancaster County

Introduction

by Joyce Eisenberg

The plain and fancy live side by side in Lancaster County, some 65 miles west of Philadelphia. This is Pennsylvania Dutch Country, where horse-drawn buggies and horn-tooting cars jockey for position on picturesque country roads.

The tourists come to see the Old Order Amish, one of the most conservative of the Pennsylvania Dutch sects. Clinging to a centuries-old way of life, the Amish shun the amenities of modern civilization, using kerosene or gas lamps instead of electric lighting, horse-drawn buggies instead of automobiles. Ironically, in turning their backs on the modern world, they have attracted the world's attention.

This bucolic region can be hectic, especially on summer weekends. Its main arteries, U.S. 30 and Route 340, are lined with souvenir shops and outlet stores. The farmers markets and family-style restaurants are often crowded with busloads of tourists. But there is still much charm here in the general stores, one-room schoolhouses, country lanes, and picture-perfect farms, many of which welcome overnight guests. There are pretzel factories to tour, quilts to buy, and a host of attractions for railroad buffs. The trick is to visit the top attractions and then get off the beaten path. If possible, plan your trip for early spring, fall, or Christmas season, when it is less crowded.

Note: Although many restaurants, shops, and farmers markets close Sunday for the Sabbath, commercial attractions are open.

Pennsylvania Dutch is a collective phrase for 25 Amish and Mennonite sects. Despite their name, they aren't Dutch at all. Rather, they are descendants of German and Swiss immigrants who came to the Lancaster area to escape religious persecution. "Dutch" is a corruption of "Deutsch," meaning German.

The Mennonite movement, named after its leader Menno Simons, began in Switzerland in the 16th century, the time of the Reformation. It was a radical religious group that advocated nonviolence, separation of church and state, adult baptism, and individual freedom in choosing a religion. Nicknamed Anabaptists, the Mennonites were persecuted and killed by the thousands for not conforming to either Catholic or Protestant tenets. In 1710, eight families led by Mennonite Bishop Hans Herr accepted William Penn's invitation to settle in Lancaster County.

In 1693, Swiss Mennonite Bishop Jacob Amman, whose stricter beliefs and interpretation of church tenets had attracted a following, broke off from the movement. His followers, the Amish, also settled in Lancaster. Today, there are 109,000 Amish people living in North America; Lancaster County has the second-largest Amish community in the nation, with 16,000 people. (Holmes County, Ohio, is first.) That the number of Amish has doubled in the last two decades suggests that theirs is still a viable alternative lifestyle.

The Amish religion and way of life stress separation from the world, caring for others of the faith, and self-sufficiency. What may appear as odd behavior results from religious convictions based on Biblical interpretation. The Amish, who reject compulsory school attendance and military registration, do not accept social-security benefits or purchase life or property insurance. Barn-raising is probably the best example of the Amish spirit. If a new family barn is needed, hundreds of men gather to supply the labor to build it while the women cook the meals. The job is completed in a day or two.

Old Order Amish send their children to one-room schoolhouses with eight grades to a room. They avoid larger public schools to prevent the exposure of their children to the influence of "outsiders." The Supreme Court has ruled that Amish children need not attend school beyond the eighth grade.

Telephones, television, radio, and electric appliances are not permitted. Farmers work with teams of mules to plow, plant, and harvest their crops. Families ride in horse-drawn buggies. Men and women wear plain clothing which has remained unchanged for centuries.

Although some changes have been thrust upon them by the government, the Amish do change and update some rules themselves. Some have telephones in their barns or on the edge of their property for emergency use only; many will accept a ride in an automobile or take public transportation. They live a lively, rich life of discipline and caring. They seek to be at peace with themselves, their neighbors, their surroundings, and their God.

Although the Amish are a prime attraction, they are not the only lure to Lancaster County. Lancaster (which the English named after Lancashire) is an intriguing city to explore. Very residential, with blocks of charming row houses, it served as the nation's capital for one day during the American Revolution when Congress fled Philadelphia after the Battle of Brandywine. It is also the nation's oldest inland city, dating from 1710. Historic sites in the area include Wheatland, the home of James Buchanan, Pennsylvania's only contribution to the White House.

One can spend a full day following Oregon Pike (Rte. 272) northeast from the Landis Valley Museum, an exhibit devoted to rural life before 1900. Ephrata Cloister provides a look at a religious communal society of the 1700s. And Main Street in Lititz, founded in 1756, is a charming place for a stroll.

Western Lancaster County, which includes the towns of Marietta, Mount Joy, and Columbia, is a quieter part of the county where visitors can bicycle down winding lanes, sample local wines and authentic Mennonite cooking, and explore friendly uncrowded villages. Its history is rooted in the Colonial period. The residents are of Scotch and German descent, and architecture varies from log cabins to Victorian homes. There are a number of good restaurants, inns, and farms which accept guests.

If you've brought your children as far as Lancaster, you may want to continue north to Hershey, the "Chocolate Town" founded in 1903 by Milton S. Hershey. Here the street lights are shaped like giant Hershey Kisses and the number one attraction is Hersheypark, an 87-acre theme park with kiddie rides and thrill rides, theaters and live shows. Hershey's Chocolate World offers tours into the simulated world of chocolate production.

Essential Information

Getting Around

By Car From Philadelphia, take the Schuylkill Expressway (I–76) west to the Pennsylvania Turnpike. Lancaster County attractions are accessible from Exits 20, 21, and 22. For a more scenic route, follow U.S. 30 (Lancaster Pike) west from Philadelphia. It's about 65 miles; allow 90 minutes.

By Bus **Greyhound/Trailways** (tel. 215/931–4000) has three runs daily from Philadelphia to the RCS Bus Terminal, 22 West Clay Street, in Lancaster. The ride takes two hours and 20 minutes.

By Train **Amtrak** (tel. 215/824–1600 or 800/872–7245) has regular service from Philadelphia's 30th Street Station to the Lancaster Amtrak station, 53 McGovern Avenue. Trips take 70 minutes.

Guided Tours

Amish Country Tours (Rte. 340 between Bird-in-Hand and Intercourse, tel. 717/392–8622) has a variety of large bus or minivan tours. Most popular are the two- and four-hour Amish farmlands trips. Featured are stops at a one-room schoolhouse, wine tasting and food tasting, and shopping for crafts. Also available are tours to Hershey.

Brunswick Tours (2034 Lincoln Hwy. E, tel. 717/397–7541) provides private guides who will tour with you in your car.

The Mennonite Information Center (2209 Millstream Rd., Lancaster, tel. 717/299–0954) has local Mennonite guides who will join you in your car. These knowledgeable guides will lead you to country roads, produce stands, and craft shops, and also acquaint you with their religion.

Rutts Tours (3466 W. Main St., Route 340, Intercourse, tel. 717/768–8238) has guides who will join you in your car.

For an aerial tour, try **Glick Aviation** at Smoketown Airport (Mabel Ave. off Rte. 340, Smoketown, tel. 717/394–6476). Fifteen-minute flights in a four-seater plane (pilot plus three) provide a splendid view of rolling farmlands.

You can rent or purchase a cassette tape for the self-guided **Auto Tape Tour of Pennsylvania Dutch Country.** Minimum driving time is two to three hours. *Available at Dutch Wonderland, Holiday Inn East, and National Wax Museum, tel. 717/291–1888.*

Tapetours begins at the Pennsylvania Dutch Convention & Visitors Bureau on Greenfield Road. The 28 stops take about three hours. *Available from Brunswick Tours (see above) and Bird-In-Hand Family Inn, Rte. 340, tel. 717/299–8901.*

Important Addresses and Numbers

Tourist Information **The Pennsylvania Dutch Convention & Visitors Bureau** (Greenfield Rd. exit of U.S. 30 E, Dept. 2064, 501 Greenfield Rd., Lancaster 17601, tel. 717/299–8901) has many brochures and maps, direct phone connections to local hotels, and a 14-minute multi-image slide presentation, "There Is a Season," a visual journey through picturesque Pennsylvania Dutch Country which serves as a good introduction to the area. *Open daily 9–5, later in summer.*

The Mennonite Information Center (2209 Millstream Rd., Lancaster 17602–1494, tel. 717/299–0954) serves mainly to "interpret the faith and practice of the Mennonite Church to all who inquire." It has information on local inns and Mennonite guest homes as well as a film about the Amish and Mennonite people, shown every half-hour. *Open Mon.–Sat. 8–5.*

Emergencies   Dial 911 for assistance, or go to one of the three emergency rooms in the city of Lancaster: **Community Hospital of Lancaster** (1100 E. Orange St., tel. 717/397–3711), **Lancaster General Hospital** (555 N. Duke St., tel. 717/299–5511), **St. Joseph's Hospital** (250 College Ave., tel. 717/291–8211).

Pharmacy   **Weis Pharmacy** (1603 Lincoln Hwy. E, Lancaster, tel. 717/394–9826). *Open Mon.–Fri. 9–9, Sat. 10–6, Sun. 10–4.*

Exploring Lancaster County

Most visitors come to Pennsylvania Dutch Country to get a glimpse of the Amish and their lifestyle. Below are suggestions for a one-day tour which will allow you to accomplish that goal, plus suggested itineraries for additional touring. Train lovers will appreciate the Strasburg attractions; history and architecture buffs will enjoy the sites in and around the city of Lancaster. There is also information on a tour following Oregon Pike north from Lancaster and some suggestions for seeing the western part of Lancaster County.

Day 1

Numbers in the margin correspond with points of interest on the Lancaster County map.

❶ People's Place, a "people-to-people interpretation center," provides an excellent introduction to the Amish, Mennonites, and Hutterites. A 30-minute multiscreen slide show titled "Who Are the Amish?" features close-ups of Amish life and perceptive narration. Geared toward children, **Amish World** is a hands-on exhibit on transportation, dress, schools, the effects of growing old, and mutual aid. Children can try on bonnets and play in the "feeling box." Don't miss the collection of wood sculptures by Aaron Zook. "Hazel's People," a feature film starring Geraldine Page and set in the Mennonite community, is shown Monday through Saturday from April through October at 6 and 8 PM; separate admission fee. *Rte. 340, Intercourse, tel. 717/768–7171. Admission: $4.25 adults, $2.10 children. Open Mon.–Sat. 9:30–9 Apr.–Oct., until 5 in winter.*

❷ Following Route 340 west past Bird-in-Hand will bring you to **Abe's Buggy Rides.** Abe chats about the Amish during a 2-mile spin down country roads in an Amish family carriage. *No phone. Price: $8 adults, $4 children 12 and under. Open Mon.–Sat., 8–dusk.*

For lunch (actually, they serve dinner all day) try one of the family-style Pennsylvania Dutch restaurants (**Amish Barn** or **Plain & Fancy** on Rte. 340; **Good 'N Plenty** on Rte. 896). You'll share a table with about a dozen other customers and be treated to hearty regional fare, including traditional "sweets and sours." There's no menu; they just bring out the food (*See* Chapter 6). Although it doesn't serve family style, **Bird-in-Hand Family Restaurant** on Rte. 340 is an excellent place to sample local specialties.

Several furnished farmhouses offer a simulated, up-close look at how the Amish live. Note that these are commercial, not Amish-run, enterprises.

❸ The Amish Homestead house and farm tour provides perhaps the most complete introduction to Amish life. You'll learn about Amish origins, worship, clothing, courtship, marriage and honeymoon rituals, the wearing of beards, and burial. The house and farm are occupied by the Dunkard family and are in full operation. A 40-minute tour covers five rooms of the 1744 farmhouse and farm buildings. There are acres of growing crops and a vegetable garden. *2034 Lincoln Hwy. E (U.S. 30),*

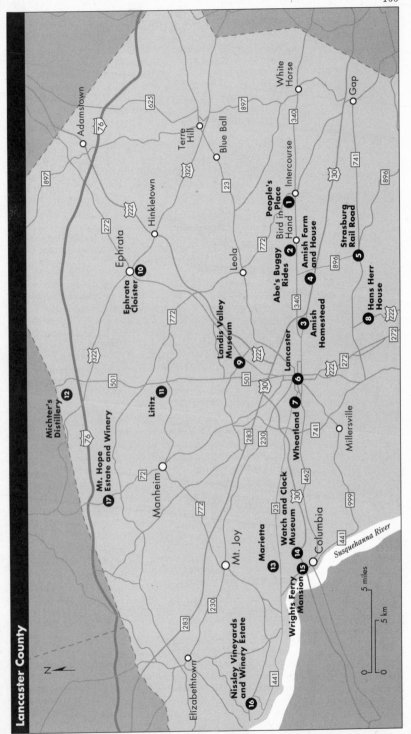

Lancaster County

N

Adamstown

Elizabethtown

441

283

230

Mt. Joy

72

Manheim

Lititz 11

Michter's Distillery 12

Mt. Hope Estate and Winery 17

897

76

272

322

Ephrata
Ephrata Cloister 10

Hinkletown

222

501

772

Nissley Vineyards and Winery Estate 16

441

Marietta 13

Watch and Clock Museum 14

Wrights Ferry Mansion 15

Columbia

23

30

462

441

Susquehanna River

999

Millersville

741

Wheatland 7

Lancaster 6

Landis Valley Museum 9

222

501

30

272

222

625

Terre Hill

322

Blue Ball

23

Leola

772

People's Place 1

Bird in Hand

Abe's Buggy Rides 2

Amish Homestead 3

Amish Farm and House 4

340

897

White Horse

340

Intercourse

30

896

896

272

Hans Herr House 8

Strasburg Rail Road 5

741

896

222

272

Gap

0   5 miles

0   5 km

Lancaster, tel. 717/392–0832. Admission: $3.75 adults, $1.75 children 6–11. Open daily 9–4, until 7 in summer.

4 **The Amish Farm and House** offers half-hour tours through a 10-room circa 1805 house furnished in the Old Order Amish style. A map guides visitors to the farmstead's animals, waterwheel, and barns. *2395 Lincoln Hwy. E (U.S. 30), Lancaster, tel. 717/394–6185. Admission: $3.90 adults, $2 children 5–11. Open daily 8:30–4, until 6 in summer.*

Save an hour or two to explore the country roads on your own. Many Amish farms (they're the ones with windmills and green blinds) are clustered in the area between Ephrata and New Holland. Drive the side roads between routes 23 and 340; visit the roadside stands and farms where hand-painted signs entice you with quilts or farm-fresh produce and eggs. Drive in and chat with the Amish—they always welcome polite inquiries. For take-home goodies and gifts, stop at a farmers market.

Time Out To sample the local ice cream, order one of the 20 farm-fresh flavors at **Lapp Valley Farm.** It also sells homemade root beer and has animals to entertain the children. *Mentzer Rd., between New Holland and Intercourse (from Intercourse, follow Rte. 340 1 mi east, turn left on New Holland Rd., left on Peters Rd., and right on Mentzer Rd.), tel. 717/354–7988. Open Mon.–Thurs. noon–dark, Fri. and Sat. 8 AM–7 PM, or later.*

Day 2. Strasburg

Train lovers could easily spend an entire day in Strasburg. To get from U.S. 30 to Strasburg, head south on Route 896 and turn left on Route 741.

5 **The Strasburg Rail Road** is a scenic 9-mile excursion from Strasburg to Paradise on a rolling antique chartered in 1832 to carry milk, mail, and coal. Passengers can chug along in the open coach featured in *Hello Dolly.* Called America's oldest short line, the wooden coaches are pulled by an iron steam locomotive. You can buy the makings for a picnic at the Strasburg Country Store (rtes. 896 and 741) and alight at Groff's Grove in Paradise for a picnic lunch. *Rte. 741, Strasburg, tel. 717/687–7522. Round-trip: $5 adults, $2.50 children 3–11. Open daily May–Oct., weekends only Nov., March, April. Closed mid-Dec.–March. Mon.–Sat. 10–7, Sun. noon–7 in summer, shorter hours the rest of year.*

Across the road from the Strasburg Rail Road, the **Railroad Museum of Pennsylvania** features 13 colossal engines built between 1888 and 1930; 12 railroad cars including a Pullman sleeper that operated from 1855 to 1906; sleighs; and railroad memorabilia documenting the history of Pennsylvania railroading. *Rte. 741, Strasburg, tel. 717/687–8628. Admission: $3 adults, $1.50 children 6–17. Open Mon.–Sat. 9–5, Sun. noon–5. Closed Mon. from Nov.–April.*

On a smaller scale, antique and 20th-century model trains are on display at the **Toy Train Museum,** the showplace for the Train Collectors Association. There are three operating layouts plus hundreds of locomotives and cars in display cases, a nostalgia film, and many "push-me" buttons. *Paradise La., just north of Rte. 741, Strasburg, tel. 717/687–8976. Admis-*

sion: $2.25 adults, 75¢ children 7–12. Open daily, 10–5, May–Oct., weekends only Apr.–mid-Dec.

Just down the road at the **Red Caboose Motel** R-5 cabooses have been converted into motel units and a casual restaurant. **Ed's Buggy Rides** depart from the motel for 20- to 30-minute horse-drawn-carriage rides along scenic back roads. *Rte. 896, 1½ mi south of U.S. 30, Strasburg, tel. 717/687–0360. Rides: $6 adults, $3 children 10 and under. Open daily 9–5.*

If you fancy fancy cars, **Gast Classic Motorcars Exhibit** has a changing display of 50 antique, classic, sports, and celebrity cars. *Rte. 896, Strasburg, tel. 717/687–9500. Admission: $4 adults, $2 children 7–12. Open daily 9–9, 9–5 weekdays Nov.–Apr.*

Day 3. Lancaster

6 If you have another day to spend in Pennsylvania Dutch Country, tour the city of **Lancaster** and surrounding attractions or follow Oregon Pike north along the route described below.

The Historic Lancaster Walking Tour, a two-hour stroll through the heart of this charming old city, is conducted by costumed guides who impart lively anecdotes about local architecture and history. *Tours leave from S. Queen and Vine Sts., near Penn Sq., tel. 717/392–1776. Price: $3 adults, $2.50 senior citizens, $1.25 children 6–12. Tours Mon.–Sat. 10 and 1:30, Sun. 1:30 Apr. through Oct., by reservation only the rest of the year.*

Built in 1742, **Central Market** is one of the oldest covered markets in the country. This is where the locals shop for fresh fruit and vegetables, meats (try the Lebanon bologna), and baked goods such as sticky buns and shoofly pie. You can pick up food for a picnic. *Penn Sq., tel. 717/291–4740. Open 6–4:30 Tues. and Fri., 6–2 on Sat.*

The **Lancaster Newspapers Newseum** (28 S. Queen St., tel. 717/291–8600) has a series of exhibits of newspaper front pages and printing equipment on view from the street. It is open 24 hours a day but is most dramatic at night.

The Old City Hall, reborn as the **Heritage Center Museum,** shows the work of Lancaster County artisans and craftsmen—clocks, furniture, homemade toys, *fraktur* (ornate paintings), and Pennsylvania long rifles. Some exhibits are on display permanently, while some exhibits change. *King and Queen Sts., tel. 717/299–6440. Donation requested. Open Tues.–Sat. 10–4. Closed Dec.–Apr.*

Rock Ford Plantation and Kauffman Museum show antiques and folk art. The antiques are in a 1792 Georgian-style house once owned by Edward Hand, one of George Washington's generals; the Zoe and Henry Kauffman collection of pewter, brass, firearms, and furniture is displayed in the restored barn. *Lancaster County Park at 881 Rock Ford Rd., tel. 717/392–7223. Admission: $2.50 adults, $1 children 6–18. Guided hour-long tours. Open Apr.–Nov., Tues.–Sat. 10–4, Sun. noon–4. Closed Dec.–March.*

7 **Wheatland** was the home of the only president from Pennsylvania, James Buchanan. The restored 1828 Federal mansion displays the 15th president's furniture just as it was during his lifetime. A one-hour tour includes an entertaining profile of the only bachelor to occupy the White House. *1120 Marietta Ave. (Rte. 23), 1½ mi west of Lancaster, tel. 717/392–8721. Admission: $3.75 adults, $2.75 students, $1.50 children under 12. Open daily 10–4:15, Apr.–Nov. Closed mid-Dec.–March.*

8 Artist Andrew Wyeth's ancestors were members of the Herr family and the **Hans Herr House** is the subject of several Wyeth paintings. Today, the house is owned by the Lancaster Mennonite Historical Society, which aims to correct misconceptions about the Mennonite religion with exhibits in its Visitors Center. Half-hour tours cover the grounds and the 1719 sandstone house, a former Mennonite meeting place. The house is considered the best example of medieval German architecture in North America. *1849 Hans Herr Dr., 5 mi south of Lancaster off U.S. 222, tel. 717/464–4438. Admission: $2.50 adults, $1 children 7–12. Open Mon.–Sat. 9–4, Apr.–Dec. Closed Jan.–March.*

9 Follow Oregon Pike (Rte. 272) north from Lancaster to the **Landis Valley Museum,** an outdoor museum of Pennsylvania rural life and folk culture before 1900. Owned by brothers Henry and George Landis, the farm is now operated by the Pennsylvania Historical and Museum Commission. Informative and friendly guides are stationed in many of the 22 buildings to answer questions and give demonstrations of spinning and weaving, pottery making, and tinsmithing, the products of which are for sale in the Weathervane Shop. *2451 Kissel Hill Rd. (just off Oregon Pike), Lancaster, tel. 717/569–0401. Self-guided tours May–Sept., guided tour Oct.–Apr. Admission: $3 adults, $2 senior citizens, $1.50 children 6–17. Open Tues.–Sat. 9–5, Sun. noon–5.*

10 In the 1730s, a radical religious communal society took root in the town of Ephrata. A living example of William Penn's Holy Experiment, the monastic Protestants of the **Ephrata Cloister** lived an ascetic life of work, study, and prayer. They ate one meal a day of grain, fruit, and vegetables, and encouraged celibacy (the last sister died in 1813). The society was best known for a cappella singing, fraktur (ornate paintings), medieval German architecture, and its publishing center. Robed guides lead half-hour tours of three restored buildings; then visitors can tour the stable, print shop, and craft shop by themselves. *Rtes. 272 and 322, Ephrata, tel. 717/733–6600. Admission: $3 adults, $2 senior citizens, $1.50 children 6–17. Open Mon.–Sat. 9–5, Sun. noon–5. Vorspiel, a musical drama depicting cloister life, is presented Fri. and Sat. nights, Aug. 1–Labor Day. Doors open at 6:30 for tour and show. Admission: $7 adults, $6 senior citizens, $4 children 6–17. Reservations suggested.*

11 The town of **Lititz,** west of Ephrata, was founded by Moravians who settled in Pennsylvania to do missionary work among the Indians. It's a lovely town with a tree-shaded main street lined with picturesque 18th-century cottages and specialty shops selling antiques, crafts, clothing, and gifts. Around the main square are the Moravian communal residences, a church dating from 1787, and a hospital that treated the wounded during the Revolutionary War. Pick up a Historical Foundation walking tour brochure at the General Sutter Inn (*see below*).

Time Out **The General Sutter Inn** (Main St. and Rte. 501, tel. 717/626–
2115) was named after the man who founded Sacramento in
1839, 10 years before the discovery of gold on his California
property started the gold rush. A Victoriana lover's delight,
this inn has a pretty coffee shop and a more formal restaurant.
In summer, you can linger on the brick patio.

At the nation's oldest pretzel bakery, the **Julius Sturgis Pretzel
House,** you can see pretzels twisted by hand and baked in brick
ovens the same way Julius Sturgis did it in 1861. At the end of
the 20-minute guided tour, visitors can try their hand at the almost extinct art of pretzel twisting. *219 E. Main St., Lititz, tel.
717/626–4354. Admission: $1. Open Mon.–Sat. 9:30–4:30.*

The first thing you'll notice in Lititz is the smell of chocolate. It
emanates from the **Wilbur Chocolate Company's Candy Americana Museum and Factory Candy Outlet** (48 N. Broad St.,
Lititz, tel. 717/626–1131), which features a candy-making demonstration (with free samples) and a small museum of candy-
related memorabilia.

⓬ At **Michter's Distillery,** however, you may not sample the whiskey that warmed Washington's troops at Valley Forge. (There
are no samples in the whiskey business.) Michter's is the nation's oldest operating distillery (established 1753) and a
National Historic Landmark. There are half-hour tours of a
19th-century facility and the modern plant where smooth sip-
ping whiskey is made by the old-fashioned pot still sour mash
process. The highlight of the tour is the tiny copper still which
produces a barrel of whiskey a day, the smallest legal still in the
country. *Rte. 501 north of Lititz to Michter's and Distillery
Rds., Schaefferstown, tel. 717/949–6521. Admission: $1
adults, children under 14 free. Open Mon.–Sat. 10–5, Sun.
noon–5. Last tour at 4:15*

Western Lancaster County

Some visitors avoid the crowds and commercialism of eastern
Lancaster County by staying in the sleepy towns along the Sus-
quehanna River—Columbia, Marietta, Maytown, Bainbridge,
Mount Joy, and Elizabethtown.

With architecture ranging from log cabins to more recent Fed-
⓭ eral and Victorian homes, 48% of the town of **Marietta** is listed
on the National Historic Register. However, most visitor attractions are located in neighboring Columbia.

⓮ **The Watch and Clock Museum of the National Association of
Watch and Clock Collectors** displays a large and varied collection of timepieces, specialized tools, and related items from the
primitive to the modern. There's a 19th-century calendar clock
and a German Black Forest organ clock with 94 pipes. *514 Poplar St., Columbia, tel. 717/684–8261. Admission: $1.50 adults,
50¢ children 6–17. Open Tues.–Sat. 9–4.*

⓯ **Wrights Ferry Mansion** is the former residence of English
Quaker Susanna Wright, a silkworm breeder known as the
bluestocking of the Susquehanna. The 1738 stone house showcases Philadelphia furniture and accessories in the early 18th-
century William and Mary and Queen Anne styles. *38 S. 2nd
St., Columbia, tel. 717/684–4325. Admission: $3 adults, $1.50
students 6–18. Open May–Oct., Tues., Wed., Fri., Sat. 10–3.*

Two wineries operate in the western part of the county. At the
16 52-acre **Nissley Vineyards and Winery Estate,** you can review
the grape-growing and wine-making process. The tour ends
with a wine tasting; grape juice is offered to minors. *Northwest
of Columbia near Bainbridge, R.D. 1, tel. 717/426-3514. The
self-guided tour is free. Open Mon.-Sat. 10-5, Sun. 1-4.*

17 At the **Mt. Hope Estate and Winery,** you tour not vineyards but
an elegant circa 1800 mansion with turrets, hand-painted 18-
foot ceilings, Egyptian marble fireplaces, gold-leaf wallpaper,
and crystal gas chandeliers. Tours are led by costumed guides
and followed by a formal wine tasting of Mt. Hope Wines. There
are lovely estate gardens for strolls. *North of Manheim on Rte.
72, ½ mi from Exit 20 of the Pennsylvania Turnpike, tel. 717/
665-7021. Admission: $4 adults, $1.50 children 6-11. Open
Mon.-Sat. 10-5, Sun. 11-5, one hour later in summer.*

The **Pennsylvania Renaissance Faire** (tel. 717/665-7021) runs
weekends from July to mid-October on the grounds of the Mt.
Hope Estate and Winery. The winery is transformed into a
16th-century English village with human chess matches,
medieval games, jousting and fencing tournaments, street performances, craft demonstrations, jesters, and puppeteers.

What to See and Do with Children

Abe's or **Ed's Buggy Rides** (*see* Exploring, *above*).
Dutch Wonderland. With 44 acres of games and rides the
amusement park is ideally suited for families with younger children. Most rides are tame. The rides are supplemented by
diving shows, puppet shows, and bands on weekends. *U.S. 30,
east of Lancaster, tel. 717/291-1888. Admission: $9 for 5 rides;
$12.75 for unlimited rides. Open daily 10-6 or later, Memorial
Day-Labor Day. Weekends only Easter-Memorial Day, Labor Day-Oct. 31.*
Hershey's Chocolate World. An automated car takes you
through the chocolate-making process, from a cacao plantation
to a chocolate factory. *Park Blvd., Hershey, tel. 717/534-4900.
Admission free. Open daily 9-4:45, until 6:45 in summer.*
Hersheypark is a dream come true for chocoholics who love
rides. Who could resist a towering Hershey Kiss and a Hershey
Bar that walks? In addition to the more than 45 rides, there are
five theaters with musical performances, a wildlife park
(ZooAmerica), and shopping in Tudor Square. *Rte. 743 and
U.S. 422, Hershey, tel. 717/534-3900. Admission including
ZooAmerica: $17.95 adults, $14.95 children 4-8. Reduced evening rates. Open daily 10-10, Memorial Day-Labor Day;
weekends only in Sept. and May.*
Indian Echo Caverns is one of the largest caves in the north-
eastern United States. A 45-minute guided tour explores the
underground wonderland. Bring a sweater; no strollers are
allowed. *Off U.S. 322, Hummelstown, tel. 717/566-8131. Admission: $5 adults, $2.50 children 4-11. Open daily 9-6 in
summer, shorter hours the rest of the year.*
National Wax Museum. Wax figures represent important people in Lancaster County history. Visitors view scenes from
daily life and watch a simulated barn raising. *U.S. 30, east of
Lancaster, tel. 717/393-3679. Admission: $3.90 adults, $2.60
children 5-11. Open daily 9-6, or later, until 9 in summer.*
People's Place *(see* Exploring, *above*).

Strasburg Rail Road *(see* Exploring, *above).*
Toy Train Museum *(see* Exploring, *above).*

Off the Beaten Track

Choo Choo Barn, Traintown, USA, is a family hobby which got out of hand. What started in 1945 as a single train chugging around the Groff family Christmas tree is now a 1,700-square-foot display of Lancaster County in miniature with 13 O-gauge electric trains and more than 130 animated figures and vehicles. Every five minutes a house catches on fire and fire engines turn on their hoses to extinguish the blaze; flag bearers march in a Memorial Day parade; animals perform in a three-ring circus. Periodically, the overhead lights dim and it is nighttime; streetlights glow and locomotive headlights pierce the darkness. *Rte. 741, Strasburg, tel. 717/687–7911. Admission: $2.75 adults, $1.50 children 5–12. Open May–Oct., daily 10–5 (later in summer); Nov., Dec., Apr., weekends 11–5. Closed Jan.–March.*

The **Green Dragon Farmers Market and Auction** is an old traditional agricultural market held weekly during which livestock and agricultural commodities are auctioned in the morning. Local Amish and Mennonite farmers tend many of the 450 indoor and outdoor stalls selling meats, fruits, vegetables, fresh-baked pies, and dry goods. The state's largest farmers market also has a flea market and an evening auction of small animals. Try the sticky buns at Rissler's Bakery and the sausage sandwiches at Newswanger's. *R.D. 4 just off Rte. 272, Ephrata, tel. 717/738–1117. Open Fri. 9 AM–10 PM. Bring cash.*

Shopping

Crafts

Although craftspeople in the Lancaster County area produce
fine handiwork, folk art, quilts, and needlework, much of the
best work is sold to galleries nationwide and never shows up in
local shops. Among the few places to see fine local crafts are the
Weathervane Shop at the Landis Valley Museum (2451 Kissel
Hill Rd., Lancaster, tel. 717/569–9312). Craftsmen sell the
wares they make in on-site demonstrations—tin, pottery,
leather, braided rugs, weaving, and chair-caning.

The Tin Bin (Landis Valley Rd. and Rte. 501, Neffsville, tel.
717/569–6210) features handmade tinware and pottery, and reproductions of 18th-century lighting devices. **Foltz Pottery**
(Peartown Rd., Reinholds, tel. 215/267–3016) is famous for Ned
Foltz's traditional Pennsylvania redware pottery. Call for directions and appointment. For antique quilts made in
Lancaster County, try **Pandora's** (Rte. 340 just east of U.S. 30,
tel. 717/299–5305) or **Witmer's Quilt Shop** (Rte. 23 W, New Holland, tel. 717/656–3411). Though pricey, old quilts have proven
to be good investments.

Kitchen Kettle Village (Rte. 340, Intercourse, tel. 717/768–
8261) consists of 28 shops showcasing local crafts, including de-
coy carving; furniture making; leather tooling; relish, jam, and
jelly making; and tin punching. Sample the homemade fudge
and funnel cakes. Closed Sunday.

Outlets

It appears that Lancaster is trying to compete with Reading as
the Factory Outlet Capital of the Universe. U.S. 30 is lined
with outlets: Some are factory stores which offer first-quality
goods at large discounts; others call themselves outlets but
don't have real bargains. It's a good idea to find out the retail
prices of whatever you want before you leave home. The Pennsylvania Dutch Visitors Bureau publishes an *Outlet Shopping
Guide.*

Antiques

On Sundays, antiques hunters frequent the huge antiques
malls located on Route 272 between Adamstown and Denver, 2
miles east of Pennsylvania Turnpike Exit 21. As many as 5,000
dealers may turn up on summer festival Sundays. **Renninger's
Antique and Collector's Market** (tel. 215/267–2177), **Barr's Auctions** (tel. 215/267–2861), and **Black Angus** (tel. 215/484–4385)
all feature indoor and outdoor sales. Dealers display old books
and prints, Victorian blouses, corner cupboards, pewter and
local stoneware, and lots of furniture. Barr's is open on Saturdays, also. Nearby **Shupp's Grove** (Rte. 897, Denver, tel. 215/
484–4115) is a smaller outdoor market. *Open Saturday and
Sunday spring through fall.*

Farmers Markets

Farmers markets offer the most unusual shopping experiences
in the area. The **Central Market** in Lancaster (*see* Exploring,

above) and **Green Dragon Farmers Market and Auction** in Ephrata (*see* Off the Beaten Track, *above*) are the best; if you can't shop there, try **Bird-in-Hand Farmer's Market** (Rte. 340, Bird-in-Hand, tel. 717/393–9674), a conveniently located market with produce stands, baked goods, gift shops, and outlets. Open Wednesday, Friday, and Saturday. **Meadowbrook Farmer's Market** (Rte. 23, Leola, tel. 717/656–2226) is popular for its edible goodies as well as its flea-market items and country store. Open Friday and Saturday.

Outdoor Activities and Participant Sports

Ballooning

Great Adventure Balloon Club offers a bird's-eye view of Pennsylvania Dutch Country. As part of the crew, you help inflate the balloon, maneuver the controls, and land the craft in a farmer's field. You spend an hour airborne, about three hours total. A chase van drives you back to the starting point. *Rheems exit of Rte. 283, Mount Joy, tel. 717/653–2009. Price: $135 per person. Open daily year-round, weather permitting. 1-day advance reservation required.*

Bicycling

Bucks County Bicycle Tours (211H W. Callowhill Rd., Perkasie, tel. 215/257–6077) arranges two- to four-day bicycle tours (group rides and self-guided) of the Lancaster area from May to October. On week nights, riders stay at an Amish farm or Colonial B&B. On weekends, lodging is at a New Order Amish farm. A variety of rental bicycles is available.

New Horizon's Bicycle Adventures (3495 Horizon Dr., Lancaster, tel. 717/285–7607) rents 15-speed mountain bikes. If you want to ride on your own, you can pick up bikes and maps with suggested routes. There are also 12- to 44-mile guided tours past Amish farms and through covered bridges. A refreshment van follows; the agency will make lodging reservations and transfer your luggage.

Camping

The Pennsylvania Dutch Visitors Bureau has a complete list of area campgrounds. Some of the best include:

Flory's Cottages and Camping, which has camper sites, one- and two-bedroom cottages, and mobile homes. *One-half mi north of U.S. 30 on Ronks Rd., Ronks, tel. 717/687–6670. Game room, playground.*

Mill Bridge Village and Campresort, which is attached to a restored 18th-century village. *One-half mi south of U.S. 30 on Ronks Rd., tel. 717/687–8181. Snack shop, summer entertainment, free buggy rides.*

Spring Gulch Resort Campground, which has 200 shaded sites on a property equipped with a variety of recreational options. *Rte. 897 between Rtes. 340 and 322, New Holland, tel. 717/354–3100. Lake and pool for swimming, miniature golf, tennis and volleyball courts, fishing, game room, square dances, exercise classes.*

White Oak Campground (tel. 717/687–6207), which is on a quiet country road 4 miles south of Strasburg. *Call for directions. Playground, game room, Saturday-night auction.*

Golf

The **Sheraton Lancaster Golf Resort and Convention Center** (U.S. 30, Lancaster, tel. 717/299–5500) has 27 holes for regulation golf; carts are not required.

Horseback Riding

The **Forest Ridge Stables** offers leisurely guided 45-minute horseback rides on wooded trails. In summer it has hour-long horse-drawn-carriage rides through Amish farmlands. *296 S. Vintage Rd. 2½ mi south of U.S. 30, Paradise, tel. 717/442–4259. Open Memorial Day–Labor Day, daily 11–5; spring and fall, by appt. weekends only; closed Dec.–Feb.*

Dining and Lodging

Dining

Like the German cuisine that influenced it, Pennsylvania Dutch meals are hearty and are prepared with ingredients from local farms. To sample regional fare, eat at one of the several bustling restaurants in the area where diners sit with perhaps a dozen other people and the food is passed around in bowls family style. Meals are plentiful and basic—fried chicken, ham, roast beef, dried corn, buttered noodles, mashed potatoes, chowchow, bread, pepper cabbage, shoofly pie—and that's only a partial listing. Entrées are accompanied by traditional "sweets and sours," vegetable dishes made with a vinegar-and-sugar dressing. This is the way the Amish, who hate to throw things out, preserve leftover vegetables. Lancaster County has numerous smorgasbords and reasonably priced family restaurants along with a number of Continental and French restaurants in contemporary settings and quaint historic inns. Unless otherwise noted, liquor is served.

Category	Cost*
Very Expensive	over $30
Expensive	$20–$30
Moderate	$10–$20
Inexpensive	under $10

per person for a 3-course meal, without wine, tax (6%), or service

Lodging

Lancaster County lodgings are much like the people themselves—plain or fancy. You can rough it in one of the many campgrounds in the area, meet a family by staying in their B&B or on their farm, or indulge yourself at a full-frills resort. A good selection of moderately priced motels cater to families. The Pennsylvania Dutch Visitors Bureau has a listing of all area B&Bs and farms that welcome guests. Rates are highest in summer; at most hotels off-season rates are greatly reduced. Unless otherwise indicated, all rooms have private bath and hotels are open year-round.

Category	Cost*
Very Expensive	over $100
Expensive	$80–$100
Moderate	$60–$79
Inexpensive	under $60

double occupancy, based on peak (summer) rates, without room tax (6%)

The following credit card abbreviations are used: AE, American Express; CB, Carte Blanche; DC, Diners Club; MC, MasterCard; V, Visa.

Bird-in-Hand

Dining **Amish Barn Restaurant.** Pennsylvania Dutch cuisine is served family style, which means generous helpings of meat and produce, breads, and home-baked pies. Apple dumplings are a specialty. An à la carte menu is offered as well but no liquor is served. *Rte. 340 between Bird-in-Hand and Intercourse, tel. 717/768–8886. Reservations advised on summer weekends. Dress: informal. AE, DC, MC, V. Open Apr.–Nov. daily; Dec.–Jan. weekends only; Feb.–March closed Tues. and Wed. Moderate.*

Plain and Fancy Farm. This family-style restaurant serves Pennsylvania Dutch cuisine without a menu in a barn. Bake shop and gift shops are on the premises. No liquor is served. *Rte. 340 between Bird-in-Hand and Intercourse, tel. 717/768–8281. Reservations advised in summer. Dress: informal. AE, CB, DC, MC, V. Closed Sun. Breakfast served July–Aug. only. Moderate.*

★ **Bird-in-Hand Family Restaurant.** This family-owned restaurant enjoys a good reputation for its hearty Pennsylvania Dutch home cooking. The menu is à la carte. There is a lunch buffet weekdays and a breakfast buffet on Saturday. No liquor is served. *Rte. 340, just west of N. Ronks Rd., tel. 717/768–8266. Reservations not required. Dress: informal. No credit cards. Closed Sun. Inexpensive.*

Lodging **Bird-in-Hand Family Inn.** Plain but comfortable rooms in a one-story, family-owned property. The restaurant is attached. *Box B, 2740 Old Philadelphia Pike, 17505, tel. 717/768–8271 or 800/537–2535 out of state; call collect in state. 100 rooms. Facilities: tennis courts, playground, indoor and outdoor pool. AE, DC, MC, V. Moderate.*

Denver

Dining **Zinn's Country Diner.** Local specialties are served here 24 hours a day, every day. On the property are a gift shop, 27-hole miniature golf course, playground, and park. Antiques malls are nearby. No liquor is served. *Rte. 272 north at Pennsylvania Turnpike Exit 21, tel. 215/267–2210. No reservations required. Dress: informal. No credit cards. Inexpensive.*

Lodging **Howard Johnson Lodge.** The lodge has contemporary rooms with balcony or patio overlooking spacious grounds. It is convenient to antiques malls. *Rte. 272, 1 mi north of Pennsylvania Turnpike Exit 21. Box 343, 17517, tel. 215/267–7563 or 800/654–2000. 70 rooms. Facilities: restaurant, outdoor pool, basketball, playground, fitness stations. Close to Zinn's miniature golf. AE, CB, DC, MC, V. Expensive.*

East Petersburg

Dining **Haydn Zug's** offers Continental dining in an 1850s house with
★ tasteful Williamsburg furnishings. Its specialties include rack of lamb, roast pheasant, and shrimp Orleans (wild rice baked with seasoned crabmeat, jumbo shrimp, and Swiss cheese). James Beard wrote about the cheesy chowder; *Bon Appetit*

profiled the establishment. *Rte. 72 and State St., Lancaster, tel. 717/569–5746. Reservations advised. Dress up, but jackets not required. AE, CB, DC, MC, V. Very Expensive.*

Ephrata

Dining   **The Restaurant at Doneckers.** Classic and country French cuisine is served downstairs amid Colonial antiques and upstairs in a country garden. It is known for its chateaubriand for two, sautéed whole Dover sole, veal Oscar, and salmon. The service is fine; the wine cellar is extensive. From 4 to 10 its menu features lighter fare. *333 N. State St., tel. 717/738–2421. Reservations advised. Dress: casual. AE, CB, DC, MC, V. Closed Wed. Expensive.*

Lodging   **Guesthouses at Doneckers.** Three turn-of-the-century homes have been tastefully furnished with French country antiques and decorated by hand-stenciling. They have light and airy rooms, five with Jacuzzis. Complimentary Continental-plus breakfast is served. *318–324 N. State St., 17522, tel. 717/733–8696. 19 rooms, 17 with private bath. The 1777 House, 6 blocks away, has 10 rooms with private bath. AE, CB, DC, MC, V. Inexpensive–Very Expensive.*

★   **Smithton Inn.** The B&B is in a historic former stagecoach inn with six lovingly furnished guest rooms and one four-room suite. The rooms have handmade antiques, fireplaces, and canopy beds. Two rooms with whirlpool; third floor has skylights, cathedral ceiling, Franklin stove fireplace. Nice touches abound: oversize goose-down pillows, nightshirts, magazines, and fresh flowers. Outside there's a lily pond, fountain, gazebo, and lovely garden. Full breakfast is included. *900 W. Main St., 17522, tel. 717/733–6094. 6 rooms. Well-behaved children and pets welcome. 2-night minimum stay on weekends and holidays. AE, MC, V. Inexpensive–Very Expensive.*

Hershey

Lodging   **Hotel Hershey.** This gracious Spanish-style hotel surrounded by a golf course and a landscaped garden is a quiet and sophisticated resort with lots of options for recreation. The guest rooms have Colonial furniture. AP, MAP, and EP available. *Box BB, 17033, tel. 717/533–2171 or 800/533–3131. 250 rooms. Facilities: restaurant, indoor/outdoor pool, tennis, riding stables, golf. AE, DC, MC, V. Very Expensive.*

Hershey Lodge & Convention Center. This bustling, expansive resort caters to families and has two casual restaurants where kids can be kids. *W. Chocolate Ave. and University Dr., 17033, tel. 717/533–3311 or 800/533–3131. 455 rooms. Facilities: 3 restaurants, indoor and outdoor pools, lighted tennis courts, chip-and-putt golf, bicycle rental, playground, nightclub with dance band, movie theater. AE, CB, DC, MC, V. Very Expensive.*

Intercourse

Dining   **Kling House.** The Kling family home has been converted into a charming, casual restaurant serving American cuisine. Swordfish, teriyaki chicken, and snitz and knepp entrées come with complimentary appetizer of red-pepper jam and cream cheese with crackers. The soups are homemade, and the desserts are luscious. A children's menu is available. *Kitchen Kettle Village, Rtes. 340 and 772, tel. 717/768–8261. Reservations advised. Dress: casual. MC, V. Closed Sun. Dinner served Sat. nights only. Moderate.*

Lancaster

Dining **Windows on Steinman Park.** French-Continental cuisine is presented in elegant surroundings—lots of marble, fresh flowers, and huge windows overlooking an inviting red brick courtyard. Its specialties include Caesar salad, Dover sole, sautéed veal medallions, and poached salmon with champagne butter. The menu is à la carte. For entertainment, piano music is provided nightly. *16–18 W. King St., tel. 717/295–1316. Reservations advised. Jackets required. AE, DC, MC, V. Very Expensive.*

Hoar House. Victorian decor and antiques set the mood for such Continental dishes as roast stuffed duckling with Grand Marnier sauce, veal Oscar, and baked seafood in phyllo topped with a mushroom and white wine sauce. The grazing menu offers half portions at half price. The lounge has a disc jockey on Wednesday through Friday nights. *10 S. Prince St., tel. 717/397–0110. Reservations suggested. Most men wear jackets. AE, MC, V. Closed Mon. Expensive.*

★ **The Log Cabin.** Steak, lamb chops, and seafood are prepared on a charcoal grill in this 1928 expanded log cabin which was a speakeasy during Prohibition. The atmosphere is elegant and the setting is embellished with an impressive art collection. *11 Lehoy Forest Dr. (off Rte. 272), Leola (5 mi north of Lancaster), tel. 717/626–1181. Jackets and reservations suggested. AE, CB, DC, MC, V. Closed Sun. Expensive.*

Market Fare. The cuisine is American, and steaks, seafood, and veal are served in a cozy dining room with upholstered armchairs and 19th-century paintings. Steamed seafood in parchment, pasta with bay scallops, and pasta with crab and tomatoes are specialties. A light menu is also available. The café upstairs offers light breakfast, quick lunch, and carryout. *Market and Grant Sts. (across from the Central Market), tel. 717/299–7090. Reservations required on weekend. Dress: casual. AE, DC, MC, V. Expensive.*

Olde Greenfield Inn. Continental cuisine and a fine wine cellar form part of the attraction in this gracious 190-year-old restored farmhouse. House specialties include chicken and scallops à l'orange and chicken Fernando (chicken breast stuffed with crabmeat and bacon and topped with mornay sauce). Lighter dinner entrées are also available. A piano player is in the lounge on weekends. Guests can dine on the patio. *595 Greenfield Rd., tel. 717/393–0668. Reservations suggested. Dress: casual. AE, MC, V. Closed Sun. night. Expensive.*

Lancaster Dispensing Co. Soups, salads, sandwiches, and nachos are served until midnight in this stylish Victorian pub. The selection of imported beers is extensive. Thursday through Saturday live music is played. *33–35 N. Market St., tel. 717/299–4602. No reservations. Dress: informal. AE, MC, V. Inexpensive.*

Lodging **Sheraton Lancaster Golf Resort and Conference Center.** This sprawling family resort has been completely renovated since Sheraton took over in 1988, and now sports plush spaces and a striking marble lobby. Its contemporary rooms have dark cherry-wood furnishings; activities are limitless. *2300 Lincoln Hwy. E (Rte. 30) 17602, tel. 717/ 299–5500 or 800/233–0121. 330 rooms. Facilities: 2 restaurants, 4 pools, 27 holes of golf, 12 tennis courts, bike rental, minifarm, miniature golf, supervised children's programs, DJ in lounge for dancing, piano bar. MAP and EP available. AE, DC, MC, V. Very Expensive.*

★ **Best Western Eden Resort Inn.** Spacious contemporary rooms (request a room at poolside) and attractive grounds contribute to a pleasant stay here. It has a stunning tropical indoor pool and whirlpool under a retractable roof. The award-winning chef in Arthur's is noted for seafood and pasta; the Sunday buffet brunch is excellent. There's fine dining in the skylit Eden courtyard; fun food is presented in Garfield's. The lively disco is open until 2 AM; Encore provides live entertainment. *222 Eden Rd. (U.S. 30 and Rte. 272), 17601, tel. 717/569–6444 or 800/ 528–1234. 275 rooms including residential-style Club Suites with full kitchens and fireplaces. Facilities: 2 movie theaters, indoor and outdoor pool, lighted tennis courts. AE, CB, DC, MC, V. Expensive.*

King's Cottage. This elegant Spanish mansion has been transformed into a B&B furnished with antiques and 18th-century English reproductions. Full breakfast is included. It's only two miles from the heart of downtown Lancaster. *1049 E. King St., 17602, tel. 717/397–1017. 5 rooms. Children over 12 only. 2-night minimum on weekends. MC, V. Expensive.*

Olde Hickory Inn. A quiet one-story motel where many rooms open onto a spacious lawn with a pool, the Olde Hickory Inn sports attractive oak furnishings. There's dancing to live music on the patio on summer weekends. The inn is across from the Landis Valley Museum. *2363 Oregon Pike, 17601, tel. 717/569–0477 or 800/255–6859. 82 rooms. Facilities: restaurant, outdoor pool, volleyball, playground, access to Olde Hickory Racquet Club, shops nearby. AE, MC, V. Expensive.*

Willow Valley Family Resort and Conference Center. This mom-and-pop operation has blossomed into a large and stylish family resort. The striking new skylit atrium lobby is surrounded by attractive rooms. There are moderately priced rooms, but the ones overlooking the atrium are the most attractive and most expensive. Since it is Mennonite owned, there is no liquor permitted on the premises. *2416 Willow St. Pike, 17602, tel. 717/ 464–2711 or 800/444–1714. 353 rooms. Facilities: 3 restaurants, 9-hole golf course, lighted tennis courts, small lake for boating, adjacent gift mall, indoor and outdoor pools, whirlpool. AE, CB, DC, MC, V. Expensive.*

★ **Continental Inn.** The attractive two-story motel next to Dutch Wonderland is ideal for families. Request a room overlooking the pool, away from the highway. There is live music nightly. *2285 Lincoln Hwy. E (U.S. 30), 17602, tel. 717/299–0421. 165 rooms. Facilities: restaurant, 4 lighted tennis courts, basketball, indoor and outdoor pool, whirlpool, sauna, game room, 4-screen movie theater adjacent, baby-sitting available. AE, MC, V. Moderate.*

Howard Johnson Lodge. This above-average Howard Johnson's was totally renovated in 1987. Ask for a quiet room overlooking the grassy courtyard. *2100 Lincoln Hwy. E (U.S. 30), 17602, tel. 717/397–7781 or 800/654–2000. 112 rooms. Facilities: cocktail lounge, restaurant, indoor pool. AE, DC, MC, V. Moderate.*

Ramada Inn-Lancaster. This quiet, red-brick hotel a bit off the beaten track, recently refurbished, is a good base for visitors seeking Ephrata and Lititz attractions. *N. Oregon Pike (Rte. 272), 17601, tel. 717/656–2101. 120 rooms. Facilities: restaurant, lounge with live entertainment for dancing, indoor pool, indoor tennis court, outdoor pool. AE, DC, MC, V. Moderate.*

Lititz

Lodging   **General Sutter Inn.** The oldest (1764) continuously run inn in
★   the state is a Victoriana lover's dream reminiscent of "Grandma's house." Its decor ranges from Pennsylvania folk art to Louis XIV sofas and marble-topped tables. Children are welcome. *14 E. Main St. (Rte. 501), 17543, tel. 717/626–2115. 14 rooms, including 2 family suites. Facilities: 2 dining rooms, cocktail lounge. AE, MC, V. Moderate.*

Marietta

Dining   **Railroad House.** This historic 1920s hotel on the east bank of the Susquehanna River serves classic Continental cuisine upstairs and a light tavern menu downstairs, including crepes, stir-fries, and pasta. There is also a handsome copper-topped bar. Eleven guest rooms are available. *W. Front and S. Perry Sts., tel. 717/426–4141. Reservations advised. Dress: casual. MC, V. Lunch only Sunday. Moderate–Expensive.*

Mount Joy

Dining   **Cameron Estate Inn.** American and French country cuisine are served in a candlelit, Federal-style dining room of a country inn. Specialties include boneless duck in a peach sauce and crispy pecan-topped trout. *Donegal Springs Rd., tel. 717/653–1773. Reservations required. Dress: casual, but no jeans. AE, DC, MC, V. Very Expensive.*

★   **Groff's Farm.** Abe and Betty Groff's restaurant has received national attention for hearty Mennonite farm fare served in a restored 1756 farmhouse. Candlelight, fresh flowers, original Groff Farm country fabrics, and wall coverings contribute to the homey ambience. House specialties include chicken Stoltzfus, farm relishes, and cracker pudding. Dinner begins with chocolate cake. Lunch is à la carte, dinner à la carte or family style. *650 Pinkerton Rd., tel. 717/653–2048. Reservations required for dinner, suggested at lunch. Dinner seatings at Tues. –Fri. 5 and 7:30, Sat. 5 and 8. Dress: casual, but no shorts. AE, DC, MC, V. Closed Sun. and Mon. Expensive.*

Bube's Brewery. The only intact, pre-Prohibition brewery in the United States contains a museum and three unique restaurants. **The Bottling Works** in the original bottling plant of the brewery serves steaks, light dinners, pizza, and subs. *No reservations. Dress: informal.* **Alois's** offers prix fixe six-course French dinners in a Victorian hotel attached to the brewery. *Reservations required. Dress: casual.* **The Catacombs** serves traditional steak and seafood dishes in the brewery aging cellars 43 feet below street level. *Reservations are required. Jackets are preferred. An outdoor beer garden is open in summer. 102 N. Market St., tel. 717/653–2056. AE, DC, MC, V. Alois's closed Mon. Inexpensive–Expensive.*

Lodging **Cameron Estate Inn.** This sprawling Federal red-brick mansion
★ set on 15 wooded acres was the summer home of Simon
Cameron, Abraham Lincoln's first secretary of war. The rooms
are equipped with Oriental rugs, antique and reproduction furniture, and canopy beds; seven have working fireplaces. The
lovely porch overlooks the grounds. Continental breakfast is
included. *Donegal Springs Rd., 17552, tel. 717/653–1773. 18
rooms, 16 with private bath. Facilities: restaurant, access to
tennis courts and swimming pool nearby. No children under
12. AE, DC, MC, V. Moderate–Expensive.*

Paradise

Dining **Miller's Smorgasbord.** Miller's presents a lavish spread with a
★ good selection of Pennsylvania Dutch foods. Breakfast is sensa-
tional here with omelets, pancakes, and eggs cooked to order,
fresh fruits, pastries, bacon, sausage, potatoes, and much
more. It's one of the few area restaurants open on Sundays.
*2811 Lincoln Hwy. E (U.S. 30), tel. 717/687–6621. No reserva-
tions. Dress: casual. Breakfast weekends only Dec.–May. AE,
MC, V. Moderate.*
Paradise Village Inn. Steaks, seafood, and some Pennsylvania
Dutch dishes are served in this atmospheric 1796 inn. Homemade soups (Dutch pepperpot, Oriental vegetable, and others)
are ladled from a black caldron set in a walk-in fireplace; the
salad bar occupies an old watering trough. *U.S. 30, tel. 717/
687–8007. Reservations advised on weekends. Dress: casual.
AE, DC, MC, V. Moderate.*

Ronks

Lodging **Cherry Lane Motor Inn.** The family-owned motel is quiet, away
from the highway. *84 N. Ronks Rd., 17572, tel. 717/687–7646.
42 rooms. Facilities: outdoor pool, farm animals, coffee shop
serves breakfast May–Oct., picnic area. AE, MC, V. Moderate.*

Smoketown

Dining **Good 'N Plenty.** An Amish farmhouse has been remodeled into
a bustling, family-style restaurant that seats and serves more
than 500. Pennsylvania Dutch cuisine. *Rte. 896 (1 mi north of
U.S. 30), tel. 717/394–7111. No reservations. Dress: informal.
No credit cards. Closed Sun. and mid-Dec.–Jan. Moderate.*

Lodging **Mill Stream Motor Lodge.** This popular motel has been redecorated recently. Request a rear room, overlooking the stream. It
is owned by Mennonites; hence no alcohol is served. *Rte. 896,
17576, tel. 717/299–0931. 52 rooms. Facilities: restaurant
serves breakfast and lunch. 2-night minimum on weekends.
AE, MC, V. Moderate.*

Strasburg

Dining **Iron Horse Restaurant.** This charming, rustic, candlelit restaurant is housed in the original 1780s Hotel Strasburg. Best bets
are the catch-of-the-day, the daily veal special, the homemade
breads, and, for dessert, the great, warm apple pie. There's
live entertainment on weekends and an extensive wine list. *135*

E. Main St. (Rte. 741), tel. 717/687–6362. Reservations suggested on weekends. Dress: casual. AE, MC, V. Expensive.

Washington House Restaurant. This restaurant at the Historic
Strasburg Inn offers fine candlelight dining in three Colonial-
style dining rooms. The American menu features Cornish game
hen, flounder stuffed with crabmeat, and filet Mignon. The
lunch buffet is bountiful. Rte. 896 (Historic Drive), tel. 717/687–
7691. Reservations accepted for inn guests only. Dress: casual.
AE, CB, DC, MC, V. Moderate.

Lodging   **Historic Strasburg Inn.** The Colonial-style inn is set on 58
peaceful acres. The rooms come with double beds only. Full
breakfast is included. Rte. 896 (Historic Dr.), 17579, tel. 717/
687–7691 or 800/872–0201. 103 rooms. Facilities: restaurant,
tavern, outdoor pool, bicycles, volleyball. AE, CB, DC, MC, V.
Expensive.

★   **Timberline Lodges.** Beautiful lodges nestled on a hillside put
you close enough to Strasburg to hear the train whistles but far
away enough to hear the birds. The lodges, which sleep from
two to eight people, have stone fireplaces, balconies, TV, and
furnished kitchens. 44 Summit Hill Dr., 17579, tel. 717/687–
7472. 11 lodges and 5 motel units. Facilities: restaurant, outdoor pool, game room. 2-night minimum on weekends. AE,
CB, DC, MC, V. Motel inexpensive; lodge expensive.

Hershey Farm. The one-story motel overlooks a pond and a
farm. Ask for one of the crisp, new rooms with king-size beds
and large dressing areas. Breakfast is included, except Sundays. Box 89 (Rte. 896), 17579, tel. 717/687–8635. 58 rooms.
Facilities: outdoor pool. Adjoins Hershey Farm restaurant, ice
cream barn, bakery, and gift shops. MC, V. Moderate.

Strasburg Village Inn. This historic circa 1787 house has rooms
elegantly appointed in the Williamsburg style. Most have canopy or poster beds; two have Jacuzzis. A sitting/reading room is
on the second floor; an old-fashioned porch overlooks Main
Street. Full breakfast in the adjacent ice cream parlor is included. 1 W. Main St., 17579, tel. 717/687–0900 or 800/541–
1055. 11 rooms. AE, MC, V. Moderate–Expensive.

Red Caboose Motel. The motel consists of 37 railroad cabooses
that have been converted into a string of rooms: a unique place
to stay, especially for railroad buffs. Half a caboose sleeps two;
a family of four gets a whole car (one double bed, two bunks).
TV sets are built into pot-bellied stoves. Box 102, Paradise La.
(off Rte. 741), 17579, tel. 717/687–6646. 43 units, with 8 effi-
ciencies. Facilities: restaurant, playground, buggy rides. AE,
MC, V. Inexpensive.

Wrightsville

Dining   **Accomac Inn.** A stone building with a magnificent Susquehanna River setting, the inn offers American cuisine with French
flair. Tableside cooking is featured with dishes such as tenderloin flambéed with brandy and bananas Foster. Specialties
include chicken de Gaulle (chicken breast with white asparagus, crabmeat, and hollandaise) and baked Alaska. Queen
Anne furnishings are reminiscent of Williamsburg; the wine
list boasts 150 selections. Across Susquehanna River from
Marietta (take Rte. 30 west to Wrightsville exit, turn right and
follow signs), tel. 717/252–1521. Reservations suggested. Most
men wear jackets. AE, DC, MC, V. Very Expensive.

Farm Vacations

A number of farm families open their homes to visitors and allow them to observe, and even participate in, day-to-day farm life. Your hosts may teach you how to milk a cow and feed chickens. They serve you breakfast with their family, and invite you to church services. Make reservations weeks in advance: Most farms are heavily booked during the summer tourist season.

Jonde Lane Farm. Breakfast with the family is served every day but Sunday at this working dairy and poultry farm. There are three guest rooms including one family room which can sleep up to seven people; two shared baths. Ponies, goats, chickens, and cats are conspicuous. *Box 657 (Rte. 7), Manheim 17545, tel. 717/665–4231. No credit cards. Inexpensive.*

Morning Meadows Farm. Pigs and heifers populate this picturesque farm in Marietta. The one guest room has a working fireplace. Full or Continental breakfast is served. The game refuge is two blocks away. *RD 1, Box 129, Marietta 17547, tel. 717/426–1425. No credit cards. Inexpensive.*

Rayba Acres. This 100-acre working dairy farm in Paradise also has some sheep and kittens. Guests can help with the milking. No breakfast is served. *183 Black Horse Rd., Paradise 17562, tel. 717/687–6729. 6 rooms, 2 with private bath. Phones in guest rooms. MC, V. Inexpensive.*

Rocky Acre Farm. Sleep in a 200-year-old stone farmhouse. This is a dairy farm with horses to ride, dogs, and kittens. Guests can go fishing in the creek. A full hot breakfast is served daily. *1020 Pinkerton Rd., Mt. Joy 17552, tel. 717/653–4449). 5 rooms, 3 with bath, and 2 efficiency apartments. No credit cards. Inexpensive.*

Verdant View Farm. Don and Virginia Ranck's 1896 farmhouse sits on about 94 acres devoted to dairy and crop farming. Guests use four rooms on the second floor, one with a private bath. Hearty breakfasts are served in the family dining room every day but Sunday. *429 Strasburg Rd., Paradise 17562, tel. 717/687–7353. Closed Nov.–Easter. No credit cards. Inexpensive.*

The Arts

Theater

Dutch Apple Dinner Theater (510 Centerville Rd. at U.S. 30, Lancaster, tel. 717/898–1900). A candlelight buffet plus Broadway musicals and comedies are the draws in this 300-seat theater. Recent seasons have included *Fiddler on the Roof*, *Best Little Whorehouse in Texas*, and *South Pacific*. It has matinees and dinner shows. Call for reservations.

The Fulton Opera House (12 N. Prince St., Lancaster, tel. 717/397–7425). This restored 19th-century Victorian theater is America's oldest theater in continuous use, and a National Landmark. The company features family theater as well as a music and theater series that includes opera, big-band concerts, and Broadway shows.

11 Excursions

Brandywine Valley

by Joyce Eisenberg

The Brandywine River flows lazily from West Chester, Pennsylvania, to Wilmington, Delaware. Although in spots it's more a creek than a river, it has nourished many of the valley's economic and artistic endeavors and has inspired the du Ponts and the Wyeths, the families most often associated with the Brandywine Valley.

The Wyeths, who captured the beauty of the local landscape on canvas, and the du Pont family, who recontoured it with grand gardens, mansions, and mills, have bequeathed much to visitors in this scenic region 25 miles south of Philadelphia. The Brandywine Valley actually incorporates parts of three counties in two states: Chester and Delaware counties in Pennsylvania, and New Castle County in Delaware.

This is the kingdom of the du Ponts, the French bureaucratic family (originally named du Pont de Nemours) whose patriarch, Pierre-Samuel du Pont, escaped with his family from post-Revolutionary France and settled in northern Delaware. The Du Pont company was founded in 1802 by his son Éleuthère Irénée (E. I.), who made the family fortune first in gunpowder and iron, and later in chemicals and textiles.

E. I. and five generations of du Ponts lived in Eleutherian Mills, the stately family home on the grounds of a black-powder mill that has been transformed into the Hagley Museum. The home, from which Mrs. Henry du Pont was driven after accidental blasts at the powder works, was closed in 1921. Louise du Pont Crowninshield, a great-granddaughter of E. I., restored the house fully before opening it to the public.

Louise's brothers were busy, too. Henry Francis was filling his country estate, Winterthur, with furniture by Duncan Phyfe, silver by Paul Revere, decorative objects, and interior woodwork salvaged from entire homes built between 1640 and 1840. More than 200 rooms were added to display his outstanding collection of American decorative arts.

Pierre devoted his life to horticulture. He bought a 1,000-acre 19th-century arboretum and created Longwood Gardens, where he entertained his many friends and relatives. Today, 350 acres of the meticulously landscaped gardens are open to the public. Displays range from a tropical rain forest to a desert; acres of heated conservatories, where flowers are in bloom year-round, create eternal summer. Pierre also built the grand Hotel du Pont in downtown Wilmington adjacent to company headquarters. No expense was spared; more than 18 French and Italian craftsmen labored for two years carving, gilding, and painting.

Alfred I. du Pont's country estate, Nemours, was named after the family's ancestral home in north-central France. It encompasses 300 acres of French gardens and a mansion in the Louis XVI style.

The Brandywine Valley is also Wyeth country, where three generations of artists have found landscapes worthy of their talents. Although American realist Andrew Wyeth is the most famous local artist, the area's artistic tradition started long before when artist/illustrator Howard Pyle started a school in the valley. He had more than 100 students, including Andrew's father, N. C. Wyeth; Frank Schoonover; Jessie Willcox Smith; and Harvey Dunn. It was that tradition which inspired Andrew and his son Jamie.

In 1967, local residents formed the Brandywine Conservancy to prevent industrialization of the area and pollution of the river. In 1971, they opened the Brandywine River Museum in a preserved 19th-century gristmill. It celebrates the Brandywine School of artists in a setting much in tune with their world.

The valley is also the site of one of the more dramatic turns in the American Revolution, the Battle of Brandywine, and an offbeat museum which celebrates the mushroom. The region is dotted with antique shops, fine restaurants, cozy country inns, and reliable bed-and-breakfasts.

Getting Around

By Car Take U.S. 1 south from Philadelphia; Brandywine Valley is about 25 miles from Philadelphia and many attractions are on U.S. 1. To reach Wilmington, pick up U.S. 202 south just past Concordville, or take I–95 south from Philadelphia.

By Bus From Philadelphia, **Greyhound/Trailways** (tel. 215/931–4000) has about 10 daily departures to the Wilmington terminal at 101 North French Street. The trip takes one hour.

By Train **Amtrak** (tel. 215/824–1600 or 800/872–7245) has frequent service from Philadelphia's 30th Street Station to the Wilmington Station at Martin Luther King Jr. Boulevard and French Street on the edge of downtown. It's a 25-minute ride.

Guided Tours

Colonial Pathways (tel. 215/388–2654) guides escort you—in your car—for full-day excursions. You plan the itinerary.

My World Travel (tel. 215/358–3744) offers half- and full-day guided tours in a six-passenger van. Itineraries are flexible. Reserve at least one week ahead.

Important Addresses and Numbers

Tourist Information The Tourist Information Center for the Brandywine Valley (U.S. 1 north of Kennett Sq., tel. 215/388–2900 or 800/228–9933) in the Longwood Meeting House at the entrance to Longwood Gardens has information on attractions, lodging, and restaurants. Open daily 10–6. The center is run by the **Chester County Tourist Bureau,** which also has offices at 117 West Gay Street, West Chester, PA 19380, tel. 215/344–6365.

For good road maps and visitors' guides, contact the **Delaware County Convention and Visitors Bureau** (602 E. Baltimore Pike, Media, PA 19063, tel. 215/565–3680) and the **Greater Wilmington Convention and Visitors Bureau** (1300 Market St., Suite 504, Wilmington, DE 19801, tel. 302/652–4088).

Exploring

Numbers in the margin correspond with points of interest on the Brandywine Valley map.

If you start early enough, you can tour the valley's top three attractions—the Brandywine River Museum, Longwood Gardens, and Winterthur—in one day. If you have more time to spend in the valley, you can stop in to see the additional sites in Pennsylvania and then move on to Delaware.

1 **Franklin Mint Museum,** a private mint that creates heirloom-quality collectibles, displays uniquely designed and minted coins, jeweled masterpieces from the House of Igor Carl Fabergé, paintings by Andrew Wyeth and Norman Rockwell, and sculpture in porcelain, crystal, pewter, and bronze. *U.S. 1, Franklin Center, PA 19063, tel. 215/459–6168. Admission free. Open Tues.–Sat. 9:30–4:30, Sun. 1–4:30.*

2 **Brandywine Battlefield State Park,** in Chadds Ford, is a popular stop for history buffs. Nearby is the site of the Battle of Brandywine, where British General William Howe and his troops defeated George Washington on September 11, 1777. The Continental Army then fled to Lancaster, leaving Philadelphia vulnerable to British troops. The Visitors Center has audiovisual materials and displays about the battle. On the site are two restored farmhouses that once sheltered Washington and Lafayette. This is a lovely spot for a picnic. *U.S. 1, Chadds Ford, PA 19317, tel. 215/459–3342. Admission: $1 adults, 75¢ senior citizens, 50¢ children 6–17. Open Tues.–Sat. 9–5, Sun. noon–5.*

3 In a converted Civil War–era gristmill, the **Brandywine River Museum** showcases the art of Chadds Ford native Andrew Wyeth, a major American realist, and his family: his father, N. C. Wyeth, illustrator of many children's classics; his sisters Henriette and Carolyn; and his son Jamie. The collection emphasizes still life, landscape painting, and American illustration. Glass-walled lobbies display the river and countryside which inspired the Brandywine School. The museum uses a new system of filters, baffles, and blinds to direct natural light. Outside the museum visit a garden with regional wildflowers and follow a nature trail along the river. Lunch is served in a cafeteria-style restaurant. *U.S. 1 and Rte. 100, Chadds Ford, PA 19317, tel. 215/388–7601. Guided gallery tours weekdays with reservations. Admission: $4 adults, $2.50 senior citizens, $2 student, children under 6 free. Open daily 9:30–4:30.*

4 **Longwood Gardens** has established an international reputation for its colorful gardens featuring flowers and blossoming shrubs. Without an estate, these ultimate estate gardens were created by Pierre-Samuel du Pont. Fabulous seasonal attractions include magnolias and azaleas in spring, roses and water lilies in summer, fall foliage and harvest motifs, and winter camellias, orchids, and palms. Bad weather is no problem as 3½ acres of exotic foliage, cacti, ferns, and bonsai are housed in heated conservatories. Illuminated fountain displays Tuesday, Thursday, and Saturday evenings at 9:15 in summer. The restaurant is open for lunch daily, and dinner on nights of late closing. *U.S. 1, Kennett Square, PA 19348, tel. 215/388–6741. Admission: $8 adults, $1.50 children 6–14. Open daily 10–5, plus some evenings in summer and at Christmastime.*

5 **Phillips Mushroom Place** is a small museum devoted exclusively to a fungus—the mushroom. Mushrooms are Pennsylvania's number one cash crop and most are grown in Kennett Square. The history, lore, and growing process of mushrooms is ex-

Brandywine Valley

plained with dioramas, exhibits, and slides. The gift shop sells a variety of mushrooms. *U.S. 1, ½ mi south of Longwood Gardens, Kennett Square, PA 19348, tel. 215/388–6082. Admission: $1.25 adults, 50¢ children 7–12. Open daily 10–6.*

6 Henry Francis du Pont housed his 50,000 objects of decorative art in a nine-story mansion called **Winterthur.** The 1640–1840 furniture, silver, paintings, and textiles are displayed in period room settings. Surrounding the museum are 200 acres of English-style landscaped lawns, gardens, and virgin forest. Yuletide at Winterthur (Nov. 15–Dec. 31) showcases the holiday traditions of early America. A restaurant serves lunch. *Rte. 52, Winterthur, DE 19735, 5 mi south of U.S. 1, tel. 302/888–4600. Children under 12 not permitted on reserved tours. Admission for unreserved 45-min guided museum tour: $9 adults, $7.50 senior citizens and children 12–16. Adults pay $8 to $12.50 for a variety of prepaid, reserved tours. Garden tram tour ($2.50) runs mid-April–Oct. Open Tues.–Sat. 9–5, Sun. noon–5.*

7 Whereas many Brandywine Valley attractions are du Pont pleasure palaces, **Hagley on the Brandywine** offers a glimpse of the du Ponts at work. A restored, mid-19th-century mill community on 230 landscaped acres, the Hagley is the site of the first Du Pont black-powder mills. Making gunpowder and explosives was dangerous work and the museum depicts and demonstrates that enterprise in the powder-yard stone mills and in a restored workers' community. The tour includes stops at Eleutherian Mills, an 1803 Georgian-style home which was furnished by five generations of du Ponts, and a French Renaissance-style garden. A bus transports visitors through the property. Allow about two hours for your visit. The coffee shop is open for lunch except in winter. *Rte. 141 between Rte. 100 and U.S. 202, Wilmington, DE 19807, tel. 302/658–2400. Admission: $8 adults, $6.50 senior citizens, $3 children 6–14. Open Apr.–Dec., daily 9:30–4:30; Jan.–Mar., Sat. and Sun. 9:30–4:30. In winter, weekday tours at 1:30.*

⑧ Nemours Mansion and Gardens, a 300-acre country estate built for Alfred I. du Pont in 1910, is a modified Louis XVI château showcasing European and American furnishings, rare rugs, tapestries, and art. The surrounding gardens, reminiscent of Versailles, are landscaped with fountains, pools, and statuary. Allow two hours for the house tour and bus tour of the gardens. *Rockland Rd., off Rte. 141 between Rte. 100 and U.S. 202, Wilmington, DE 19899, tel. 302/651–6912. Admission: $8; visitors must be over 16. Open May through Nov. Tours Tues.–Sat. 9, 11, 1, and 3; Sun. at 11, 1, and 3. Reservations recommended.*

⑨ Delaware Art Museum. The museum's main assets include the works of Howard Pyle, a Wilmington native and "father of American illustration," as well as paintings by his accomplished students—N. C. Wyeth, Frank Schoonover, and Maxfield Parrish. It also houses the largest American collection of 19th-century English pre-Raphaelite paintings and decorative arts; *2301 Kentmere Pkwy., Wilmington, DE 19806, tel. 302/571–9590. Admission free. Open Tues. 10–9, Wed.–Sat. 10–5, Sun. noon–5.*

In contrast to the opulent French-inspired du Pont homes is **⑩ Rockwood,** a quietly elegant English-style country house and a fine example of rural Gothic architecture. Built in 1851 by Joseph Shipley, a Quaker merchant, the house is now a museum filled with 17th- to 20th-century American, European, and Oriental decorative arts and furnishings. There is a guided tour of the mansion and an unguided tour of the gardens. *610 Shipley Rd., Wilmington, DE 19706, tel. 302/571–7776. Admission: $3 adults, $2.50 senior citizens, $1 children 5–16. Open Tues.– Sat. 11–3.*

Dining and Lodging

Dining It seems that while almost every restaurant in the Brandywine Valley serves what is called Continental-American cuisine, most also feature local specialties—fresh seafood from the Chesapeake Bay and dishes made with Kennett Square mushrooms.

Category	Cost*
Very Expensive	over $40
Expensive	$25–$40
Moderate	$15–$25
Inexpensive	under $15

per person for a 3-course meal, without wine, tip, or tax (6%)

Lodging Many Brandywine Valley accommodations call themselves bed-and-breakfasts because they provide beds and serve breakfast, but they are far from the typical B&B—which is usually a room in a private home—and are more accurately characterized as inns or small hotels.

Unless otherwise indicated, all rooms have private bath and the hotel is open year-round.

Category	Cost*
Very Expensive	over $100
Expensive	$80–$100
Moderate	$60–$80
Inexpensive	under $60

double occupancy, without tax (6%)

The following credit card abbreviations are used: AE, American Express; CB, Carte Blanche; DC, Diners Club; MC, MasterCard; V, Visa.

Chadds Ford
Dining

Chadds Ford Inn. Continental-American dishes such as two-textured duck and tenderloin of pork in puff pastry are featured in a lively former rest stop on the Wilmington–Philadelphia–Lancaster commerce route. Generous portions are served in a Colonial setting featuring candlelight, stone hearths, and Wyeth prints. The downstairs dining rooms are more formal. This popular lunch spot is close to the Brandywine River Museum. *Rte. 100 and U.S. 1, tel. 215/388–7361. Reservations advised. Dress: casual. AE, CB, DC, MC, V. Expensive.*

Lodging
★

Brandywine River Hotel. This small, modern, two-story hotel opened in summer 1988 across the highway from the Brandywine River Museum. Tasteful Queen Anne furnishings, classic English chintz, and florals create a homey feeling. Ten suites have fireplaces and Jacuzzis. Continental breakfast is served in a lovely dining room. *Rte. 100 and U.S. 1, Chadds Ford, PA 19317, tel. 215/388–1200. 40 rooms. AE, DC, MC, V. Expensive.*

Glen Mills
Lodging
★

Sweetwater Farm. A handsome 18th-century fieldstone farmhouse has been lovingly restored into a homey inn serving hearty breakfasts. A shaded porch lined with rockers overlooks the farm; no other houses are in sight. Rooms have handmade quilts, fresh flowers, fragrant potpourri, and authentic period furnishings, including some canopy beds. Rooms in the newer section (circa 1800) of the house are larger; loft suites are favorites. *Linda Kaat, Box 86, Glen Mills, PA 19342, tel. 215/459–4711. 9 rooms, 6 with private bath, and 5 cottages. Facilities: outdoor pool, horses and other farm animals. 2-night minimum stay requested on weekends. AE, MC, V. Very Expensive.*

Kennett Square
Dining
★

Longwood Inn. Live Maine lobsters, homemade crab cakes, Chesapeake seafood dishes, and mushroom specialties are served in a relaxed Williamsburg-style setting. The inn serves early-bird dinners; a good choice for lunch. *815 E. Baltimore Pike (U.S. 1), ½ mi from Longwood Gardens, tel. 215/444–3515. Reservations suggested for dinner. Dress: informal. AE, DC, MC, V. Moderate.*

Lodging **Longwood Inn.** A small, family-owned motel ½ mile south of Longwood Gardens offers lower-priced accommodations with simple, traditional furnishings. The inn was totally renovated in 1988. *815 E. Baltimore Pike, Kennett Square, PA 19348, tel. 215/444-3515. 28 rooms. Facilities: restaurant, lounge. AE, CB, DC, MC, V. Inexpensive.*

Meadow Spring Farm. Anne Hicks's farmhouse, built in 1836, is a gallery for her family's antiques, dolls, and teddy bears. Rooms have Amish quilts and televisions. A full country breakfast is served daily on the glassed-in porch. Children are welcome here. *201 E. Street Rd., 19348, tel. 215/444-3903. 6 rooms, 3 with bath. Facilities: outdoor pool, hot tub in solarium, game room with pool table and Ping-Pong, pond for fishing, farm animals. No credit cards. Inexpensive–Moderate.*

Mendenhall **Mendenhall Inn.** Continental and American cuisine is served in
Dining this 1790s Quaker mill building with its old beams still intact. Crab imperial, prime rib, and game are featured. For lunch, request a table with a courtyard view; at Saturday dinner, ask for the Mill Room upstairs. *Rte. 52 1 mi south of U.S. 1, tel. 215/388-1181. Reservations advised for lunch, required for dinner. Jacket and tie required, except in tavern. AE, DC, MC, V. Closed Mon. Expensive.*

Lodging **Fairville Inn.** Halfway between Winterthur and Longwood
★ Gardens, Ole and Patti Retlev's inn offers bright, airy rooms furnished with Queen Anne and Hepplewhite reproductions. There's a main house, built in 1826; a remodeled barn; and a carriage house. Request a room in the back of the property, away from traffic. The main house has a striking living room with a large fireplace. The Fairville serves complimentary light breakfast and afternoon tea. Not suitable for children under 10. *Rte. 52 (Kennett Pike), Box 219, 19357, tel. 215/388-5900. 15 rooms and suites. AE, MC, V. Expensive–Very Expensive.*

Thornton **Pace One.** A 250-year-old barn with poplar beams and stone
Dining walls features imaginative country specialties such as pork chops stuffed with cornbread and sausage and marinated, broiled fish. Chocolate fondue and a double chocolate mint pie head the list of tempting desserts. A friendly, casual spot. *Glen Mills and Thornton Rds., tel. 215/459-3702. Reservations advised. Dress: informal. AE, DC, MC, V. Expensive.*

West Chester **Dilworthtown Inn.** Fresh seafood from the Chesapeake, local
Dining quail and partridge, and smoked pheasant are served at this completely restored 1758 inn. Vegetables and herbs are grown in the garden across the road. A Korean chef prepares Continental favorites using French techniques. The wine cellar is stocked with over 14,000 bottles. *Old Wilmington Pike and Brinton's Bridge Rd., tel. 215/399-1390. Reservations advised. Jacket required. AE, CB, DC, MC, V. Closed for lunch. Expensive.*

Wilmington **Green Room.** For years Philadelphians have trekked to Wil-
Dining mington to celebrate special occasions in the famous Hotel du
★ Pont restaurant. Classic French cuisine is served in Edwardian splendor under a gold-encrusted ceiling with massive Spanish chandeliers and high French windows. Harp music accompanies formal dinners. *Hotel du Pont, 11th and Market Sts., tel. 302/594-3100. Reservations advised. Jackets required. AE, CB, DC, MC, V. Very Expensive.*

Lodging **Hotel du Pont.** The hotel is an elegant 12-story building with an old-world feel built in 1913 by Pierre-Samuel du Pont. The lobby has a spectacular gold-encrusted ceiling, polished marble walls, and carved oak and walnut paneling. Rooms feature antique reproductions and original art; request a newly renovated room. *11th and Market Sts., 19899, tel. 302/594–3100 or 800/441–9019. 276 rooms. Facilities: 2 restaurants serving French-Continental and American cuisine, lobby lounge, theater next door. AE, CB, DC, MC, V. Very Expensive.*

Valley Forge

Valley Forge National Historical Park preserves the moment in American history when George Washington's Continental Army endured the bitter winter of 1777–1778. Although the park's 3,500 acres of rolling hills offer serenity and quiet beauty, it is doubtful that Washington enjoyed any peaceful nights as he struggled with the morale problems that beset his troops.

The army had just lost the battles of Brandywine, White Horse, and Germantown. While the British occupied Philadelphia, Washington's soldiers were forced to endure horrid conditions—blizzards that iced up the rivers, inadequate food and clothing, damp quarters, and disease. Many men deserted and although no battle was fought at Valley Forge, 2,000 American soldiers died.

But the troops won one victory that winter—a war of the will. The forces slowly regained strength and confidence under the leadership of Prussian drillmaster Friedrich von Steuben. In June 1778, Washington led his troops away from Valley Forge in search of the British. Fortified, the Continental Army was able to carry on the fight for five years more.

For the day-tripper interested in early-American history, a visit to the monuments, markers, huts, and headquarters in Valley Forge National Historical Park, 18 miles from Center City, Philadelphia, is illuminating. If the weather is fine, consider renting a bicycle or packing a lunch and picnicking at one of three park sites. Other nearby attractions include Mill Grove, the home of naturalist John James Audubon, and The Court and The Plaza, one of the nation's largest shopping complexes.

If you stay overnight in Valley Forge, check the schedule for the **Valley Forge Music Fair** (tel. 215/644–5000). This theater-in-the-round presents top names in entertainment, with recent performances by Dolly Parton, the Pointer Sisters, and Chuck Mangione. The **People's Light and Theater Company** in nearby Malvern (tel. 215/644–3500), a pioneer of the regional theater movement, offers classics and avant-garde productions from April through December.

Getting Around

By Car Take the Schuylkill Expressway (I–76) west from Philadelphia to Exit 25 (Goddard Blvd.). Take Route 363 to North Gulph Road and follow signs to Valley Forge National Historical Park. Exit 25 also provides easy access to The Court and The Plaza shopping complex.

By Bus **Greyhound/Trailways** (tel. 215/931–4000) buses leave Philadelphia almost hourly for the Valley Forge Shopping Center on U.S. 202 (1 mile north of The Plaza). The trip takes 30 to 50 minutes.

The **SEPTA** (tel. 215/574–7800) no. 45 bus leaves from 16th Street and John F. Kennedy Boulevard for King of Prussia Plaza. From there take the no. 99 "Royersford" bus which goes through Valley Forge National Historical Park. The no. 99 bus departs hourly.

Guided Tours

The Valley Forge National Historical Park Bus Tour (tel. 215/783–7700) is a narrated minibus tour that originates from the park Visitor Center (rtes. 23 and 363). Passengers can alight, visit sites, and reboard. Tours are scheduled from May through October; times vary.

Important Addresses and Numbers

Tourist **Valley Forge Convention and Visitors Bureau** (Box 311, Norris-
Information town, PA 19404, tel. 215/278–3558). Call or write for information packet.

Valley Forge Country Funline (tel. 215/275–4636) offers information about special events and exhibits 24 hours a day.

Exploring

Numbers in the margin correspond with points of interest on the Valley Forge map.

❶ **Valley Forge National Historical Park,** administered by the National Park Service, is the site of the 1777–1778 winter encampment of General George Washington and the Continental Army. Stop first at the Visitor Center for a 15-minute orientation film, exhibits, and a map for a 10-mile, unguided auto tour of the 10 park attractions. Stops include reconstructed huts of the Muhlenberg Brigade, and the National Memorial Arch, which pays tribute to those soldiers who suffered through the infamous winter. Other sites include the bronze equestrian statue on the encampment of General Anthony Wayne and his Pennsylvania troops; Artillery Park, where the soldiers stored their cannons; and the Isaac Potts House, which served as Washington's headquarters. A park employee is stationed here to answer questions. From May through October, you can purchase an auto-tour cassette tape for $7 (plus $7.50 to rent a cassette player).

The park contains 6 miles of paved trails for jogging or bicycling, and two hiking trails. Single- and five-speed bicycles are available for rental by the hour from Memorial Day to Labor Day, weekends only in April, May, and September. Visitors can picnic at any of three designated areas. At the Washington Headquarters stop, there is a snack bar for fast-food lunches. A leisurely visit to the park will take no more than half a day. *Rtes. 23 and 363, Box 953, Valley Forge, PA 19481, tel. 215/783–7700. Admission to historic houses: $1 adults 17–61. Open daily 8:30–5, extended hours in summer. Closed Christmas.*

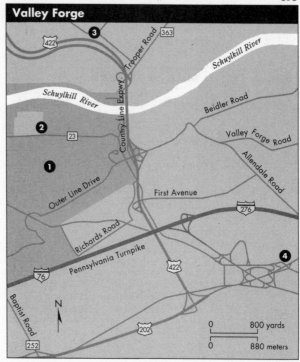

Valley Forge

❷ The **Valley Forge Historical Society Museum** tells the Valley Forge story with military equipment and Colonial artifacts plus a large collection of items that belonged to Martha and George Washington. The nearby gift shop sells homemade goodies such as Martha's 16-Bean Soup and strawberry jam. *Next to the Washington Memorial Chapel on Rte. 23, tel. 215/783–0535. Admission: $1.50 adults, $1 senior citizens, 50¢ children 2–12. Open Mon.–Sat. 9:30–4:30, Sun. 1–4:30. Closed Christmas and Easter.*

❸ **Mill Grove** was the first American home of Haitian-born artist and naturalist John James Audubon. Built in 1762, the house is now a museum furnished in the style of the early 1800s and displays all of Audubon's major works. The collection includes reproductions, original prints, his paintings of birds and wildlife, and the double-elephant folio of his *Birds of America*. The attic has been restored to a studio and taxidermy room. The Audubon Wildlife Sanctuary has 6 miles of marked hiking trails along Perkiomen Creek. *Audubon and Pawlings Rds., Box 25, Audubon PA 19407, tel. 215/666–5593. Admission free. Museum open Tues.–Sat. 10–4, Sun. 1–4; grounds open Tues.–Sun. dawn–dusk. Closed Thanksgiving, Christmas, and New Year's Day.*

❹ For lunch or an afternoon of browsing, head for the **Court and Plaza** at King of Prussia, one of the nation's largest shopping complexes. These two adjacent malls contain more than a dozen restaurants, 300 shops and boutiques, and a half-dozen major department stores, including Bloomingdale's and a stunning new branch of Philadelphia's own Strawbridge and Clothier. The shops cater to the affluent surrounding Main Line community. *Rte. 202 and N. Gulph Rd., tel. 215/265–5727. Open Mon. –Sat. 10– 9, Sun. 11–5.*

Dining and Lodging

King of Prussia
Dining

Kennedy Supplee Mansion. New American cuisine is served in a circa 1852 Italian Renaissance mansion that has been handsomely restored, overlooking Valley Forge National Historical Park. *1100 W. Valley Forge Rd., tel. 215/337–3777. Reservations required. Jackets required. AE, CB, DC, MC, V. No lunch weekends. Very Expensive (over $40).*

★ **Bocconcini.** Updated northern Italian specialties (angel hair pasta with goat cheese and sun-dried tomatoes; veal medallions topped with lobster gratin) are served amid majestic marble columns and hanging vines interlaced on cherrywood ceiling beams. Panna Cotta, a cold cream soufflé, is the winning dessert. The lunch menu has lighter fare, including salads and sandwiches. *Radisson Hotel Valley Forge, N. Gulph Rd. and 1st Ave., tel. 215/265–1500. Reservations advised. Jackets required for dinner, suggested for lunch. AE, CB, DC, MC, V. Expensive ($25–$40).*

Lily Langtry's. This lavishly appointed Victorian-era restaurant/cabaret serves American and Continental dishes, but the campy Las Vegas-style entertainment—corny comedians, scantily clad showgirls, and some fine singers, dancers, and ice skaters—is the real draw here. *Sheraton Valley Forge Hotel, N. Gulph Rd. and First Ave., tel. 215/337–LILY. Reservations required. Jackets suggested. AE, CB, DC, MC, V. Closed Mon. Moderate ($15–$25).*

Lodging

Radisson Hotel Valley Forge. The six-story Radisson, opened in early 1988, and the Sheraton Valley Forge flank the Valley Forge Convention Center and share several restaurants and nightclubs. Contemporary rooms here are minisuites with Jacuzzis for two and numerous telephones and TV sets. *N. Gulph Rd. and First Ave., 19406, tel. 215/265–1500 or 800/333–3333. 160 rooms. Facilities: restaurant, dinner theater, disco, health club, outdoor pool. AE, CB, DC, MC, V. Very Expensive (over $100).*

★ **Sheraton Valley Forge Hotel.** A bustling high rise catering to groups and couples escaping to Jacuzzi-equipped fantasy theme suites—a prehistoric cave, a wild-and-woolly jungle, the outer-space-like "Outer Limits." *N. Gulph Rd. and 1st Ave., 19406, tel. 215/337–2000 or 800/325–3535. 327 rooms, including 72 fantasy suites. Facilities: restaurants, dinner theater, disco, health club, outdoor pool. AE, CB, DC, MC, V. Very Expensive (over $100).*

McIntosh Inn. Very basic accommodations but you can't stay anywhere for less in the Valley Forge area. Though bedspreads look a bit worn, the hotel is clean and almost always fully occupied. *Rte. 363 and Goddard Blvd., 19406, tel. 215/768–9500. 212 rooms. AE, MC, V. Inexpensive (under $60).*

Reading

Reading (RED-ing), founded by William Penn's sons Thomas and Richard, was a 19th-century industrial city best known as the terminus of the Reading Railroad. Today, Reading has another claim to fame. It promotes itself as the "Outlet Capital of the World" and entices bargain hunters with promises of savings up to 80% off retail.

This method of merchandising began when local factories and mills started selling overruns and seconds to employees. Eventually, small stores sprang up inside the factories. About 6 million visitors a year, many coming in bus excursions from all over the East Coast, now visit some 260 "outlets" located within a 4-mile radius. The stores sell clothing for the whole family, pretzels, candy, luggage, jewelry, shoes, pet food, even tropical fish. Designer labels, including Ralph Lauren, Laura Ashley, and Liz Claiborne, are discounted. A large number of outlets are grouped together in six former factory complexes.

It's easy to get caught up in the buying frenzy as you browse through racks marked $10 and under, but not all the buys are bargains. If an item is marked "irregular," look it over carefully. It may be fine or it might have holes in the sleeves. There is no sales tax on clothing in Pennsylvania.

Reading is an easy 75-minute drive from Philadelphia and the major outlets can be scanned in a day. Most outlet complexes have cafeterias or food courts. If you want another day to shop or sightsee, you have more overnight options since the success of the outlet stores has spawned revitalization of the local hotel and restaurant industries.

Sitting prettily atop Mt. Penn on Skyline Drive is the Pagoda, a seven-story building of Japanese design, which provides an expansive view of the city. Skyline Drive is a meandering road with miles of unspoiled vistas. The Daniel Boone Homestead, a renovation of the frontiersman's home, and the Mary Merritt Doll Museum, make good diversions after a shopping spree.

Getting Around

By Car Take the Schuylkill Expressway (I–76) west from Philadelphia to the Pennsylvania Turnpike. Go west to Exit 22, take I–176 north to U.S. 422 and then west into downtown Reading.

By Bus **Greyhound/Trailways** (tel. 215/931–4000) has almost hourly runs to the Intercity Bus Terminal, Third and Court streets, in Reading. Most buses make the trip in 90 minutes, although some locals take up to three hours. Check the schedule carefully.

Important Addresses and Numbers

Tourist Information **Berks County Pennsylvania Dutch Travel Association** (Sheraton Berkshire Inn, Rte. 422 west, Papermill Rd. Exit, Wyomissing, PA 19610, tel. 215/375–4085). Open weekdays 9–5, Saturday 9–2. Request outlet map and guide.

Exploring

Numbers in the margin correspond with points of interest on the Reading map.

1 If you can't wait to load up your shopping bag, stop at the **Manufacturers Outlet Mall** when you exit the Pennsylvania Turnpike in Morgantown (Exit 22). "MOM" looks like any mod-

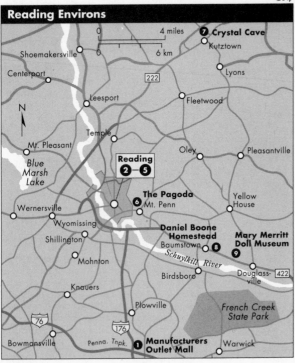

Reading Environs

ern suburban enclosed shopping mall and has more than 75 stores on one level including Van Heusen, Munsingwear, Izod, Levi-Strauss and Johnston & Murphy. Attached to the mall is a 200-room luxury hotel and convention center; if you need to nap, shower, or change, you can rent a "day room" for $35. The food court serves lunch and dinner. *Exit 22, Pennsylvania Turnpike, tel. 215/286–2000. Open Mon.–Sat. 10–9, Sun. noon–5.*

2 The **Vanity Fair Factory Outlet Complex** offers some of the best buys and the largest variety of goods in the city. Situated on what was once the world's largest hosiery mill, the complex originally sold surplus hosiery, sleepwear, and lingerie. Today it consists of nine major buildings on more than 900,000 square feet. The VF Factory Outlet offers a vast selection of Lee jeans, women's sleepwear, and lingerie from Vanity Fair and Lollipop, and Jantzen and Jansport activewear at half price. Upstairs are Jonathan Logan and Laura Ashley. Other buildings contain Carter's Childrenswear, Black & Decker hardware, and Freeman Shoes. Reading China and Glass has 100,000 square feet of glassware, housewares, furniture, and linens. *Park Rd. and Hill Ave., Wyomissing, tel. 215/378–0408. Cafeteria and food court. Shuttle buses take shoppers to and from the parking lot. Open weekdays 9–9, Sat. 9–6, Sun. noon–5.*

3 After VF, the **Reading Outlet Center** may make you feel claustrophobic. The former silk-stocking mill in the heart of the city now houses more than 60 shops on four floors plus stores in nearby buildings. There are lots of stairs to climb and the long

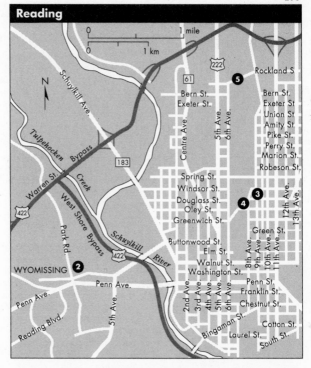

Reading

hallways are narrow and not well marked. Items for sale range from toys and cosmetics to sporting goods and wine. There's a Polo/Ralph Lauren outlet, Fashion Flair's Izod Lacoste clothes, Maidenform, J. G. Hook, and Corning. Liz Claiborne occupies a new site nearby at 832 Oley Street. *801 N. 9th St., tel. 215/373-5495. Freight elevator for handicapped and for parents with strollers. Restaurant. Open Mon.–Wed. 9:30–6, Thurs.–Sat. 9:30–8, Sun. noon–5.*

4 A block away from the Reading Outlet Center, the smaller **Big Mill Outlet** is housed in a former shoe factory. Long hallways and stairs make shopping here a bit of a trial but sometimes the bargains make it all worthwhile. Among the 20 stores are Gitano (sportswear), Delta Hosiery Mill Outlet, Jordache Shoetown, Stone Mountain handbags, and Adolfo (sportswear). *8th and Oley Sts. tel. 215/378-9100. Small food court. Open Mon.–Wed. 9:30–6, Thurs.–Sat. 9:30–8, Sun. 11–5.*

5 **Outlets on Hiesters Lane** is a grouping of three outlet buildings along one city block at the northern end of downtown Reading. Except for a linen outlet and the dinnerware at the Mikasa Factory Store, most stores sell coats, clothes, and shoes. There's Burlington Coat Factory Warehouse, Flemington Fashion Outlet, and the Sweater Mill. *Corner of Hiesters La. and Kutztown Rd., tel. 215/921-9394. Most stores are open Mon.–Sat. 9:30–5:30, Sun. noon–5.*

6 **The Pagoda,** a seven-story Japanese castle attached to the top of Mt. Penn by 10 tons of bolts, offers a panoramic view of the Reading area. *Skyline Dr., tel. 215/372-0553. Admission: 25¢*

adults, children under 12 free. Open weekdays noon–4, weekends noon–6; in summer, weekdays until 8, weekends until 9.

7 **Crystal Cave** 45-minute guided walking tours wind through illuminated stalactites and stalagmites in distinctive formations like the "ice cream cone," "totem pole," and innumerable others. *From Reading, take U.S. 222 north 15 mi to Kutztown exit; follow signs; tel. 215/683-6765. Admission: $5 adults, $3 children 5–11. Open weekdays 9–5, spring weekends 9–6, one hour later in summer. Closed Dec.–Feb.*

8 The **Daniel Boone Homestead,** 10 miles east of Reading, is where the great frontiersman lived until the age of 16. The rebuilt homestead has been furnished to typify rural life in this part of the state. Offered are a half-hour house tour and unguided tours of the blacksmith shop, sawmill, and barn. *Daniel Boone Rd. off U.S. 422, tel. 215/582-4900. Admission: $1.50 adults, $1 senior citizens, 50¢ children 6–17. Open Tues.–Sat. 9–5, Sun. noon–5. Closed Mon. except Memorial Day, Labor Day and July 4.*

9 It's a small world at the **Mary Merritt Doll Museum** where you'll find rare dolls—rag dolls, French bisque dolls, mechanical dolls, and more—crafted between 1725 and 1900. Also on display are toys, exquisitely fashioned miniature period rooms, and elaborate dollhouses. **Merritt's Museum of Childhood** has an eclectic collection of Pennsylvania Dutch fraktur, tin and iron toys, Colonial lighting devices, and early baby carriages. *Both on Rte. 422 in Douglassville, 1 mi east of Boone Homestead, tel. 215/385-3809. Admission: $2 adults, $1.75 senior citizens, $1.50 children 5–12. Open Mon.–Sat. 10–5, Sun. 1–5. Closed major holidays.*

Dining

★ **Joe's.** This family-owned restaurant has attracted national attention for unusual dishes enriched by the exotic accents of wild and domestic mushrooms (cepes, morels, slippery jacks, woodblewits and boletes, among others), most of which are handpicked by the Czarnecki family. Wild mushroom soup is a don't-miss item. Jack Czarnecki wrote *Joe's Book of Mushroom Cookery*, the definitive mushroom cookbook. *7th and Laurel Sts., tel. 215/373-6794. Reservations requested on weekends. Jackets preferred. AE, CB, DC, MC, V. Closed Sun. and Mon. Very expensive (over $40).*

The Peanut Bar. Free peanuts (throw the shells on the floor), video games, and good burgers and fries make this 1930s-style tavern/restaurant a fun outing. It is also known for fried cheese balls and Buffalo chicken wings, seafood, steaks, and salads. *332 Penn St., tel. 215/376-7373. Reservations suggested. Dress: informal. AE, DC, MC, V. Closed Sun. Moderate ($15–$25).*

Arner's. Family restaurants—three locations—with the look and feel of spruced-up diners serve American favorites such as pork chops, fried seafood, veal parmigiana, and homemade pastries and pies. The bountiful salad bar and daily specials make this a hard-to-beat bargain. *9th and Exeter Sts., Reading, tel. 215/929-9795; Howard Blvd., Mt. Penn, tel. 215/779-6555. Bern Rd., Berkshire Mall, tel. 215/372-6101. No reservations. Dress: informal. No credit cards. Inexpensive (under $15).*

Lodging

Sheraton Berkshire Inn. A $10 million renovation has made this an exceptionally attractive property with a striking Art Deco lobby and marble-tile floors. It's worth the extra $10 a night to upgrade from a standard room to an extra-large executive room in the tower. *U.S. 422 W, on Papermill Rd., Wyomissing 19610, tel. 215/376–3811 or 800/325–3535. 257 rooms, 4 bi-level suites. Facilities: 2 restaurants, nightclub, indoor pool, game room, fitness center. AE, CB, DC, MC, V. Expensive ($80–$100).*

Inn at Reading. Housed in a well-kept, elegant complex, the inn is furnished in the Colonial style. All of its guest rooms were renovated in 1988. Large rooms feature remote-control cable TV and traditional cherrywood furnishings, including some four-poster beds. Request a room close to the lobby. The Publick House restaurant serves excellent meals. *1040 Park Rd. and Warren St., Wyomissing 19610, tel. 215/372–7811. 250 rooms. Facilities: restaurant, live entertainment in lounge, gift shop, outdoor pool, playground. AE, DC, MC, V. Moderate ($60–$80).*

Hampton Inn. This small hotel has stylish contemporary rooms but no dining or recreational facilities. The spacious King Special, just $5 more than a double, has a separate sitting area, king-size bed, and remote-control cable TV. Complimentary Continental breakfast is served. *1800 Papermill Rd., Wyomissing 19610, tel. 215/374–8100 or 800/HAMPTON. 127 rooms. AE, DC, MC, V. Inexpensive (under $60).*

Index

Personal Itinerary

Departure *Date*

Time

Transportation

Arrival *Date*   *Time*

Departure *Date*   *Time*

Transportation

Accommodations

Arrival *Date*   *Time*

Departure *Date*   *Time*

Transportation

Accommodations

Arrival *Date*   *Time*

Departure *Date*   *Time*

Transportation

Accommodations

Personal Itinerary

Arrival *Date*   *Time*

Departure *Date*   *Time*

Transportation

Accommodations

Arrival *Date*   *Time*

Departure *Date*   *Time*

Transportation

Accommodations

Arrival *Date*   *Time*

Departure *Date*   *Time*

Transportation

Accommodations

Arrival *Date*   *Time*

Departure *Date*   *Time*

Transportation

Accommodations

Personal Itinerary

Arrival *Date*   *Time*

Departure *Date*   *Time*

Transportation

Accommodations

Arrival *Date*   *Time*

Departure *Date*   *Time*

Transportation

Accommodations

Arrival *Date*   *Time*

Departure *Date*   *Time*

Transportation

Accommodations

Arrival *Date*   *Time*

Departure *Date*   *Time*

Transportation

Accommodations

Addresses

Name	*Name*
Address	*Address*
Telephone	*Telephone*
Name	*Name*
Address	*Address*
Telephone	*Telephone*
Name	*Name*
Address	*Address*
Telephone	*Telephone*
Name	*Name*
Address	*Address*
Telephone	*Telephone*
Name	*Name*
Address	*Address*
Telephone	*Telephone*
Name	*Name*
Address	*Address*
Telephone	*Telephone*
Name	*Name*
Address	*Address*
Telephone	*Telephone*
Name	*Name*
Address	*Address*
Telephone	*Telephone*

Addresses

Name	*Name*
Address	*Address*
Telephone	*Telephone*
Name	*Name*
Address	*Address*
Telephone	*Telephone*
Name	*Name*
Address	*Address*
Telephone	*Telephone*
Name	*Name*
Address	*Address*
Telephone	*Telephone*
Name	*Name*
Address	*Address*
Telephone	*Telephone*
Name	*Name*
Address	*Address*
Telephone	*Telephone*
Name	*Name*
Address	*Address*
Telephone	*Telephone*
Name	*Name*
Address	*Address*
Telephone	*Telephone*

Notes

Notes

Fodor's Travel Guides

U.S. Guides

Alaska
Arizona
Atlantic City & the
 New Jersey Shore
Boston
California
Cape Cod
Carolinas & the
 Georgia Coast
The Chesapeake Region
Chicago
Colorado
Disney World & the
 Orlando Area

Florida
Hawaii
Las Vegas
Los Angeles, Orange
 County, Palm Springs
Maui
Miami,
 Fort Lauderdale,
 Palm Beach
Michigan, Wisconsin,
 Minnesota
New England
New Mexico
New Orleans

New Orleans (Pocket
 Guide)
New York City
New York City (Pocket
 Guide)
New York State
Pacific North Coast
Philadelphia
The Rockies
San Diego
San Francisco
San Francisco (Pocket
 Guide)
The South

Texas
USA
Virgin Islands
Virginia
Waikiki
Washington, DC

Foreign Guides

Acapulco
Amsterdam
Australia, New Zealand,
 The South Pacific
Austria
Bahamas
Bahamas (Pocket
 Guide)
Baja & the Pacific
 Coast Resorts
Barbados
Beijing, Guangzhou &
 Shanghai
Belgium &
 Luxembourg
Bermuda
Brazil
Britain (Great Travel
 Values)
Budget Europe
Canada
Canada (Great Travel
 Values)
Canada's Atlantic
 Provinces
Cancun, Cozumel,
 Yucatan Peninsula

Caribbean
Caribbean (Great
 Travel Values)
Central America
Eastern Europe
Egypt
Europe
Europe's Great
 Cities
France
France (Great Travel
 Values)
Germany
Germany (Great Travel
 Values)
Great Britain
Greece
The Himalayan
 Countries
Holland
Hong Kong
Hungary
India,
 including Nepal
Ireland
Israel
Italy

Italy (Great Travel
 Values)
Jamaica
Japan
Japan (Great Travel
 Values)
Kenya, Tanzania,
 the Seychelles
Korea
Lisbon
Loire Valley
London
London (Great
 Travel Values)
London (Pocket Guide)
Madrid & Barcelona
Mexico
Mexico City
Montreal &
 Quebec City
Munich
New Zealand
North Africa
Paris
Paris (Pocket Guide)
People's Republic of
 China

Portugal
Rio de Janeiro
The Riviera (Fun on)
Rome
Saint Martin &
 Sint Maarten
Scandinavia
Scandinavian Cities
Scotland
Singapore
South America
South Pacific
Southeast Asia
Soviet Union
Spain
Spain (Great Travel
 Values)
Sweden
Switzerland
Sydney
Tokyo
Toronto
Turkey
Vienna
Yugoslavia

Special-Interest Guides

Health & Fitness
 Vacations
Royalty Watching

Selected Hotels of
 Europe

Selected Resorts and
 Hotels of the U.S.
Shopping in Europe

Skiing in North America
Sunday in New York